D1356377

Evans' TV Trivia

Evans' TV Trivia

Jeff Evans

Collins

First published in 2005 by HarperCollins Publishers

HarperCollins Publishers
77–85 Fulham Palace Road
London
W6 8JB

www.collins.co.uk

Reprint 10 9 8 7 6 5 4 3 2 1 0

ISBN 0-00-720778-6

A catalogue record for this book is available from the British Library

Printed and bound in Great Britain by Clays Ltd, St Ives plc.

Acknowledgements

Jeff Evans would like to thank the following people in particular for their help with the compilation of this book: Malcolm Batchelor for the Watch with Mother list; Stewart Larque at the National Grid for the TV Pick Ups; Paul at gladiatorszone.co.uk for the Gladiators info; Phil Borge at ABC for the magazine sales figures; Mike Brown at the countdownpage.com for the Dictionary Corner stats; Louise Dorey at ITV Sales for help with programme sponsorship; Laurence Bray and Greta McMahon at the Channel 4 press office; and Alun Powell for his many suggestions and encouragement over a pint or three. Thanks also to Martin Toseland at HarperCollins for taking up the idea so positively.

A Few Opening Lines

Evening all.
Dixon of Dock Green

*From Norwich,
it's the quiz of the week.*
Sale of the Century

Here's a house, here's a door.
Play School

It's Friday, it's five to five and it's ...
Crackerjack

*Stand by for action!
Anything can happen in the next half-hour.*
Stingray

*There is nothing wrong
with your television set.*
The Outer Limits

Wakey, wakey!
The Billy Cotton Band Show

Yes, it's number one, it's ...
Top of the Pops

Hello there!
Blue Peter

Britain's Best Sitcom

In 2003–4 the BBC organised a national poll of the greatest ever British situation comedy. The ten shortlisted candidates (in final finishing order) and the celebrities who advocated their cause were as follows:

	SITCOM	CELEBRITY
1	Only Fools and Horses	David Dickinson
2	Blackadder	John Sergeant
3	The Vicar of Dibley	Carol Vorderman
4	Dad's Army	Phill Jupitus
5	Fawlty Towers	Jack Dee
6	Yes, Minister	Armando Iannucci
7	Porridge	Johnny Vaughan
8	Open All Hours	Clarissa Dickson-Wright
9	The Good Life	Ulrika Jonsson
10	One Foot in the Grave	Rowland Rivron

....

Blue Peter Own Goal

In November 1983 viewers of the children's magazine show Blue Peter were shocked to hear that the programme's ornate garden (lovingly tended by Percy Thrower) near Television Centre had been trashed by vandals. Some years later football fans were even more shocked when England striker Les Ferdinand admitted that he'd been part of the teenage gang involved and had helped his mates to scale the fence.

....

TV on TV (Fictitious TV Stations)

TV COMPANY	PROGRAMME
Chanel 9	The Fast Show
Channel 3	Wild Palms
Eagle Television	Hilary
EBC (Emu's Broadcasting Company)	EBC
Globelink	Drop the Dead Donkey
KBBL	The Simpsons
K-MUP TV	Muppets Tonight!
Krankie Television	Krankies Television
KYTV	KYTV
Megalith Television	Jemima Shore Investigates
Network 23	Max Headroom
Outer Hebrides Broadcasting Corporation	Naked Video
PPC TV	Pinky and Perky
WJM-TV	The Mary Tyler Moore Show

Puppets and Their People

PUPPET	HUMAN COMPANION
Fred Barker	Muriel Young, Howard Williams, Wally Whyton
Ollie Beak	Muriel Young, Howard Williams, Wally Whyton
Basil Brush	Howard Williams, David Nixon, Rodney Bewes, Derek Fowlds, Roy North, Billy Boyle, Doug Ridley, Stephen (Christopher Pizzey)
Edd the Duck	Andy Crane, Andi Peters
Emu	Rod Hull
Gordon the Gopher	Phillip Schofield
Muffin the Mule	Annette Mills
Otis the Aardvark	Kirsten O'Brien, Richard McCourt
Pinky and Perky	John Slater, Roger Moffat, Jimmy Thompson, Bryan Burdon, Fred Emney
Pussy Cat Willum	Muriel Young, Wally Whyton
Sooty	Harry Corbett, Matthew Corbett, Richard Cadell
Spit the Dog	Bob Carolgees
Tingha and Tucker	'Auntie' Jean Morton
Tinker	Alan Taylor
Zig and Zag	Ian Dempsey

One Large Audience for Mankind

It is estimated that Apollo XI astronaut Neil Armstrong's first step onto the surface of the moon on 21 July 1969 was watched by a worldwide television audience of 723 million.

The Longest-Running Programmes Still on UK TV*

	PROGRAMME	FIRST BROADCAST
1	Panorama	11 November 1953
2	What the Papers Say	5 November 1956
3	The Sky at Night	24 April 1957
4	Grandstand	11 October 1958
5	Blue Peter	16 October 1958
6	Coronation Street	9 December 1960
7	Survival	1 February 1961
8	Songs of Praise	1 October 1961
9	Top of the Pops	1 January 1964
10	Horizon	2 May 1964

* Programmes continuously on air since their first broadcast, although screenings may be sporadic during each year.

Hullabaloo and Custard

It was a strange move when, in 1964, the BBC decided to promote its innovative, new channel, BBC 2, with two cartoon mascots. The image of a mother kangaroo (Hullabaloo) and her joey (Custard) was hardly in keeping with the largely cultural and educational output of the new network, but perhaps their creator, Desmond Marwood, knew something we didn't. BBC 2's first evening's viewing was wiped out by a power cut in West London with the result that the first proper programme to be screened on the intellectual outpost was the next morning's edition of Play School. Hullabaloo and Custard – who had been chosen to represent the old mother channel and her new offspring – were quickly dropped once David Attenborough took over as the channel's controller in 1965.

From Child Stars to Adult Performers

ACTOR	EARLY ROLE
Holly Aird	The Flame Trees of Thika (Elspeth Grant)
Christopher Beeny	The Grove Family (Lennie Grove)
Todd Carty	Grange Hill (Tucker Jenkins)
Keith Chegwin	The Wackers (Raymond Clarkson)
Charlotte Coleman	Educating Marmalade (Marmalade Atkins)
Mark Curry	Junior Showtime (presenter)
Mickey Dolenz	Circus Boy (Corky, as Mickey Braddock)
Peter Firth	Here Come the Double Deckers (Scooper)
Liza Goddard	Skippy, the Bush Kangaroo (Clancy Merrick)
Ron Howard	The Andy Griffith Show (Opie Taylor)
Bonnie Langford	Just William (Violet Elizabeth Bott)
Nicholas Lyndhurst	Anne of Avonlea (Davy Keith)
Ant McPartlin	Why Don't You...? (presenter)
Richard O'Sullivan	The Adventures of Robin Hood (Prince Arthur)
Pauline Quirke	You Must Be Joking! (presenter)
Dennis Waterman	William (William Brown)

There's No Money In It

'I will earn more from the ice creams I sell in my cinemas than I ever will from commercial TV.'

– Sidney Bernstein, founder of Granada Television

It's a Knockout Around the World

Classical Music Used as TV Theme Tunes

MUSIC	PROGRAMME
Delibes' Sous Le Dome Epais from Lakme	Screaming
Gounod's Funeral March of a Marionette	Alfred Hitchcock Presents
Holst's Mars from The Planet Suite	The Quatermass Experiment
Khachaturyan's Spartacus	The Onedin Line
Mozart's Great Mass in C Minor	A Very British Coup
Mozart's Rondo Horn Concerto No. 4 in E Flat Major	Colin's Sandwich
Prokofiev's Classical Symphony	The Flaxton Boys
Prokofiev's Peter and the Wolf	Zoo Time
Rachmaninov's Rhapsody on a Theme of Paganini	The South Bank Show
Ravel's String Quartet in F	The Camomile Lawn
Respighi's The Birds	Going for a Song
Rossini's The William Tell Overture	The Lone Ranger
Saint-Saens' Carnival of the Animals	A Bit of Fry and Laurie
Saint-Saens' Danse Macabre	Jonathan Creek
Schubert's Piano Quintet in A (Trout Quintet)	Waiting for God
Shostakovich's Prelude Opus 34 No. 15	Ever Decreasing Circles
Shostakovich's Romance	Reilly – Ace of Spies
Sibelius's Karelia Suite	This Week
Sibelius's Pelléas et Mélisande	The Sky at Night
Sousa's Liberty Bell March	Monty Python's Flying Circus
Vaughan Williams' Symphony No. 6 in E Minor	A Family at War

The Blue Peter Pets

Petra	dog*		George	tortoise
Jason	cat		Willow	cat
Patch	dog		Kari and Oke	cats
Freda	tortoise**		Lucy	dog
Shep	dog		Mabel	dog
Jack and Jill	cats		Meg	dog
Goldie	dog		Smudge	cat
Maggie and Jim	tortoises		Shelley	tortoise
Bonnie	dog			

* replacement for original Petra which died after one programme.
** originally thought to be 'Fred' (a male).

....

Soap Heaven

'Manchester produces what to me is the Pickwick Papers. That is to say Coronation Street. Mondays and Wednesdays, I live for them. Thank God, half past seven tonight and I shall be in paradise.'

– Sir John Betjeman

....

A Selection of Del Boy's Hooky Goods

CONSIGNMENT	FOOLS AND HORSES EPISODE
Pre-blessed communion wine	Miami Twice
Airport satellite dish	The Sky's the Limit
Briefcases with the combination locked inside	Big Brother
Broken lawn mower engines	Healthy Competition
Explosive adult dolls	Danger UXD
Faulty computers	The Frog's Legacy
Latvian alarm clocks	Heroes and Villains
Mobile phones that change TV channels	Little Problems
One-legged turkeys	Big Brother
Peckham Spring Water	Mother Nature's Son
Pony tail wigs	Three Men, a Woman and a Baby
A 'Queen Anne' cabinet	Yesterday Never Comes
Russian camcorders	Fatal Extraction
Self-assembly nuclear shelter	The Russians Are Coming
Unfortunately luminous paint	The Yellow Peril

Real Action Series That Led to Cartoon Copies

The Addams Family
The Adventures of Robin Hood (Rocket Robin Hood and His Merry Spacemen)
Batman
The Brady Bunch (The Brady Kids)
Buffy the Vampire Slayer (Buffy the Animated Series)
Dick Tracy (The Dick Tracy Show)
The Dukes of Hazzard (The Dukes)
Flash Gordon (The New Adventures of Flash Gordon)
Gilligan's Island (The New Adventures of Gilligan, Gilligan's Planet)
Happy Days (Fonz and the Happy Days Gang)
I Dream of Jeannie (Jeannie)
Lassie (Lassie's Rescue Rangers)
Laverne and Shirley (Laverne and Shirley in the Army)
The Lone Ranger
M*A*S*H (M*U*S*H)
Mr Bean
Mork and Mindy
My Favorite Martian (My Favorite Martians)
The New Adventures of Charlie Chan (The Amazing Chan and the Chan Clan)
The Odd Couple (The Oddball Couple)
The Partridge Family (The Partridge Family: 2200 AD)
Planet of the Apes (Return to the Planet of the Apes)
Punky Brewster (It's Punky Brewster)
Star Trek
Superman
Tarzan (Tarzan, Lord of the Jungle)
The Three Musketeers
Zorro

. . . .

End of Part One

Television's early flirtation with the British public ended abruptly on 1 September 1939, less than three years after it had started, as the country prepared to go war with Germany. The word was sent that Alexandra Palace had to switch off everything at once, as the transmitter alongside the North London building would have helped German bomber pilots to navigate. So sudden was the announcement that the BBC was even unable to finish broadcasting the Mickey Mouse cartoon on air at the time. The same cartoon – a short called Mickey's Gala Premiere – was used to re-open the channel when broadcasting was allowed to resume after the hostilities on 7 June 1946.

Actors Who Have Played British Prime Ministers on TV

PRIME MINISTER	ACTOR	PROGRAMME
Tony Blair	Steven Pacey	Jeffrey Archer: the Truth (2002)
	Michael Sheen	The Deal (2003)
	James Larkin	The Government Inspector (2005)
John Major	Keith Drinkel	Thatcher: the Final Days (1991)
Margaret Thatcher	Angela Thorne	Anyone for Denis? (1982)
	Sylvia Syms	Thatcher: the Final Days (1991)
		Half the Picture (1996)
	Patricia Hodge	The Falklands Play (2002)
	Greta Scacchi	Jeffrey Archer: the Truth (2002)
Edward Heath	Corin Redgrave	Sunday (2002)
Harold Wilson	Bill Wallis	Mrs Wilson's Diary (1969)
Harold Macmillan	Richard Vernon	Suez 1956 (1979)
	Ian Collier	Winston Churchill – the Wilderness Years (1981)
Anthony Eden	Hugh Fraser	Edward and Mrs Simpson (1978)
	Michael Gough	Suez 1956 (1979)
	Richard Easton	Churchill and the Generals (1979)
	Tony Mathews	Winston Churchill – the Wilderness Years (1981)
	Jack Fortune	Dunkirk (2004)
Clement Attlee	Patrick Stewart	Walk with Destiny (1974)
	Patrick Troughton	Edward and Mrs Simpson (1978)
	Norman Jones	Winston Churchill – the Wilderness Years (1981)
Winston Churchill	Warren Clarke	Jennie, Lady Randolph Churchill (1974)
	Richard Burton	Walk with Destiny (1974)
	Christopher Strauli	Edward the Seventh (1975)
	Wensley Pithey	Edward and Mrs Simpson (1978)
		Suez 1956 (1979)
	Robert Hardy	Winston Churchill – the Wilderness Years (1981)
		The Woman He Loved (1988)
		War and Remembrance (1988–9)
		Bomber Harris (1989)
	Howard Lang	The Winds of War (1983)
	Malcolm Terris	Mountbatten (1986)
	Bob Hoskins	World War II: When Lions Roared (1994)
	Albert Finney	The Gathering Storm (2002)
	Graham Walker	Churchill (2003)

Neville Chamberlain	Robin Bailey	Walk with Destiny (1974)
	Eric Porter	Winston Churchill – the Wilderness Years (1981)
	Christopher Good	Dunkirk (2004)
Stanley Baldwin	David Waller	Edward and Mrs Simpson (1978) The Woman He Loved (1988)
	Thorley Walters	Walk with Destiny (1974)
	Nigel Stock	A Man Called Intrepid (1979)
	Timothy West	Churchill and the Generals (1979)
	Peter Barkworth	Winston Churchill – the Wilderness Years (1981)
	Hugh Simon	Mosley (1998)
	Derek Jacobi	The Gathering Storm (2002)
	David Ryall	Bertie and Elizabeth (2002)
	Simon Russell Beale	Dunkirk (2004)
James Ramsey MacDonald	Robert James	Winston Churchill – the Wilderness Years (1981)
	Ian Richardson	Number 10 (1982)
	Ralph Riach	Mosley (1998)
David Lloyd George	Anthony Hopkins	The Edwardians (1973)
	Philip Madoc	The Life and Times of David Lloyd George (1981)
	John Stride	Number 10 (1982)
	Windsor Davies	Mosley (1998)
	Ron Cook	The Lost Prince (2003)
Herbert Asquith	Basil Dignam	Edward the Seventh (1975)
	David Markham	The Life and Times of David Lloyd George (1981)
	David Langton	Number 10 (1982)
	Frank Finlay	The Lost Prince (2003)
Henry Campbell-Bannerman	Geoffrey Bayldon	Edward the Seventh (1975)
Arthur Balfour	Adrian Ropes	Jennie, Lady Randolph Churchill (1974)
William Gladstone	Michael Hordern	Edward the Seventh (1975)
	Roland Culver	The Life and Times of David Lloyd George (1981)
	Denis Quilley	Number 10 (1982)
Benjamin Disraeli	John Gielgud	Edward the Seventh (1975)
	Ian McShane	Disraeli (1978)
	Richard Pasco	Number 10 (1982)
William Pitt the Younger	Jeremy Brett	Number 10 (1982)

The Lucrative Worst

'Because television can make so much money doing its worst, it often cannot afford to do its best.'

– Fred W Friendly, on his resignation as President of CBS News in 1966, when CBS screened a repeat of *I Love Lucy* instead of live coverage of a Senate investigation into the USA's involvement in Vietnam

Television Pubs and Bars

PROGRAMME	PUB/BAR/CLUB
Albion Market	The Waterman's Arms
All Creatures Great and Small	The Drovers
'Allo 'Allo	Café René
Ballykissangel	Fitzgerald's
Best of the West	Square Deal Saloon
Big Deal	The Dragon Club
Bless This House	The Hare and Hounds
Bootsie and Snudge	The Imperial
Born and Bred	The Signalman's Arms
Brookside	The Swan, Bar Brookie
Brush Strokes	The White Hart, Elmo Putney's Wine Bar
Buffy the Vampire Slayer	The Bronze
Cheers	Cheers
Citizen Smith	The Vigilante
Coronation Street	Rover's Return
Dead Man Weds	The Douglas Bader
Early Doors	The Grapes
EastEnders	The Queen Victoria, The Dagmar, e20, Angie's Den
Emmerdale	The Woolpack
Gangsters	The Maverick
Give Us a Break	The Crown and Sceptre
Goodnight Sweetheart	The Royal Oak
Gunsmoke	Longbranch Saloon
Heartbeat	The Aidensfield Arms
Hollyoaks	The Dog in the Pond
I Love Lucy	The Tropicana Club, The Babaloo Club
I'm Alan Partridge	The Linton Travel Tavern
The Life and Legend of Wyatt Earp	Birdcage Saloon
The Lotus Eaters	Shepherd's Bar
Love Thy Neighbour	Jubilee Social Club

McCready and Daughter	Hogan's Pub
M*A*S*H	Rosie's Bar
Men Behaving Badly	The Crown
Mickey Spillane's Mike Hammer	Light 'n' Easy Bar
Minder	The Winchester Club
Neighbours	The Waterhole, Chez Chez, Lou's Place, The Pub
The Newcomers	The Bull, The Crown
Newhart	The Stratford
Northern Exposure	The Brick
Not on Your Nellie	The Brown Cow
Oh No It's Selwyn Froggitt	Scarsdale Workingmen's Club and Institute
Only Fools and Horses	The Nag's Head
'Orrible	The Fox and Hounds
Peter Kay's Phoenix Nights	The Phoenix Club
Pobol y Cwm	The Deri Arms
Roseanne	The Lobo Lounge
The Royle Family	The Feathers
Rumpole of the Bailey	Pomeroy's Wine Bar
Second Thoughts	Harpo's Wine Bar
Secret Army	Le Candide
The Simpsons	Moe's Tavern
Steptoe and Son	The Skinner's Arms
Time Gentlemen Please	The Cowshed
Trainer	The Dog and Gun
Turtle's Progress	The Robin Hood
Two Pints of Lager and a Packet of Crisps	Archer Hotel
Up the Elephant and Round the Castle	The Freemasons Arms
Watching	The Grapes
Where the Heart Is	The Skelthwaite Arms

....

Jump the Shark

On the back of the popularity of a website of the same name, the term 'jump the shark' has become associated with TV series (particularly American) that have passed their peak. The moment when the series 'jumps the shark' is when it starts to go downhill. The origin of this odd phrase is an episode of the long-running sitcom Happy Days, in which Fonzie (Henry Winkler) accepts a challenge to waterski-leap over a shark – a sign, it was claimed, that the programme was struggling for inspiration and had seen considerably happier days.

Famous Voices Behind Animated Characters

CHARACTER	VOICE
Andy Pandy (remake)	Tom Conti
Bananaman	The Goodies
Barbapapa	Michael Flanders
Bear (Teletubbies)	Penelope Keith
Mr Benn	Ray Brooks
Bill (Bill and Ben remake)	John Thomson
Bob the Builder	Neil Morrissey
Bod	John Le Mesurier
Boot (The Perishers)	Leonard Rossiter
Harry Boyle (Wait Till Your Father Gets Home)	Tom Bosley
Bump	Simon Cadell
Chef (South Park)	Isaac Hayes
Dangermouse	David Jason
Duckman	Jason Alexander
Engie Benjy	Dec Donnelly
Fireman Sam	John Alderton
King Rollo	Ray Brooks
Kipper	Martin Clunes
Lion (Teletubbies)	Eric Sykes
The Lone Ranger	William Conrad
Maisy	Neil Morrissey
Mary, Mungo and Midge	Richard Baker
Prof. Ian McLaine (Joe 90)	Rupert Davies
Mermaid Man (Spongebob Squarepants)	Ernest Borgnine
The Mr Men	Arthur Lowe
Noah and Nelly	Richard Briers
Paddington	Michael Hordern
Penfold (Dangermouse)	Terry Scott
Roobarb	Richard Briers
Captain Scarlet	Francis Matthews
Sideshow Bob (The Simpsons)	Kelsey Grammer
Maggie Simpson (The Simpsons)	Elizabeth Taylor
Spot	Paul Nicholas
Superted	Derek Griffiths
Thomas the Tank Engine	Ringo Starr, Michael Angelis
Sheriff Tex Tucker (Four Feather Falls)	Nicholas Parsons
Wallace and Gromit	Peter Sallis
Willo the Wisp	Kenneth Williams
The Wombles	Bernard Cribbins

Who Does What in a TV Drama Crew

CREW MEMBER	ROLE
Art director	Puts into practice the thoughts of the Designer, handling colour schemes, set designs and more
Associate producer	The Producer's number two and stand-in on set
Best boy	Second-in-command to the Gaffer or Grip
Casting director	Makes initial selection of actors for the various roles and deals with actors' contracts
Composer	Writes the theme and/or incidental music
Costume designer	Establishes the style of dress for the characters
Designer	Conceives the feel, style and texture of the production
Director	Supervises the filming, organising the actors and film crew
Director of Photography	Chief cameraman, also responsible for lighting each scene
Editor	Edits the pictures, sound and music, putting scenes in running order
Executive producer	Top of the tree, but may be supervising more than one programme at a time and therefore less hands-on
First assistant director	The Director's number two, organising the shoot
Gaffer	Chief electrician
Grip	Set manager, ensuring equipment and props are in order
Location manager	Finds places where scenes can be shot and negotiates their use
Make up artist	Applies make up to the performers
Make up designer	Sets out the make up style for the production
Producer	Takes a programme from concept to production, handling the budget and pulling together the crew
Props buyer	Acquires items to furnish the set
Script editor	Works with the Writer to ensure style and continuity are maintained
Script supervisor	Keeps a record of all scenes shot
Sound recordist	Handles all aspects of recording dialogue and effects
Stunt co-ordinator	Arranges the safe shooting of falls, crashes and other dangerous incidents
Wardrobe supervisor	Supplies the garments worn by actors
Writer	Provides the script

Additionally, second and third assistant directors look after actors, props and anything else that arises, with runners and drivers assisting with logistics.

Chronology of Major UK TV Programmes

Match of the Day (22 August)
The Wednesday Play (28 October)
Crossroads (2 November)

1965 Tomorrow's World (7 July)
Thunderbirds (2 October)
Call My Bluff (17 October)
The Magic Roundabout (18 October)
Jackanory (13 December)

1966 Till Death Us Do Part (6 June)
It's a Knockout (7 August)

1967 The Forsyte Saga (7 January)
The Prisoner (29 September)

1968 Dad's Army (31 July)

1969 Holiday (2 January)
Civilisation (23 February)
On the Buses (28 February)
Nationwide (9 September)
Monty Python's Flying Circus (5 October)

1970 The Six Wives of Henry VIII (1 January)
A Question of Sport (5 January)

1971 The Two Ronnies (10 April)
Parkinson (19 June)
The Generation Game (2 October)
Upstairs, Downstairs (10 October)

1972 Newsround (4 April)
Mastermind (11 September)
Emmerdale (16 October)

1973 Last of the Summer Wine (4 January)
That's Life (26 May)

1974 Rising Damp (2 September)
Porridge (5 September)

1975 The Sweeney (2 January)
The Good Life (5 April)
Jim'll Fix It (31 May)
Fawlty Towers (19 September)
Poldark (5 October)

1976 Open All Hours (20 February)
The Fall and Rise of Reginald Perrin (8 September)
I, Claudius (20 September)
Multi-Coloured Swap Shop (2 October)

1978 Grange Hill (8 February)

CURIOUS FACT

Comedian
Steve Coogan was
once a regular on
The Krypton
Factor, acting in a
series of playlets

Chronology of Major UK TV Programmes

YEAR	PROGRAMME (DATE OF FIRST UK BROADCAST)
1979	Life on Earth (16 January)
	Antiques Roadshow (18 February)
	Question Time (25 September)
	Not the Nine O'Clock News (16 October)
	Minder (29 October)
1980	Newsnight (30 January)
	Yes Minister (25 February)
1981	Only Fools and Horses (8 September)
	Brideshead Revisited (12 October)
1982	The Boys from the Blackstuff (10 October)
	Brookside (2 November)
	The Young Ones (9 November)
1983	Breakfast Time (17 January)
	Blackadder (15 June)
	Taggart (6 September)
	Auf Wiedersehen, Pet (11 November)
1984	The Bill (16 October)
1985	EastEnders (19 February)
1986	Casualty (6 September)
	The Singing Detective (16 November)
1987	Inspector Morse (6 January)
1988	London's Burning (2 February)
1989	Agatha Christie's Poirot (8 January)
1990	One Foot in the Grave (4 January)
	Have I Got News for You (28 September)
1991	The Darling Buds of May (7 April)
	Prime Suspect (7 April)
1992	Heartbeat (10 April)
	The Big Breakfast (28 September)
	Absolutely Fabulous (12 November)
	A Touch of Frost (6 December)
1994	The Fast Show (27 September)
1995	Father Ted (21 April)
1997	Midsomer Murders (23 March)
1998	The Royle Family (14 September)
2000	Big Brother (18 July)
2001	The Office (9 July)
	Pop Idol (6 October)
2003	Little Britain (1 December)

The Great Britons

In 2002 the BBC organised a national poll of the greatest ever Britons. The ten shortlisted candidates (in final finishing order) and the celebrities who championed their cause were as follows:

	BRITON	CELEBRITY
1	Winston Churchill	Mo Mowlam
2	Isambard Kingdom Brunel	Jeremy Clarkson
3	Princess Diana	Rosie Boycott
4	Charles Darwin	Andrew Marr
5	William Shakespeare	Fiona Shaw
6	Isaac Newton	Tristram Hunt
7	Queen Elizabeth I	Michael Portillo
8	John Lennon	Alan Davies
9	Horatio Nelson	Lucy Young
10	Oliver Cromwell	Richard Holmes

The other 90 people in the top 100 chosen by viewers were (alphabetically):

Alfred the Great, Julie Andrews, King Arthur, David Attenborough, Jane Austen; Charles Babbage, Lord Baden-Powell, Douglas Bader, John Logie Baird, David Beckham, Alexander Graham Bell, Tony Benn, Tim Berners-Lee, Aneurin Bevan, Tony Blair, William Blake, William Booth, Boudicca, David Bowie, Richard Branson, Robert the Bruce, Richard Burton;

Donald Campbell, William Caxton, Charlie Chaplin, Geoffrey Chaucer, Leonard Cheshire, James Connolly, Captain James Cook, Michael Crawford, Aleister Crowley; Charles Dickens, Francis Drake; King Edward I, Edward Elgar, Queen Elizabeth II, Queen Elizabeth, the Queen Mother; Michael Faraday, Guy Fawkes, Alexander Fleming; Bob Geldof, Owain Glyndwr; George Harrison, John Harrison, Stephen Hawking, King Henry II, King Henry V, King Henry VIII, Paul Hewson (Bono); Edward Jenner; TE Lawrence, David Livingstone, David Lloyd-George, John Lydon (Johnny Rotten);

James Clerk Maxwell, Paul McCartney, Freddie Mercury, Field Marshall Bernard Montgomery, Bobby Moore, Thomas More, Eric Morecambe; Florence Nightingale; George O'Dowd (Boy George); Thomas Paine, Emmeline Pankhurst, John Peel, Enoch Powell; Walter Raleigh, Steve Redgrave, King Richard III, Cliff Richard, JK Rowling;

Robert Falcon Scott, Ernest Shackleton, George Stephenson, Marie Stopes; Margaret Thatcher, William Tindale, JRR Tolkien, Alan Turing; The Unknown Soldier; Queen Victoria; William Wallace, Barnes Wallis, James Watt, Duke of Wellington, John Wesley, Frank Whittle, William Wilberforce, Robbie Williams.

First Inductees to the Television Halls of Fame

Each year in America the Academy of Television Arts and Sciences honours up to seven people for their services to the medium with a place in its Hall of Fame. The citation is for 'persons who have made outstanding contributions in the arts, sciences or management of television, based upon either cumulative contributions and achievements or a singular contribution or achievement.' The first inductees, in 1984, were:

Lucille Ball (comedian and sitcom star)
Milton Berle (comedian and variety show host)
Paddy Chayefsky (dramatist)
Norman Lear (comedy producer)
Edward R Murrow (journalist)
William S Paley (CBS supremo)
David Sarnoff (NBC supremo)

In the UK the Royal Television Society inaugurated its own Hall of Fame in 1993 'to honour individuals who have made an unrivalled contribution over many years to the television industry – individuals who have brought to our screens their special talent, adding hugely to the delight of the audience.' The first inductees were:

Thora Hird (actress)
Lord Grade (ATV supremo)
Alan Whicker (journalist)
Jack Rosenthal (dramatist)

....

Regional Listings

In the early days of ITV a number of regional broadcasters preferred to publish their own TV listings magazines, rather than a regional edition of TV Times. The fragmentation was ended with the 1968 franchise renewal, which insisted that a single national ITV listings magazine, with regional variations, but jointly owned by the ITV companies, be published.

CONTRACTOR	PUBLICATION
ATV	TV World
Channel	The Channel Viewer*
Scottish	The Viewer
TWW	Television Weekly
Tyne Tees	The Viewer
Ulster	TV Post
Wales West and North	Wales TV and Teledu Cymru
Westward	Look Westward

* Allowed to continue after 1968 because of its important revenue for the small company.

Some Early Titles Reputedly Suggested for Monty Python's Flying Circus

Arthur Megapode's Cheap Show
Cynthia Fellatio's Flying Circus
The Full Moon Show
Gwen Dibley's Flying Circus
A Horse, a Spoon and a Basin
It's Them!
The Laughing Zoo
The Nose Show
Ow! It's Colin Plint
Owl-Stretching Time
The Plastic Mac Show
Sex and Violence
Vaseline Review
The Whizzo Easishow
The Year of the Stoat

Docu-soap Narrators

SERIES	NARRATOR(S)
A Life of Grime (environmental health)	John Peel
Airline (Britannia/easyJet)	Tony Robinson
Airport (Heathrow)	John Nettles. Liza Tarbuck
Animals in Uniform (armed forces animals)	Sandi Toksvig
Dover (port)	Stephen Tompkinson
Driving School (learner drivers)	Quentin Willson
Guns and Roses (female army recruits)	Amanda Redman
Holiday Reps (Unijet couriers)	Susan Tully
Hotel (Adelphi, Liverpool)	Andrew Sachs
Lakesiders (shopping mall)	Pauline Quirke
Love Town (Gretna)	Alison Steadman
Mersey Blues (police)	Andrew Lincoln
Molly's Zoo (Twycross)	Griff Rhys Jones
Motorway Life (M6)	Christopher Eccleston
Muscle (security guards)	Neil Pearson
Paddington Green (London district)	Ross Kemp, Todd Carty
Pleasure Beach (Blackpool funfair)	Nick Hancock
Superstore (Tesco)	Jim Broadbent
The Paras (recruit training)	Glyn Worsnip
The Zoo Keepers (Paignton)	Richard Wilson, Nick Hancock
Vets' School (trainee vets)	Christopher Timothy

The Detectives' Casefile

DETECTIVE **Insp. Roderick Alleyn**
SERIES The Inspector Alleyn Mysteries
STAR Patrick Malahide
CREATOR Ngaio Marsh
SIDEKICK Insp. Fox
BEAT London

DETECTIVE **Thomas Banacek**
SERIES Banacek
STAR George Peppard
CREATOR Anthony Wilson
SIDEKICK Jay Drury
BEAT Boston

DETECTIVE **Insp. Tom Barnaby**
SERIES Midsomer Murders
STAR John Nettles
CREATOR Caroline Graham
SIDEKICKS DS Troy, DS Scott
BEAT Midsomer

DETECTIVE **DS Jim Bergerac**
SERIES Bergerac
STAR John Nettles
CREATOR Robert Banks Stewart
SIDEKICK Charlie Hungerford
BEAT Jersey

DETECTIVE **Sexton Blake**
SERIES Sexton Blake
STAR Laurence Payne
CREATOR Harry Blyth
SIDEKICK Tinker
BEAT London

DETECTIVE **Father Brown**
SERIES Father Brown
STAR Kenneth More
CREATOR GK Chesterton
SIDEKICK Flambeau
BEAT East Anglia

DETECTIVE **George Bulman**
SERIES Bulman
STAR Don Henderson
CREATOR Kenneth Royce
SIDEKICK Lucy McGinty
BEAT London

DETECTIVE **Capt. Amos Burke**
SERIES Burke's Law
STAR Gene Barry
CREATORS Ivan Goff,
Ben Roberts
SIDEKICK Tim Tilson
BEAT Los Angeles

DETECTIVE **Cadfael**
SERIES Cadfael
STAR Derek Jacobi
CREATOR Ellis Peters
SIDEKICK n/a
BEAT Shrewsbury

DETECTIVE **Det. Christine Cagney**
SERIES Cagney and Lacey
STARS Meg Foster,
Sharon Gless
CREATORS Barney Rosenzweig,
Barbara Avedon,
Barbara Corday
SIDEKICK Mary-Beth Lacey
BEAT New York

DETECTIVE **Albert Campion**
SERIES Campion
STAR Peter Davison
CREATOR Margery Allingham
SIDEKICK Lugg
BEAT East Anglia

DETECTIVE **Frank Cannon**
SERIES Cannon
STAR William Conrad
CREATOR Quinn Martin
SIDEKICK n/a
BEAT Los Angeles

DETECTIVE **DS Caleb Cluff**
SERIES Cluff
STAR Leslie Sands
CREATOR Gil North
SIDEKICK Insp. Mole
BEAT Gunnershaw

DETECTIVE	**Lt Columbo**
SERIES	Columbo
STAR	Peter Falk
CREATORS	Richard Levinson, William Link
SIDEKICK	n/a
BEAT	Los Angeles

DETECTIVE	**Sgt Cork**
SERIES	Sergeant Cork
STAR	John Barrie
CREATOR	Ted Willis
SIDEKICK	Bob Marriott
BEAT	London

DETECTIVE	**Jonathan Creek**
SERIES	Jonathan Creek
STAR	Alan Davies
CREATOR	David Renwick
SIDEKICKS	Maddy Magellan, Carla Borrego
BEAT	East Anglia

DETECTIVE	**Sgt Cribb**
SERIES	Cribb
STAR	Alan Dobie
CREATOR	Peter Lovesey
SIDEKICK	Const. Thackeray
BEAT	London

DETECTIVE	**Det. Sonny Crockett**
SERIES	Miami Vice
STAR	Don Johnson
CREATORS	Michael Mann, Anthony Yerkovich
SIDEKICK	Det. Tubbs
BEAT	Miami

DETECTIVE	**Chief Supt Adam Dalgliesh**
SERIES	Titles vary
STARS	Roy Marsden, Martin Shaw
CREATOR	PD James
SIDEKICK	Insp. Massingham
BEAT	Norfolk

DETECTIVE	**DS Andy Dalziel**
SERIES	Dalziel and Pascoe
STAR	Warren Clarke
CREATOR	Reginald Hill
SIDEKICK	Peter Pascoe
BEAT	Wetherton

DETECTIVE	**Dangerous Davies**
SERIES	The Last Detective
STAR	Peter Davison
CREATOR	Leslie Thomas
SIDEKICK	Mod Lewis
BEAT	London

DETECTIVE	**PC George Dixon**
SERIES	Dixon of Dock Green
STAR	Jack Warner
CREATOR	Ted Willis
SIDEKICK	PC Andy Crawford
BEAT	London

DETECTIVE	**Father Dowling**
SERIES	Father Dowling Investigates
STAR	Tom Bosley
CREATORS	Ralph McInnery, Dean Hargrove, Joel Steiner
SIDEKICK	Sister Steve
BEAT	Chicago

DETECTIVE	**Jessica Fletcher**
SERIES	Murder, She Wrote
STAR	Angela Lansbury
CREATORS	Richard Levinson, William Link, Peter S Fischer
SIDEKICK	Sgt Tupper
BEAT	Cabot Cove

DETECTIVE	**DCS Christopher Foyle**
SERIES	Foyle's War
STAR	Michael Kitchen
CREATOR	Anthony Horowitz
SIDEKICKS	DS Milner, Samantha Stewart
BEAT	Hastings

DETECTIVE	**Sgt Joe Friday**
SERIES	Dragnet
STAR	Jack Webb
CREATOR	Jack Webb
SIDEKICK	Officer Smith
BEAT	Los Angeles

DETECTIVE	**DI Jack Frost**
SERIES	A Touch of Frost
STAR	David Jason
CREATOR	RD Wingfield
SIDEKICK	George Toolan
BEAT	Denton

DETECTIVE	**Mike Hammer**		DETECTIVE	**Jason King**
SERIES	Mike Hammer		SERIES	Jason King
STAR	Stacy Keach		STAR	Peter Wyngarde
CREATOR	Mickey Spillane		CREATORS	Dennis Spooner, Monty Berman
SIDEKICK	Capt. Chambers		SIDEKICK	Nicola Harvester
BEAT	New York		BEAT	London

DETECTIVE	**Jonathan Hart**		DETECTIVE	**Lt. Theo Kojak**
SERIES	Hart to Hart		SERIES	Kojak
STAR	Robert Wagner		STAR	Telly Savalas
CREATOR	Sidney Sheldon		CREATOR	Abby Mann
SIDEKICK	Jennifer Hart		SIDEKICK	Lt Crocker
BEAT	Bel-Air		BEAT	New York

DETECTIVE	**Maddie Hayes**		DETECTIVE	**Mike Longstreet**
SERIES	Moonlighting		SERIES	Longstreet
STAR	Cybill Shepherd		STAR	James Franciscus
CREATOR	Glenn Gordon Caron		CREATOR	Stirling Silliphant
SIDEKICK	David Addison		SIDEKICK	Nikki Bell
BEAT	Los Angeles		BEAT	Louisiana

DETECTIVE	**James Hazell**		DETECTIVE	**Insp. Thomas Lynley**
SERIES	Hazell		SERIES	The Inspector Lynley Mysteries
STAR	Nicholas Ball		STAR	Nathaniel Parker
CREATORS	Terry Venables, Gordon Williams		CREATOR	Elizabeth George
SIDEKICK	'Choc' Minty		SIDEKICK	DS Havers
BEAT	London		BEAT	London

DETECTIVE	**Sherlock Holmes**		DETECTIVE	**PC Hamish Macbeth**
SERIES	Titles vary		SERIES	Hamish Macbeth
STARS	Douglas Wilmer,		STAR	Robert Carlyle
	Peter Cushing, Jeremy Brett		CREATOR	MC Beaton
CREATOR	Sir Arthur Conan Doyle		SIDEKICK	Wee Jock (dog)
SIDEKICK	Dr Watson		BEAT	Lochdubh
BEAT	London			

			DETECTIVE	**JL 'Fatman' McCabe**
			SERIES	Jake and the Fatman
DETECTIVE	**Marty Hopkirk**		STAR	William Conrad
SERIES	Randall and Hopkirk (Deceased)		CREATORS	Dean Hargrove,
STAR	Kenneth Cope			Joel Steiner
CREATOR	Dennis Spooner		SIDEKICK	Jake Styles
SIDEKICK	Jeff Randall		BEAT	California/Hawaii
BEAT	London			

DETECTIVE	**Chief Robert Ironside**		DETECTIVE	**Dr Iain McCallum**
SERIES	A Man Called Ironside		SERIES	McCallum
STAR	Raymond Burr		STAR	John Hannah
CREATOR	Collier Young		CREATOR	Stuart Hepburn
SIDEKICK	Mark Sanger		SIDEKICK	Dr Angela Moloney
BEAT	San Francisco		BEAT	London

DETECTIVE	**Dep. Marshal Sam McCloud**
SERIES	McCloud
STAR	Dennis Weaver
CREATOR	Glen A Larson
SIDEKICK	Sgt Broadhurst
BEAT	New York

DETECTIVE	**Det. Steve McGarrett**
SERIES	Hawaii Five-O
STAR	Jack Lord
CREATOR	Leonard Freeman
SIDEKICK	Danny Williams
BEAT	Honolulu

DETECTIVE	**Comm. Stewart McMillan**
SERIES	McMillan and Wife
STAR	Rock Hudson
CREATOR	Leonard B Stern
SIDEKICK	Sally McMillan (wife)
BEAT	San Francisco

DETECTIVE	**Thomas Magnum**
SERIES	Magnum, PI
STAR	Tom Selleck
creators	Donald P Bellisario,
	Glen A Larson
SIDEKICKS	TC Calvin, Rick Wright
BEAT	Hawaii

DETECTIVE	**Chief Insp. Maigret**
SERIES	Maigret
STARS	Rupert Davies, Michael Gambon
CREATOR	Georges Simenon
SIDEKICK	Lucas
BEAT	Paris

DETECTIVE	**Joe Mannix**
SERIES	Mannix
STARS	Mike Connors
CREATOR	Richard Levinson, William Link
SIDEKICK	Peggy Fair
BEAT	Los Angeles

DETECTIVE	**Col. Perceval March**
SERIES	Colonel March of Scotland Yard
STAR	Boris Karloff
CREATOR	Carter Dickson
SIDEKICK	Insp. Ames
BEAT	London

DETECTIVE	**Miss Jane Marple**
SERIES	Miss Marple, Agatha Christie's
	Marple
STARS	Joan Hickson, Geraldine McEwan
CREATOR	Agatha Christie
SIDEKICK	n/a
BEAT	St Mary Mead

DETECTIVE	**Insp. Endeavour Morse**
SERIES	Inspector Morse
STAR	John Thaw
CREATOR	Colin Dexter
SIDEKICK	DS Lewis
BEAT	Oxford

DETECTIVE	**Harry Orwell**
SERIES	Harry O
STAR	David Janssen
CREATOR	Howard Rodman
SIDEKICK	Lt Quinlan
BEAT	San Diego/Santa Monica

DETECTIVE	**Hercule Poirot**
SERIES	Agatha Christie's Poirot
STAR	David Suchet
CREATOR	Agatha Christie
SIDEKICK	Capt. Hastings
BEAT	London

DETECTIVE	**Quincy**
SERIES	Quincy, ME
STAR	Jack Klugman
CREATORS	Glen A Larson, Lou Shaw
SIDEKICK	Sam Fujiyama
BEAT	Los Angeles

DETECTIVE	**DI John Rebus**
SERIES	Rebus
STAR	John Hannah
CREATOR	Ian Rankin
SIDEKICK	Jack Morton
BEAT	Edinburgh

DETECTIVE	**DI Charlie Resnick**
SERIES	Resnick
STAR	Tom Wilkinson
CREATOR	John Harvey
SIDEKICK	DS Millington
BEAT	Nottingham

DETECTIVE	**Jim Rockford**		DETECTIVE	**DCI Jim Taggart**
SERIES	The Rockford Files		SERIES	Taggart
STAR	James Garner		STAR	Mark McManus
CREATORS	Roy Huggins, Stephen J Cannell		CREATOR	Glenn Chandler
			SIDEKICKS	DS Livingstone, DS Jardin
SIDEKICK	Rocky Rockford			
BEAT	Los Angeles		BEAT	Glasgow

DETECTIVE	**PC Nick Rowan**		DETECTIVE	**Paul Temple**
SERIES	Heartbeat		SERIES	Paul Temple
STAR	Nick Berry		STAR	Francis Matthews
CREATOR	Nicholas Rhea		CREATOR	Francis Durbridge
SIDEKICK	PC Phil Bellamy		SIDEKICK	Steve Temple
BEAT	Aidensfield		BEAT	London

DETECTIVE	**Mark Saber**		DETECTIVE	**Comm. Piet Van der Valk**
SERIES	Mark Saber		SERIES	Van der Valk
STAR	Donald Gray		STAR	Barry Foster
CREATOR	Danziger Brothers		CREATOR	Nicholas Freeling
SIDEKICK	Barny O'Keefe		SIDEKICK	Kroon
BEAT	London		BEAT	Amsterdam

DETECTIVE	**Eddie Shoestring**		DETECTIVE	**Hetty Wainthropp**
SERIES	Shoestring		SERIES	Hetty Wainthropp Investigates
STAR	Trevor Eve		STAR	Patricia Routledge
CREATOR	Robert Banks Stewart		CREATOR	David Cook
SIDEKICK	Erica Bayliss		SIDEKICK	Geoffrey Shawcross
BEAT	Bristol		BEAT	Lancashire

DETECTIVE	**DS Spender**		DETECTIVE	**Insp. Reg Wexford**
SERIES	Spender		SERIES	The Ruth Rendell Mysteries
STAR	Jimmy Nail		STAR	George Baker
CREATORS	Jimmy Nail, Ian La Frenais		CREATOR	Ruth Rendell
SIDEKICK	Stick		SIDEKICK	DI Burden
BEAT	Newcastle		BEAT	Kingsmarkham

DETECTIVE	**Det. Dave Starsky**		DETECTIVE	**Lord Peter Wimsey**
SERIES	Starsky and Hutch		SERIES	Lord Peter Wimsey
STAR	Paul Michael Glaser		STAR	Ian Carmichael
CREATOR	William Blinn		CREATOR	Dorothy L Sayers
SIDEKICK	Ken Hutchinson		SIDEKICK	Bunter
BEAT	Los Angeles		BEAT	London

DETECTIVE	**Det. Lt. Mike Stone**		DETECTIVE	**DS Charles Wycliffe**
SERIES	The Streets of San Francisco		SERIES	Wycliffe
STAR	Karl Malden		STAR	Jack Shepherd
CREATOR	Carolyn Weston		CREATOR	WJ Burley
SIDEKICK	Steve Keller		SIDEKICK	DI Lucy Lane
BEAT	San Francisco		BEAT	Cornwall

Sitcoms and Society

'It doesn't help matters when prime time TV has Murphy Brown – a character who supposedly epitomizes today's intelligent, highly paid, professional woman – mocking the importance of a father, by bearing a child alone, and calling it just another "lifestyle choice".'

– US Vice-President Dan Quayle in a 1992 speech about family values

'We need a nation closer to the Waltons than the Simpsons.' – President George Bush (Snr) in a 1992 speech on family values

....

Celebrities Who Have Played Themselves in The Simpsons

Aerosmith	Mel Gibson	Rupert Murdoch
Andre Agassi	Elliott Gould	Bob Newhart
Buzz Aldrin	George Harrison	Paul Newman
Paul Anka	Stephen Hawking	Leonard Nimoy
Neil Armstrong	Hugh Hefner	Dolly Parton
The B-52s	Larry Holmes	Matthew Perry
Alec Baldwin	Bob Hope	Tom Petty
Kim Basinger	Ron Howard	Red Hot Chili Peppers
Tony Bennett	Mick Jagger	Keith Richard
Tony Blair	Elton John	Linda Ronstadt
Ernest Borgnine	Magic Johnson	Mickey Rooney
Mel Brooks	Tom Jones	Isabella Rossellini
Pierce Brosnan	Larry King	Pete Sampras
Jackson Brown	Stephen King	Brooke Shields
James Brown	Lenny Kravitz	Britney Spears
Steve Buscemi	Cyndi Lauper	Jerry Springer
James Caan	Lucy Lawless	Ringo Starr
Johnny Carson	Jay Leno	Sting
Dick Cavett	Little Richard	Elizabeth Taylor
Elvis Costello	Paul and Linda	James Taylor
David Crosby	McCartney	Justin Timberlake
Peter Frampton	Ian McKellen	U2
Joe Frazier	Bette Midler	Adam West
Richard Gere	The Moody Blues	Barry White

Reality TV Winners

BIG BROTHER	CELEBRITY BIG BROTHER	I'M A CELEBRITY ...
Craig Phillips	Jack Dee	Tony Blackburn
Brian Dowling	Mark Owen	Phil Tufnell
Kate Lawler	Bez (Mark Berry)	Kerry McFadden
Cameron Stout		Joe Pasquale
Nadia Almada		

SURVIVOR
Charlotte Hobrough
Jonny Gibb

THE X FACTOR
Steve Brookstein

POP STARS
Kym Marsh, Myleene Klass,
Suzanne Shaw, Noel Sullivan, Danny Foster
(Hear'Say)

POP STARS: THE RIVALS

Jamie Shaw, Keith Semple,	Nadine Coyle, Sarah Harding,
Daniel Pearce,	Nicola Roberts, Cheryl Tweedy,
Matthew Johnson, Anton Gordon	Kimberly Walsh
(One True Voice)	(Girls Aloud)

POP IDOL	FAME ACADEMY	CELEBRITY FAME ACADEMY
Will Young	David Sneddon	Will Mellor
Michelle McManus	Alex Parks	Edith Bowman

....

The Blackadder Timeline

SERIES	ERA
The Black Adder	15th century (Wars of the Roses)
Blackadder II	16th century (Elizabethan England)
Blackadder the Third	18th–19th century (Georgian age)
Blackadder Goes Forth	20th century (World War I)

Apart from the above series, there were also Blackadder specials:

Blackadder the Cavalier Years*	17th century (Civil War)
Blackadder's Christmas Carol	19th century (Victorian times)
Blackadder Back and Forth**	Various eras

* For Comic Relief.
** For the Millennium Dome.

Prolific TV Theme Composers and Their Best Known Works

SIMON MAY
Castaway 2000
Don't Try This at Home
EastEnders
Eldorado
Food and Drink
Great Estates
Holiday
Howards' Way
Lakesiders
Paramedics
Pet Rescue
The Russ Abbot Show
Trainer
The Vet

MIKE POST
The A-Team
Blossom
CHiPS
Hardcastle and McCormick
Hill Street Blues
Hooperman
Hunter
LA Law
Law and Order
Magnum, PI
Murder One
NYPD Blue
Quantum Leap
Rockford Files

TONY HATCH
Airline
Backs to the Land
The Champions
Codename
Crossroads
The Doctors
Emmerdale Farm
Hadleigh
Man Alive
Mr and Mrs
Neighbours
Quizball
Sportsnight
Who-Dun-It?

RON GRAINER
Comedy Playhouse
Doctor Who
Edward and Mrs Simpson
For the Love of Ada
Maigret
Man in a Suitcase
Paul Temple
The Prisoner
Shelley
South Riding
Steptoe and Son
Tales of the Unexpected
That Was the Week That Was
The Train Now Standing

....

TV's First Quiz Millionaire

The first programme to give away a £1 million cash prize was Channel 4's TFI Friday. The tea-time music and chat show, hosted by Chris Evans, ran a quiz called Someone's Going to be a Millionaire, resulting in contestant Ian Woodley claiming the big money on 24 December 1999, 11 months before Who Wants to Be a Millionaire? first dished out its top prize.

Products Promoted in Commercials by TV Personalities

TV PERSONALITY	PRODUCT
Leslie Ash	Homebase
Rowan Atkinson	Barclaycard
Danny Baker	Daz
Ronnie Barker	Sekonda watches, Hertz car hire
Lynda Bellingham	Oxo stock cubes
Cilla Black	Typhoo tea
Bernard Braden	Stork margarine
Kim Cattrall	Tetley tea
Lorraine Chase	Campari
John Cleese	Accurist watches, Sony electricals, Sainsbury's
George Cole	Leeds Building Society, Benson & Hedges cigars
Joan Collins	Cinzano
Billy Connolly	The National Lottery
Tommy Cooper	Sodastream drinks maker
Ronnie Corbett	Hertz car hire
Bing Crosby	Shell petrol
Leslie Crowther	Stork margarine
Alan Davies	Abbey National Bank
Jack Dee	John Smith's beer
Harry Enfield	Worthington beer, Mercury telecom, Dime chocolate bars
Gregor Fisher	Hamlet cigars
Dawn French	Terry's chocolate
Clement Freud	Chunky dog food
Liza Goddard	Nescafé
Sarah Greene	Nescafé
Tony Hancock	Eggs
Jeremy Hawk	Cadbury's Whole Nut
Jane Horrocks	Tesco
Karl Howman	Walls sausages, Flash floor cleaner
Patricia Hayes	Eggs
Anthony Head	Gold Blend coffee
Benny Hill	Farmer's Wife bread
Paul Hogan	Foster's lager
Anthony Hopkins	Barclays Bank
Gareth Hunt	Nescafé
Stratford Johns	Magicote paint

Griff Rhys Jones	Holsten Pils, Vauxhall cars
Peter Kay	John Smith's beer
Penelope Keith	Parker pens
Diane Keen	Nescafé
Gary Lineker	Walkers crisps
Maureen Lipman	British Telecom
Nicholas Lyndhurst	WH Smith
Sharon Maughan	Gold Blend coffee
Henry McGee	Sugar Puffs cereal
Leo McKern	Lloyds Bank
Helen Mirren	Virgin Atlantic
Warren Mitchell	Findus frozen foods
Kenneth More	Birds coffee
Morecambe & Wise	Texaco petrol
Neil Morrissey	Homebase
Ted Moult	Everest double glazing
Frank Muir	Cadbury's Fruit and Nut
Nanette Newman	Fairy Liquid detergent
Jamie Oliver	Sainsbury's
Pauline Quirke	Surf washing powder
Linda Robson	Surf washing powder
Jonathan Ross	Harp lager
Leonard Rossiter	Cinzano
Prunella Scales	Tesco
Terry Scott	Curly Wurly chocolate
Harry Secombe	Woolworth's
William Shatner	Kellogg's All Bran
Valerie Singleton	Flash floor cleaner
Sooty	Oxo stock cubes
Una Stubbs	Nescafé
Melanie Sykes	Boddingtons beer
Jimmy Tarbuck	Sharp microwaves
John Thomson	Lloyds TSB Bank
Denise van Outen	Nescafé
Johnny Vaughan	Strongbow cider
Norman Vaughan	Roses chocolates
Carol Vorderman	Benecol margarine
Dennis Waterman	Oxo stock cubes
Alan Whicker	Barclaycard
Mark Williams	Holsten Pils
Ray Winstone	Holsten Pils
Terry Wogan	Flora margarine

CURIOUS FACT

Franc Roddam, co-creator of Auf Wiedersehen, Pet, was also creator of Masterchef

The Herbs

Aunt Mint, the keen knitter
Bayleaf, the gardener
Belladonna, the evil witch
The Chives, the Onions' children/pupils
Constable Knapweed, the lawman
Dill, the manic dog
Good King Henry, Miss Jessop's husband-to-be
Lady Rosemary, Sir Basil's wife
Miss Jessop, the stickler for neatness
Mr Onion, the teacher
Mrs Onion, Mr Onion's tearful wife
Parsley, the 'very friendly' lion
Pashana Bedi, the snake charmer
Sage, the fat, feathery owl
Signor Solidago, the Italian singing teacher
Sir Basil, owner of the herb garden
Tarragon, the dragon

....

The Quiz Show Scandal

American television was rocked in the late 1950s when it was alleged that certain contestants in quiz shows were favoured over others because they had greater public appeal. It was suggested that popular participants were fed answers to ensure they returned the following week – to the great delight of programme sponsors. After several claims of cheating from disgruntled losers, the media turned the heat onto programme makers and eventually one favoured contestant, Charles Van Doren, who had won a total of $129,000 in the quiz show *Twenty-One*, admitted he had been given assistance and that his agonising and indecisiveness under the studio lights had all been an act. His story is told in the 1994 movie *Quiz Show*, starring Ralph Fiennes. The episode spelled a temporary end to big-money quiz shows in the USA.

....

The First and Last Juke Box Juries*

FIRST (1 JUNE 1959)
Pete Murray (DJ), Alma Cogan (singer), Gary Miller (singer), Susan Stranks (teenager)

LAST (27 DECEMBER 1967)
Pete Murray (DJ), Susan Stranks (no longer a teenager), Eric Sykes (comedian), Lulu (singer)

* Original David Jacobs-hosted run.

Prominent Wildlife Presenters

PRESENTER(S)	MAJOR PROGRAMME(S)
David Attenborough	Zoo Quest, Life on Earth
Nick Baker	The Really Wild Show
David Bellamy	Bellamy's Backyard Safari
Jacques Cousteau	The Undersea World of Jacques Cousteau
Armand and Michaela Denis	On Safari
Hans and Lotte Hass	The Undersea World of Adventure
Steve Irwin	The Crocodile Hunter
Simon King	A Walk on the Wildside
Steve Leonard	Steve Leonard's Ultimate Killers
Nigel Marven	Nigel Marven's Animal Detectives
Desmond Morris	Zoo Time
Johnny Morris	Animal Magic
Terry Nutkins	Animal Magic
Bill Oddie	Birding with Bill Oddie
Michaela Strachan	The Really Wild Show
Charlotte Uhlenbroek	Cousins

What's on the Other Side?

Until March 1991 the only magazines permitted to carry weekly UK TV listings information were Radio Times and TV Times. Radio Times was restricted to BBC programming and TV Times was tied to ITV schedules, so, if you wanted a complete picture of the week's viewing, you had to buy both. When these monopolies were broken, not only did these publications themselves rush to carry both BBC and ITV details but a raft of new TV listing magazines also entered the market place.

Star Trek Spin-offs and Movie Sequels

THE TV SPIN-OFFS	THE MOVIE SEQUELS
Star Trek: the Next Generation	Star Trek: the Motion Picture (1979)
Star Trek: Deep Space Nine	Star Trek II: the Wrath of Khan (1982)
Star Trek: Voyager	Star Trek III: the Search for Spock (1984)
Star Trek: Enterprise	Star Trek IV: the Voyage Home (1986)
	Star Trek V: the Final Frontier (1989)
	Star Trek VI: the Undiscovered Country (1991)
	Star Trek: Generations (1994)
	Star Trek: First Contact (1996)
	Star Trek: Insurrection (1998)
	Star Trek: Nemesis (2002)

First Night: The BBC's Opening Schedule (2 November 1936)

3.00pm Opening of the BBC Television Service. Speeches from the Postmaster General, Major GC Tryon MP; Mr RC Norman, Chairman of the BBC; and Lord Selsdon, Chairman of the Television Advisory Committee.

3.15 Interval, followed by time and weather

3.20 British Movietone News

3.30 Variety. Starring Adele Dixon, the Lai Founs, Buck and Bubbles and the Television Orchestra.

4.00 Closedown

9.00 Programme summary

9.05 Film: Television Comes to London

9.20 Picture Page. A topical magazine.

9.50 British Movietone News

10.00 Closedown

....

Names of TV Theme Tunes

PROGRAMME	THEME TUNE TITLE
The Adventures of Black Beauty	Galloping Home
Animal Magic	Las Vegas
Ask the Family	Sun Ride
The Avengers	The Shake
BBC Wimbledon Tennis	Light and Tuneful
The Benny Hill Show	Yakkety Sax
Blue Peter	Barnacle Bill
Call My Bluff	Ciccolino
Comedy Playhouse	Happy Joe
Coronation Street	Kaleidoscope No. 21
Crane	Casablanca
Crimewatch UK	Rescue Helicopter
Danger Man	High Wire
Dixon of Dock Green	An Ordinary Copper
Dr Finlay's Casebook	A Little Suite
Dr Kildare	Three Stars Will Shine Tonight
Film	I Wish I Knew (How It Would Feel to Be Free)
The Forsyte Saga (BBC)	Elizabeth Tudor
Grandstand (original)	News Scoop
Grange Hill	Chicken Man
ITN News (original)	Non Stop

The Life and Times of David Lloyd George	Chi Mai
M*A*S*H	Suicide Is Painless
Maigret	Midnight in Montmartre
Mastermind	Approaching Menace
Naked City	Somewhere in the Night
Nationwide	The Good Word
On the Buses	Happy Harry
Owen, MD	Sleepy Shores
Panorama	Aujourd'hui C'est Toi
Pebble Mill at One	As You Please
Riviera Police	Latin Quarter
Secret Army	Wall of Fear
Sportsview	Saturday Sports
Steptoe and Son	Old Ned
Take Three Girls	Light Flight
Television Top of the Form	Marching Strings
Thank Your Lucky Stars	Lunar Walk
This Is Your Life	Gala Performance
Top of the Pops	Whole Lotta Love, Yellow Pearl, The Wizard
Top Secret	Sucu Sucu
The Train Now Standing	Green Pastures
Treasure Hunt	Peak Performance
Upstairs, Downstairs	The Edwardians
Van der Valk	Eye Level
Whicker's World	West End
The World of Tim Frazer	The Willow Waltz
Z Cars	Johnny Todd

....

Top Cat and Bilko

Conceived as a feline version of The Phil Silvers Show, Top Cat (or Boss Cat as it was retitled for UK audiences, to avoid promotion of a cat food of the same name) was based around the same principle of a scheming leader and his small troop of patsies. Their respective gangs read as follows:

BILKO (MAIN CORPS):	TOP CAT:
Cpl Rocco Barbella	Benny the Ball*
Cpl Henshaw	Choo-Choo
Pte Duane Doberman	Spook
Pte Sam Fender	The Brain
Pte Dino Paparelli	Fancy-Fancy
Pte Fielding Zimmerman	

* Equivalent to Doberman and voiced by the same actor, Maurice Gosfield

Birth of a Children's TV Magazine

The first issue of Look-in, 'The Junior TV Times', appeared on 9 January 1971.
As well as a listing of ITV programmes for kids (by region), and a spread on how
to assemble the free gift (a pop-out Magpie TV studio), features in issue one
included:

Crowther in Trouble (cartoon strip)
Survival (natural history feature)
World of Sport (sporting snippets)
How! (quirky questions and answers)
Freewheelers (cartoon strip)
Stewpot (a feature on DJ Ed Stewart)
Wreckers at Dead Eye (cartoon strip)
Tony Bastable's Backchat (miscellany of items)
Please Sir! (cartoon strip)
David Nixon's Magic Box (magic tricks)
Timeslip (cartoon strip)
Magpie (news from the magazine programme)

....

The Young Ones

Rick (Rick Mayall)
Neil (Nigel Planer)
Vyvyan (Adrian Edmondson)
Mike (Christopher Ryan)

....

On the Road with Michael Palin

Routes followed by the itinerant Python.

AROUND THE WORLD IN 80 DAYS

UK · France · Switzerland · Liechtenstein · Austria · Italy · Greece · Egypt ·
Saudi Arabia · Qatar · United Arab Emirates · India · Singapore · Hong Kong ·
China · Japan · USA · France · UK

POLE TO POLE

North Pole · Greenland · Spitsbergen · Norway · Finland · Estonia · Russia ·
Turkey · Cyprus · Egypt · Sudan · Ethiopia · Kenya · Tanzania · Zambia · Zimbabwe ·
South Africa · Brazil · Chile · South Pole

FULL CIRCLE

Little Diomede · USA (Alaska) · Russia · Japan · South Korea · China · Vietnam ·
Philippines · Malaysia · Indonesia · Australia · New Zealand · Chile · Bolivia · Peru ·
Colombia · Mexico · USA · Canada · USA (Alaska) · Little Diomede (almost)

Initials in Programme Titles Explained

A&E	Always and Everyone
ALF	Alien Life Form
CATS Eyes	Covert Activities Thames Section
CHiPS	California Highway Patrols
CSI	Crime Scene Investigation
Danger UXB	Unexploded Bomb
ER	Emergency Room
GBH	Great British Holiday
Magnum PI	Private Investigator
MASH	Mobile Army Surgical Hospital
NYPD Blue	New York Police Department
The OC	Orange County
OSS	Office of Strategic Services
OTT	Over The Top
QED	Quod Erat Demonstrandum
Quincy ME	Medical Examiner
SM:TV Live	Saturday Morning Television
SWAT	Special Weapons And Tactics
The FBI	Federal Bureau of Investigation
TISWAS	Today Is Saturday Watch And Smile
V	Visitors/Victory
VR5	Virtual Reality

....

Newsreaders Who Have Worked for Both BBC and ITN

Mark Austin	Sue Carpenter	Anna Ford
Andrew Harvey	Martyn Lewis	Dermot Murnaghan
Angela Rippon	Peter Sissons	Julia Somerville

....

The Eggheads

BBC's daytime quiz show Eggheads pits a team of champion TV quizzers against pub quiz teams. The five Eggheads are:

Kevin Ashman	Mastermind champion 1995 (and series highest ever scorer), World Quizzing Champion 2004 and former Brain of Britain
CJ De Mooi	Fifteen to One winner and British Mensa chess champion
Daphne Fowler	Former Brain of Britain and Fifteen to One winner
Chris Hughes	Mastermind champion 1983
Judith Keppel	The first jackpot winner on Who Wants to be a Millionaire?

Commentators and Their Sports

COMMENTATOR	SPORT
James Allen	Formula 1
Peter Allis	Golf
Paul Allott	Cricket
John Arlott	Cricket
Wally Barnes	Football
John Barrett	Tennis
Richie Benaud	Cricket
Hamilton Bland	Swimming
Raymond Brooks-Ward	Equestrianism
Ken Brown	Golf
Martin Brundle	Formula 1
Eddie Butler	Rugby union
Harry Carpenter	Boxing, golf
Mike Cattermole	Horse racing
John Champion	Football
David Coleman	Football, athletics
Charles Colvile	Cricket
Tony Cooke	Horse racing
Steve Cram	Athletics
Ian Darke	Boxing
Barry Davies	Football, gymnastics, tennis, ice skating
Paul Dickenson	Athletics
Ray Edmonds	Snooker
Clive Everton	Snooker
Brendan Foster	Athletics
Ray French	Rugby league
Raleigh Gilbert	Horse racing
Graham Goode	Horse racing
David Gower	Cricket
Clive Graham	Horse racing
Tony Green	Darts
Tony Gubba	Football
Reg Gutteridge	Boxing, greyhound racing
John Hanmer	Horse racing
Miles Harrison	Rugby union
Simon Holt	Horse racing
Hugh Johns	Football
Brian Johnston	Cricket
Jim Laker	Cricket
Tony Lewis	Cricket

David Lloyd	Cricket
Henry Longhurst	Golf
Ted Lowe	Snooker
Dan Maskell	Tennis
Jim McGrath	Horse racing
Bill McLaren	Rugby union
Adrian Metcalfe	Athletics
Brian Moore	Football
Cliff Morgan	Rugby union
John Motson	Football
Nick Mullins	Rugby union
Jim Neilly	Boxing, rugby union
Mark Nicholas	Cricket
Barry Nutley	Motor racing
Tony O'Hehir	Horse racing
Peter O'Sullevan	Horse racing
Alan Parry	Football, athletics
John Penney	Horse racing
Ron Pickering	Athletics
John Pulman	Snooker
Idwal Robling	Football
Gerald Sindstadt	Football
Nigel Starmer-Smith	Rugby union
Stuart Storey	Athletics
Dennis Taylor	Snooker
John Taylor	Rugby union
Derek Thompson	Horse racing
Julian Tutt	Skiing
Clive Tyldesley	Football
Martin Tyler	Football
David Vine	Skiing
John Virgo	Snooker
Sid Waddell	Darts
Murray Walker	Formula 1
Kent Walton	Wrestling
Eddie Waring	Rugby league
Alan Weeks	Ice skating, football, swimming
Peter West	Cricket
Dorian Williams	Equestrianism
Julian Wilson	Horse racing
Steve Wilson	Football
Kenneth Wolstenholme	Football

CURIOUS FACT

Alex Ferguson was once played on TV by Cherie Lunghi. It was the name of her character in the 1976 political drama Bill Brand

The Pages of Picture Book

Turning the pages of Watch with Mother's Picture Book was Patricia Driscoll and later Vera McKechnie, both assisted by Sossidge, the string puppet dachshund. This is what they revealed:

A making something page
Bizzy Lizzy page (puppet adventure)
An animals page
The Jolly Jack Tars* page (puppet adventure)

* Individually, the Captain, Mr Mate, Jonathan the deckhand and Ticky the Monkey.

....

Ten Odd Titles of US Game Shows

Dough Re Me (NBC 1958–60)
Bid-cash-for-notes musical quiz.

Feather Your Nest (NBC 1954–6)
Three couples do quiz battle for furniture for their homes.

Funny Boners (NBC 1954–5)
Kids' show where incorrectly answered questions demand the performance of a silly stunt.

Haggis Baggis (NBC 1958–9)
Contestants spot the identity of a famous person by answering questions that, one-by-one, remove squares covering his/her picture.

How's Your Mother-in-Law? (ABC 1967–8)
Celebrities act as defence lawyers for three mothers-in-law, with a jury deciding which of the three they would prefer as their own.

Ladies Be Seated (ABC 1949)
A quiz and stunt show for ladies in the studio audience.

Let's Play Post Office (NBC 1965–6)
Contestants sitting in a studio post office guess a famous person's identity from clues hidden in a letter, winning the value of the stamp on the envelope ($5–100).

Messing Prize Party (CBS 1948–9)
Party games such as charades sponsored by Messing Bread Company.

Missus' Goes A-Shopping (CBS 1947–8)
Game show set in real-life supermarkets.

The Wizard of Odds (NBC 1973–4)
Contestants answer questions based on the law of averages and other statistics.

Workers' Gift to the Lady of the Manor

From early August to 24 October 1979, Britain endured its longest ever television strike. When workers at ITV withdrew their labour during an industrial dispute, it resulted in a 75-day hiatus in commercial broadcasting. Only Channel Television of the ITV companies remained on air. The BBC continued as normal and secured some of its highest ever programme ratings while the opposition was away, including an episode of the situation comedy To the Manor Born that drew a record-breaking 24 million viewers on Sunday 7 October. This was the second episode in the first series and saw leading lady Audrey fforbes-Hamilton being forced to quit her beloved Grantley Manor.

TV Witches

WITCH	SERIES
Amanda Tucker	Tucker's Witch
Bella Donna	Witches' Brew
Belladonna	The Herbs
Belor	Into the Labyrinth
Evil Edna	Willo the Wisp
Fenella	Chorlton and the Wheelies
Grandmama	The Addams Family
Grotbags	Emu's World/Grotbags
Hazel the McWitch	Rentaghost
Mildred Hubble	The Worst Witch
Prue, Piper and Phoebe Halliwell	Charmed
Sabrina Spellman	Sabrina the Teenage Witch
Samantha Stephens	Bewitched
Tabitha Stephens	Bewitched/Tabitha
The White Witch	The Lion, the Witch and the Wardrobe
Witchiepoo	HR Pufnstuf
Wizadora	Wizadora

The First 'Mini-Series'

Breaking the mould of American television in the mid-1970s was a dramatisation of Irwin Shaw's 1970 novel Rich Man, Poor Man. Made in 12 one-hour instalments, this was the first 'mini-series' in a country where the standard practice was not to make short, finite dramas, but long-running series or serials. It proved to be a massive success and led to a host of similar projects, including Roots, Captains and the Kings, 79 Park Avenue, Wheels and The Winds of War.

UK Top 40 Hits from TV Series

PROGRAMME	HIT	ARTIST(S)
The Adventures of Robin Hood	Robin Hood	Dick James
The Army Game	The Signature Tune of the Army Game	Michael Medwin, Bernard Bresslaw, Alfie Bass and Leslie Fyson
Auf Wiedersehen, Pet	That's Living Alright	Joe Fagin
Bob the Builder	Can We Fix It	Bob the Builder (Neil Morrissey)
Boon	Hi Ho Silver	Jim Diamond
Brush Strokes	Because of You	Dexy's Midnight Runners
Cilla	Step Inside Love	Cilla Black
	Something Tells Me (Something Is Gonna Happen Tonight)	Cilla Black
Connie	The Show (Theme from Connie)	Rebecca Storm
Coronation Street	Not Too Little Not Too Much	Chris Sandford
Crocodile Shoes	Crocodile Shoes	Jimmy Nail
Crossroads	Where Will You Be?	Sue Nicholls
	Born with a Smile on My Face	Stephanie De Sykes
	More Than in Love	Kate Robbins
	Summer of My Life	Simon May
	Benny's Theme	Paul Henry and the Mason Glen Orchestra
EastEnders	Every Loser Wins	Nick Berry
	Something Outa Nothing	Letitia Dean and Paul Medford
Emmerdale	Just This Side of Love	Malandra Burrows
Fame	Hi-Fidelity	Kids From Fame
	Starmaker	Kids From Fame
Fireball XL5	Fireball	Don Spencer
Follyfoot	The Lightning Tree	The Settlers
Fraggle Rock	Fraggle Rock Theme	Fraggles
Friends	I'll Be There for You	Rembrandts
Happy Days	Rock around the Clock	Bill Haley and his Comets
Harpers West One	Johnny Remember Me	John Leyton
Harry's Game	Theme from Harry's Game	Clannad

Heartbeat	Heartbeat	Nick Berry
Hill Street Blues	Theme from Hill Street Blues	Mike Post
The Hong Kong Beat	Theme from The Hong Kong Beat	Richard Denton and Martin Cook
Howards' Way	Howards' Way	Simon May Orchestra
	Always There	Marti Webb
It's Dark Outside	Where Are You Now	Jackie Trent
Juke Box Jury	Hit and Miss	John Barry Seven
The Life and Times of David Lloyd George	Chi Mai	Ennio Morricone
The Life and Times of Grizzly Adams	Maybe	Tom Pace
The Light of Experience	Doina de Jale	Georghe Zamfir
The Marriage	Starting Together	Su Pollard
Miami Vice	Miami Vice Theme	Jan Hammer
Minder	I Could Be So Good For You	Dennis Waterman
Moonlighting	Moonlighting Theme	Al Jarreau
The Muppet Show	Halfway Down the Stairs	The Muppets
Neighbours	Suddenly	Angry Anderson
No Hiding Place	No Hiding Place	Ken Mackintosh
No, Honestly	No, Honestly	Lyndsey De Paul
Not Only ... But Also ...	Goodbye-ee	Peter Cook and Dudley Moore
The Onedin Line	Theme from The Onedin Line	Vienna Philharmonic Orchestra
Owen MD	Sleepy Shores	Johnny Pearson
The Partridge Family	I Think I Love You	The Partridge Family
The Persuaders!	The Persuaders	John Barry
The Professionals	Theme from The Professionals	Laurie Johnson's London Big Band
The Protectors	Avenues and Alleyways	Tony Christie
Rawhide	Rawhide	Frankie Laine
Ready, Steady, Go!	5-4-3-2-1	Manfred Mann
Rock Follies	OK	Julie Covington, Rula Lenska, Charlotte Cornwell and Sue Jones Davies
Rupert	Rupert	Jackie Lee
The Rutles	I Must Be in Love	The Rutles
Sailor	Sailing	Rod Stewart

PROGRAMME	HIT	ARTIST(S)
Seaside Special	Summertime City	Mike Batt
Seven Faces of Woman	She	Charles Aznavour
South Park	Chocolate Salty Balls (PS I Love You)	Chef (Isaac Hayes)
Spitting Image	The Chicken Song	Spitting Image
	Santa Is on the Dole	Spitting Image
The Strange World of Gurney Slade	Gurney Slade	Max Harris
Teletubbies	Teletubbies Say Eh-Oh!	Teletubbies
The Thorn Birds	Love Theme from the Thorn Birds	Juan Martin
Tiswas	The Bucket of Water Song	The Four Bucketeers
Top of the Pops	Yellow Pearl	Phil Lynott
Top Secret	Sucu Sucu	Laurie Johnson
Van Der Valk	Eye Level	The Simon Park Orchestra
The Water Margin	The Water Margin	Peter Mac Junior/Godiego
Whatever Happened to the Likely Lads?	Whatever Happened to You	Highly Likely
White Horses	White Horses	Jacky
Who Pays The Ferryman	Who Pays the Ferryman	Yannis Markopoulos
The Wombles	The Wombling Song	The Wombles
Z Cars	Theme from Z Cars	Johnny Keating

....

Blue Peter Time Capsules

Children's magazine Blue Peter has made three attempts at safely burying a time capsule containing objects that may prove of interest some time in the future. The first was buried on 7 June 1971 and contained items like the 1970 Blue Peter annual, photographs of the presenters of the time – Valerie Singleton, John Noakes and Peter Purves – and a set of the decimal coins that were soon to be introduced. This was moved, however, because of construction work, to the Blue Peter garden in 1984, when a second capsule was buried alongside. This contained some video footage, a recording of the theme tune by Mike Oldfield and some hairs from Goldie, one of the programme's dogs. Both capsules were retrieved and opened on 4 January 2000 but the contents were found to be badly damaged by water. The most recent was buried on 11 June 1998 under the floor of the Millennium Dome in Greenwich. It is due for opening in 2050 and contains items like a football from the France 98 tournament, a photograph of Princess Diana and a Spice Girls CD.

Famous Offspring

PARENT(S)	CHILD(REN)
Ralph Bates	Daisy Bates
Ann Beach	Charlotte Coleman, Lisa Coleman
Tony Britton	Fern Britton
Beverly Callard	Rebecca Callard
Jasper Carrott	Lucy Davis
Judith Chalmers	Mark Durden-Smith
Harry H Corbett	Susannah Corbett
Nigel Davenport and Maria Aitken	Jack Davenport
Richard Dimbleby	David Dimbleby, Jonathan Dimbleby
Tony Doyle	Susannah Doyle
Julia Foster	Ben Fogle
Edward Fox and Joanna David	Emilia Fox
Hughie Green	Paula Yates
Jimmy Hanley and Dinah Sheridan	Jenny Hanley
Rosemary Harris	Jennifer Ehle
Jeremy Hawk	Belinda Lang
Ronald Lacey	Rebecca Lacey
Roger Lloyd Pack	Emily Lloyd
Judy Loe and Richard Beckinsale	Kate Beckinsale
Magnus Magnusson	Sally Magnusson, Jon Magnusson
Kay Mellor	Gaynor Faye
Cliff Michelmore	Guy Michelmore
John Mills	Juliet Mills, Hayley Mills
Nanette Newman	Emma Forbes
Bill Owen	Tom Owen
Donald Pleasence	Angela Pleasence
Ted Ray	Robin Ray, Andrew Ray
Corin Redgrave	Jemma Redgrave
Diana Rigg	Rachael Stirling
William Roache	Linus Roache
Derek Royle	Carol Royle, Amanda Royle
Phil Silvers	Cathy Silvers
Sylvia Sims	Beatie Edney
Donald Sinden	Jeremy Sinden, Mark Sinden
Aaron Spelling	Tori Spelling
Jimmy Tarbuck	Liza Tarbuck
Eric Thompson and Phyllida Law	Emma Thompson, Sophie Thompson
Patrick Troughton	Michael Troughton, David Troughton
Timothy West and Prunella Scales	Sam West
Patrick Wymark	Jane Wymark

The Biggest Time-Waster

'Well, gentlemen, you have now invented the biggest time-waster of all time. Use it well.'

– Isaac Shoenberg of EMI in 1934, after a demonstration of the company's first electronic television camera

. . . .

TV Systems and Countries

There are three incompatible television operating systems in use around the world: NTSC (National Television System Committee, a 525-line system developed in the USA), PAL (Phase Alternate Line, a 625-line system developed in Germany) and SECAM (Séquential Couleur à Mémoire, a different 625-line system developed in France). The following list indicates which systems are in use in which countries.

COUNTRY	TV SYSTEM	COUNTRY	TV SYSTEM
Albania	PAL	Hungary	PAL
Argentina	PAL	Iceland	PAL
Australia	PAL	India	PAL
Austria	PAL	Indonesia	PAL
Bahamas	NTSC	Iran	SECAM
Bahrain	PAL	Iraq	SECAM
Barbados	NTSC	Ireland	PAL
Belgium	PAL	Israel	PAL
Bermuda	NTSC	Italy	PAL
Bolivia	NTSC	Jamaica	NTSC
Brazil	PAL	Japan	NTSC
Bulgaria	SECAM	Jordan	PAL
Canada	NTSC	Kenya	PAL
Chile	NTSC	Kuwait	PAL
China	PAL	Libya	SECAM
Colombia	NTSC	Luxembourg	PAL
Cuba	NTSC	Madagascar	SECAM
Cyprus	PAL	Malaysia	PAL
Czech Republic	PAL	Malta	PAL
Denmark	PAL	Mauritius	SECAM
Egypt	SECAM	Mexico	NTSC
Finland	PAL	Monaco	SECAM
France	SECAM	Morocco	SECAM
Gambia	PAL	Netherlands	PAL
Germany	PAL	New Zealand	PAL
Greece	PAL	North Korea	SECAM

Norway	PAL	Sweden	PAL
Pakistan	PAL	Switzerland	PAL
Paraguay	PAL	Syria	SECAM
Peru	NTSC	Tahiti	SECAM
Philippines	NTSC	Taiwan	NTSC
Poland	PAL	Thailand	PAL
Portugal	PAL	Trinidad	NTSC
Romania	PAL	Tunisia	SECAM
Russia	SECAM	Turkey	PAL
Saudi Arabia	SECAM	United Arab Emirates	PAL
Seychelles	PAL	United Kingdom	PAL
Singapore	PAL	Uruguay	PAL
South Africa	PAL	USA	NTSC
South Korea	NTSC	Venezuela	NTSC
Spain	PAL	Yugoslavia	PAL
Sri Lanka	PAL	Zimbabwe	PAL

....

Some Celebrity Visitors to The Flintstones' World

CHARACTER (BASED ON)
Ann-Margrock (Ann-Margret)
Stony Curtis (Tony Curtis)
Conrad Hailstone (Conrad Hilton)
Perry Masonry (Perry Mason)
Sassie (Lassie)
Ed Sullystone (Ed Sullivan)

....

Comedy Quizzes

QUIZ	HOST(S)	SUBJECT
29 Minutes of Fame	Bob Mortimer	Celebrities
The Best Show in the World ... Probably	Tony Hawks	Advertising
Bygones	Danny Baker	Nostalgia
Have I Got News for You	Angus Deayton	Current affairs
If I Ruled the World	Clive Anderson	Politics
It's Only TV But I Like It	Jonathan Ross	Television
Jumpers for Goal Posts	Simon Day	Football
Never Mind the Buzzcocks	Mark Lamarr	Pop music
Ps and Qs	Tony Slattery	Etiquette
QI	Stephen Fry	General knowledge
Shooting Stars	Vic Reeves, Bob Mortimer	General knowledge
They Think It's All Over	Nick Hancock	Sport
Tibs and Fibs	Tony Slattery	Medical matters

The National Museum

The National Museum of Photography, Film & Television, based in Bradford, was founded in 1983, and this treasure trove of television memorabilia now attracts around 750,000 visitors every year. The earliest television footage is housed here, along with a collection of over 1,000 TV receivers, a large number of cameras and a fine archive of television advertising. Visitors can learn about milestones in the history of television, or try their hands at reading the news or operating a TV camera. The TV Heaven section offers the chance to view an episode of an historic programme, with around 1,000 classic choices available, and regular talks are scheduled, with topics covered varying from Watch with Mother and Top of the Pops to children's drama series and notable single plays. What's more, the Museum is free!

Notable TV Addresses

ADDRESS	RESIDENTS	SERIES
000 Cemetery Ridge	The Addams Family	The Addams Family
10 Stigwood Avenue, Brooklyn	The Huxtables	The Cosby Show
19 Riverbank	The Meldrews	One Foot in the Grave
23 Railway Cuttings, East Cheam	Anthony Aloysius Hancock	Hancock's Half Hour
24 Sebastopol Terrace, Acton	Eric and Hattie	Sykes
29 Acacia Road	Bananaman	Bananaman
30 Kelsall Street, Liverpool	The Boswells	Bread
32 Windsor Gardens, London	The Browns	Paddington
34 Claremount Avenue, London	Edina Monsoon	Absolutely Fabulous
52 Festive Road, London	Mr Benn	Mr Benn
66 Sycamore Street	The Larkins	The Larkins
77 Sunset Strip	Stu Bailey and Jeff Spencer	77 Sunset Strip
165 Eaton Place, Belgravia, London	The Bellamys	Upstairs, Downstairs
173 Essex Drive, Denver	The Carringtons	Dynasty
221B Baker Street	Sherlock Holmes	Sherlock Holmes
345 Stone Cave Road, Bedrock	The Flintstones	The Flintstones
518 Crestview Drive, Beverly Hills	The Clampetts	The Beverly Hillbillies
565 North Clinton Drive, Milwaukee	The Cunninghams	Happy Days
607 South Maple Street, Springfield	The Andersons	Father Knows Best
623 East 68th Street, New York	The Ricardos	I Love Lucy
698 Candlewood Lane, Cabot Cove	Jessica Fletcher	Murder, She Wrote
698 Sycamore Road, San Pueblo	The Partridge Family	The Partridge Family
704 Hauser Street, Queens	The Bunkers	All in the Family
742 Evergreen Terrace, Springfield	The Simpsons	The Simpsons
805 St Claud Road, Bel-Air	The Bankses	The Fresh Prince of Bel-Air

933 Hillcrest Drive, Beverly Hills	The Walshes	Beverly Hills 90210
1049 Park Avenue, New York	Oscar and Felix	The Odd Couple
1164 Morning Glory Circle, Westport	The Stevenses	Bewitched
1313 Mockingbird Lane, Mockingbird Heights	The Munsters	The Munsters
1630 Revello Drive, Sunnydale	The Summerses	Buffy the Vampire Slayer
1901 Elliott Bay Towers, Seattle	Dr Frasier Crane	Frasier
2354 Pacific Coast Highway (mobile home)	Jim Rockford	The Rockford Files
4222 Clinton Way/Avenue, Los Angeles	The Bradys	The Brady Bunch
Apartment D, 119 North Weatherly Avenue, Minneapolis	Mary Richards	The Mary Tyler Moore Show
Apartment 5A, 129 West 81st Street, New York	Jerry Seinfeld	Seinfeld
Birch Avenue, Putney	The Abbotts	Bless This House
Blossom Avenue	The Buckets	Keeping Up Appearances
Grantleigh Manor	Richard DeVere	To the Manor Born
Hillsdown Avenue, Hampstead	The Glovers	Father, Dear Father
Mews Cottage, Old Drum Lane, Shepherd's Bush	The Steptoes	Steptoe and Son
Nelson Mandela House, Peckham	The Trotters	Only Fools and Horses
Parochial House, Craggy Island	Father Ted Crilly	Father Ted
Southfork Ranch, Braddock County	The Ewings	Dallas
The Avenue, Surbiton	The Goods	The Good Life
Wayne Manor, Gotham City	Bruce Wayne	Batman

....

Professional Occupations of the Walmington-on-Sea Home Guard (Dad's Army)

CHARACTER	OCCUPATION
Capt George Mainwaring	Bank manager
Sgt Arthur Wilson	Chief bank clerk
L/Cpl Jack Jones	Butcher
Pte Frank Pike	Bank clerk
Pte James Fraser	Undertaker
Pte Joe Walker	Black marketeer
Pte Charles Godfrey	Retired men's outfitter
Pte Cheeseman	Newspaper reporter
Pte Sponge	Farmer

ARP Warden William Hodges was the town's greengrocer.

Ten Strange Titles for TV Series

Badger by Owl-Light (Drama: BBC 1, 1982)
Elephant's Eggs in a Rhubarb Tree (Children's Comedy: ITV, 1971)
It's Awfully Bad for Your Eyes, Darling (Sitcom: BBC 1, 1971)
No Soap, Radio (Sitcom: ABC, 1982)
Souvenirs of Sidmouth (Variety: BBC 2, 1982)
The House of Gristle (Children's Comedy: BBC 1, 1994)
The Mulberry Accelerator (Drama: BBC, 1955)
The Saturday Banana (Children's Entertainment: ITV, 1978)
Wdyjsoytsagadslbi? (Why Don't You Just Switch off Your Television Set and Go and
Do Something Less Boring Instead?; Children's Entertainment: BBC 1, 1973–95)
When Uncle Klaas Fell Over (Drama: BBC 1, 1969)

....

Stars and Their Cars

STAR	CAR
The A-Team	GMC G Series van
Baretta	The Blue Ghost (Chevrolet Sedan)
Batman	Batmobile (converted Lincoln Continental)
Inspector Barnaby (Midsomer Murders)	Ford Mondeo, Rover 75
Mr Bean	Mini Cooper
Jim Bergerac (Bergerac)	Triumph
The Beverly Hillbillies	Oldsmobile
Sexton Blake	The Grey Panther (Rolls-Royce)
George Bulman	Citroen 2CV
Amos Burke (Burke's Law)	Rolls-Royce
Albert Campion (Campion)	Lagonda
Frank Cannon (Cannon)	Lincoln Continental
Columbo	Peugeot 403
Sonny Crockett (Miami Vice)	Ferrari Testarossa
Dr Paul Dangerfield (Dangerfield)	Land Rover Discovery
The Dukes of Hazzard	General Lee (Dodge Charger)
Basil Fawlty (Fawlty Towers)	Austin 1100
James Herriot (All Creatures Great and Small)	Morris 8 Tourer
Michael Knight (Knight Rider)	KITT (converted Pontiac Firebird TransAm)
Theo Kojak (Kojak)	Buick Regal
Jules Maigret (Maigret)	Citroen Traction Avant/Light 15
Thomas Magnum (Magnum, PI)	Ferrari 308
Robert McCall (The Equalizer)	Jaguar XJ6
The Monkees	Monkeemobile (converted Pontiac GTO)
Inspector Morse	Jaguar Mark II

The Munsters	Koach (converted Model T Ford)
Number 6 (The Prisoner)	Lotus Seven, Mini Moke
The Partridge Family	Chevrolet School Bus
Emma Peel (The Avengers)	Lotus Elan
Lady Penelope (Thunderbirds)	Rolls-Royce
The Persuaders	Aston Martin DBS (Brett Sinclair), Ferrari Dino (Danny Wilde)
The Professionals	Ford Capri
Purdey	Triumph TR7 (The New Avengers)
Jack Regan (The Sweeney)	Ford Granada
Jim Rockford (The Rockford Files)	Pontiac Firebird
Eddie Shoestring (Shoestring)	Ford Cortina Estate
Dave Starsky (Starsky and Hutch)	Ford Torino
John Steed (The Avengers)	Vintage Bentley
Adam Strange (The Strange Report)	Black cab
Simon Templar (The Saint)	Volvo P1800
Paul Temple	Rolls-Royce
Del Boy Trotter (Only Fools and Horses)	Reliant Regal Supervan III, Ford Capri Ghia
Z Cars	Ford Zephyr Mark 4

....

Home Entertainment

'Television is an invention that permits you to be entertained in your own living room by people you wouldn't have in your home.' – David Frost, speaking on CBS in 1971

....

The Patron Saint of Television

Pope Pius XII (1876–1958) was a man of his times. Fascinated by the arrival of television and its potential as a powerful means of communication, he decided to bestow the new medium with its own patron saint – albeit a saint that lived 700 years before television was invented. St Clare was St Francis of Assisi's most adherent follower, leaving home at the age of 19 in the year 1212 to join his religious fellowship. In appointing Clare the patron saint of television in 1958, Pope Pius reflected upon a moment in Clare's life when, too ill to attend church, she was granted a vision by God in which she was able miraculously to witness the service while still confined to her sickbed. This early instance of television (literally, from the Greek and Latin meaning 'far seeing') confirmed to the Pope that St Clare was the most fitting person to fulfil this unusual duty.

Situations for Comedy

SITUATION	EXAMPLE COMEDY
AA patrol	The Last Salute
Advertising agency	The Creatives
Airline cabin	The High Life
Bakery	All Night Long
Bank	The Peter Principle
Barber shop	Desmond's
Bingo hall	Eyes Down
Bistro	Robin's Nest
Boarding house	Rising Damp
Book shop	Black Books
Boxing gym	Punch Drunk
Brass band	Oh Happy Band!
Bus depot	On the Buses
Cab firm	Taxi
Café	Pilgrim's Rest
Canteen	dinnerladies
Car park	Pay and Display
Caravan park	Romany Jones
Cinema	Potter's Picture Palace
Clothes factory	The Rag Trade
Convent	The Flying Nun
Corner shop	Open All Hours
Country hotel	Grace and Favour
Cricket club	Outside Edge
Dairy	Bottle Boys
Department store	Are You Being Served?
Desert island	Gilligan's Island
Dessert factory	The Fall and Rise of Reginald Perrin
Divorced persons' group	Dear John
Driving school	L for Lester
EEC department	The Gravy Train
English language class	Mind Your Language
Farm	Sunnyside Farm
Fish market	Down the 'Gate
Florist's	Bloomers
Football club	Atletico Partick
French court	Let Them Eat Cake
Funeral director's	In Loving Memory
Furniture maker's	A Little Big Business
Garage	Chico and the Man

Garden	The Gnomes of Dulwich
Gentlemen's club	Bootsie and Snudge
Golf club	The Nineteenth Hole
Heaven	Dead Ernest
Holiday camp	Hi-De-Hi!
Home Guard platoon	Dad's Army
Hospital ward	Only When I Laugh
House of Commons	Yes Minister
Houseboat	Sink or Swim
Indian restaurant	Tandoori Nights
Junk yard	Steptoe and Son
Leisure Centre	The Brittas Empire
MI5	The Piglet Files
Minicab firm	Roger Roger
Model agency	Les Girls
Motorcycle couriers	Roy's Raiders
Newspaper	Nelson's Column
Office smoking room	The Smoking Room
Old people's home	Waiting for God
Outer space	Red Dwarf
Parochial house	Father Ted
Pickle factory	Nearest and Dearest
Pirate ship	Captain Butler
Police station	The Thin Blue Line
Prison	Porridge
Prisoner of War camp	Hogan's Heroes
Promotions agency	The Glamour Girls
Public bar	Early Doors
Public convenience	In for a Penny
Public School	Whack-O!
Publishing house	Executive Stress
Radio station	WKRP in Cincinnati
Railway station	Oh Doctor Beeching!
Refuse depot	The Dustbinmen
Repertory company	Rep
Restaurant	Chef!
River police	Duck Patrol
Roman Britain	Chelmsford 123
Roman town	Up Pompeii!
Royal Air Force	Get Some In!
Royal Navy	HMS Paradise
Rugby League team	All Our Saturdays
Salvation Army citadel	Hallelujah!

Situations for Comedy

SITUATION	EXAMPLE COMEDY
Sanatorium	Get Well Soon
Seaside hotel	Fawlty Towers
Seaside pier	High and Dry
Secondary Modern School	Please Sir!
Secret services	Get Smart
Social Club	Peter Kay's Phoenix Nights
Solicitor's office	Is It Legal?
Spacecraft	Red Dwarf
Spanish holiday resort	Duty Free
Stately home	Land of Hope and Gloria
Supermarket	Tripper's Day/Slinger's Day
Tailor's shop	Never Mind the Quality, Feel the Width
Teaching hospital	Doctor in the House
The Army	The Army Game
Travel agency	Men of the World
TV chat show	The Larry Sanders Show
TV newsroom	Drop the Dead Donkey
University	Honey for Tea
US Army platoon	The Phil Silvers Show
US Cavalry outpost	F Troop
US High School	Head of the Class
War hospital	M*A*S*H
Wartime concert party	It Ain't Half Hot Mum
Wax museum	Hope It Rains
Women's Land Army	Backs to the Land
World War I trenches	Blackadder Goes Forth

....

The Wacky Racers

CAR NO.	NAME	CREW
00	The Mean Machine	Dick Dastardly and Muttley
1	The Boulder Mobile	Rock and Gravel Slag
2	Creepy Coupé	The Gruesome Twosome
3	Ring-a-Ding Convert-a-Car	Prof. Pat Pending
4	Crimson Haybailer	The Red Max
5	Compact Pussycat	Penelope Pitstop
6	The Army Surplus Special	The General, Sgt Blast and Pte Pinkley*
7	The Bulletproof Bomb	Clyde and the Ant Hill Mob
8	Arkansas Chugabug	Luke and Blubber Bear
9	Turbo Terrific	Peter Perfect
10	The Buzz Wagon	Rufus Ruffcut and Sawtooth

* Also noted in places as Pte Meekley

Important Initials in TV History

ABC	American Broadcasting Company
ABC	Associated Broadcasting Company
ATV	Associated Television
BBC	British Broadcasting Corporation
BSB	British Satellite Broadcasting
CBS	Columbia Broadcasting System
CNN	Cable News Network
EBU	European Broadcasting Union
GMTV	Good Morning Television
HBO	Home Box Office
HTV	Harlech Television
IBA	Independent Broadcasting Authority
ITA	Independent Television Authority
ITC	Incorporated Television Programme Company
ITC	Independent Television Commission
ITN	Independent Television News
ITV	Independent Television
LWT	London Weekend Television
MTV	Music Television
NBC	National Broadcasting Company
ORACLE	Optional Reception of Announcements by Coded Line Electronics
S4C	Sianel Pedwar Cymru
TBS	Turner Broadcasting System
TNT	Turner Network Television
TSW	Television South West
TTT	Tyne Tees Television
TVS	Television South
TWW	Television Wales and West
UTV	Ulster Television
WWN	Wales West and North
YTV	Yorkshire Television

....

Social Menace

'It's a potential social menace of the first magnitude.'

– Lord Reith, on the arrival of commercial broadcasting in the UK

Citizens of Balamory

The 50 Greatest Comedy Sketches

As selected by viewers for the Channel 4 programme broadcast on 3 April 2005.

1 Lou and Andy (Swimming Pool): Little Britain
2 Petshop/Dead Parrot: Monty Python's Flying Circus
3 Tubbs and Edward (Road Men): The League of Gentlemen
4 Vicky Pollard (Swimming Pool): Little Britain
5 Four Candles: The Two Ronnies
6 Going for an English: Goodness Gracious Me
7 Acorn Antiques: Victoria Wood, As Seen on TV
8 Breakfast: The Morecambe and Wise Show
9 Ted and Ralph (Drinking Game): The Fast Show
10 Good Aids/Bad Aids: Brass Eye
11 The Slobs (Brown Baby): Harry Enfield and Chums
12 The Spanish Inquisition: Monty Python's Flying Circus
13 Silence of the Lambs: French and Saunders
14 Papa Lazarou (The Circus Comes to Town): The League of Gentlemen
15 Ministry of Silly Walks: Monty Python's Flying Circus
16 Previn Plays Greig: The Morecambe and Wise Show
17 The Only Gay in the Village (Dafydd's Coming Out): Little Britain
18 The Pool: The Day Today
19 Michael Jackson's Crib: Bo Selecta!
20 Suit You! Tailors (New Job): The Fast Show
21 Masterchef: The Smell of Reeves and Mortimer
22 Singing Match: Smack the Pony
23 Job Seekers (The Interview): The League of Gentlemen
24 History Today: The Mary Whitehouse Experience
25 Mastermind: The Two Ronnies

26 One Leg Too Few: Beyond the Fringe
27 Two Soups: Victoria Wood, As Seen on TV
28 Gerald the Talking Gorilla: Not the Nine O'Clock News
29 Mr Cholmondley-Warner (Women Know Your Limits): Harry Enfield's Television Programme
30 Stoneybridge Olympic Bid: Absolutely
31 Nudge Nudge: Monty Python's Flying Circus
32 Craig David on Tour: Bo Selecta!
33 Constable Savage: Not the Nine O'Clock News
34 Singing in the Rain: The Morecombe and Wise Show
35 Alan Partridge (At the Races): The Day Today
36 The Dagenham Dialogues: Not Only... But Also...
37 Thatcher and Cabinet: Spitting Image
38 Damn It!: A Bit of Fry and Laurie
39 Saying Goodbye: Smack the Pony
40 Class Sketch: The Frost Report
41 The Pandas (Japanese Tourists): Who Dares, Wins ...
42 Cissy and Ada, Babysitting: The Les Dawson Show
43 Two Flies: Alas Smith and Jones
44 Jockey Safari: Big Train
45 A La Carte: The Tommy Cooper Hour
46 The Four Yorkshiremen: At Last the 1948 Show
47 Slade in Residence (Christmas Day): The Smell of Reeves and Mortimer
48 Rod Stewart's Bum: The Kenny Everett Television Show
49 The Lumberjack Song: Monty Python's Flying Circus
50 Smashie and Nicey (Radio Quiet): Harry Enfield's Television Programme

....

Good Enough for the North

'What's good enough for London will be good enough for the North. They'll want something different in addition, and I think we'll provide it.'

– Sidney Bernstein, Chairman of Granada TV, speaking before the launch of ITV in the North

....

The Play School 'Windows'

Round   Square   Arched

What They Did for Us

Adam Hart-Davis's populist BBC histories of technology:

What the Romans Did for Us (2000)
What the Victorians Did for Us (2001)
What the Tudors Did for Us (2002)
What the Stuarts Did for Us (2002)
What the Ancients Did for Us (2005)

Celebrity Catchphrases

CATCHPHRASE	CELEBRITY (PROGRAMME)
A bobby dazzler	David Dickinson (Bargain Hunt)
And this is me	Mike Yarwood
As it happens	Jimmy Savile
Awight?	Michael Barrymore
Before your very eyes	Arthur Askey
Boom, boom!	Basil Brush
Can we talk?	Joan Rivers
Cheap as chips	David Dickinson (Bargain Hunt)
Come on down	Leslie Crowther (The Price is Right)
Didn't he do well?	Bruce Forsyth (The Generation Game)
Get down Shep	John Noakes (Blue Peter)
Good game! Good game!	Bruce Forsyth (The Generation Game)
Goody, goody gumdrops	Humphrey Lestocq (Whirligig)
Hallo my darlings	Charlie Drake
Hello, good evening and welcome	David Frost
Hello possums	Dame Edna Everage
Here is your starter for ten	Bamber Gascoigne (University Challenge)
How tickled I am	Ken Dodd
How's about that then?	Jimmy Savile
I mean that most sincerely, friends	Hughie Green (Opportunity Knocks)
I thang yew	Arthur Askey
I wanna tell you a story	Max Bygraves
I'm in charge	Bruce Forsyth (Sunday Night at the London Palladium)
It's Friday. It's five to five. It's Crackerjack	Crackerjack hosts
It's good but it's not right	Roy Walker (Catchphrase)
It's the way I tell 'em	Frank Carson
I've started so I'll finish	Magnus Magnusson (Mastermind)
Izzy Wizzy, let's get busy	Harry Corbett (The Sooty Show)
Just like that	Tommy Cooper

Look at the muck in here	Larry Grayson
May your god go with you	Dave Allen
Nice to see you, to see you, nice	Bruce Forsyth
Not a lot	Paul Daniels
Now that's magic	Paul Daniels
Oi'll give it foive	Janice Nicholls (Thank Your Lucky Stars)
Please yourselves	Frankie Howerd
Rock on Tommy	Bobby Ball
Same to you, fella	Bob Newhart
See what you say and say what you see	Roy Walker (Catchphrase)
Settle down now	Ken Goodwin
She knows, you know	Hilda Baker
Shut that door!	Larry Grayson
Smashing! Super!	Jim Bowen (Bullseye)
Stop messing about	Kenneth Williams
Swinging ... dodgy	Norman Vaughan
Terr-i-fic	Mike Reid
There's more	Jimmy Cricket
There's no answer to that	Eric Morecambe
This is what they want	Chris Tarrant (Tiswas)
Titter ye not!	Frankie Howerd
To me, to you	Chuckle Brothers
Up and under	Eddie Waring
Wakey Wakey!	Billy Cotton
Watching us, watching you	Game for a Laugh presenters
We don't want to give you that	Chris Tarrant (Who Wants to be a Millionaire)
We really want to see those fingers	Vic Reeves and Bob Mortimer (Shooting Stars)
What do points make? Prizes!	Bruce Forsyth (Play Your Cards Right)
What do you think of it so far? Rubbish!	Eric Morecambe
What's on the end of the stick, Vic?	Vic Reeves and Bob Mortimer (Vic Reeves Big Night Out)
You can't see the join	Eric Morecambe
You get nothing for a pair, not in this game	Bruce Forsyth (Play Your Cards Right)
You lucky people	Tommy Trinder
You wouldn't let it lie	Vic Reeves

....

First TV President

The first President of the United States to appear on television was Franklin D Roosevelt, when he made an official address at the opening of the World's Fair in New York on 30 April 1939.

The Noggin the Nog Sagas

The Saga of Noggin the Nog (1959)
Noggin and the Ice Dragon (1961)
Noggin and the Flying Machine (1963)
Noggin and the Omruds (1964)
Noggin and the Firecake (1965, remade in 1982)
Noggin and the Pie (1982)

Real Life Wives and Husbands (Past and Present)

WIFE	HUSBAND	WIFE	HUSBAND
Maria Aitken	Nigel Davenport	Dawn French	Lenny Henry
Gracie Allen	George Burns	Fiona Fullerton	Simon MacCorkindale
Loni Anderson	Burt Reynolds	Jill Gascoine	Alfred Molina
Rosalind Ayres	Martin Jarvis	Liza Goddard	Colin Baker ,
Barbara Bain	Martin Landau		Alvin Stardust
Glynis Barber	Michael Brandon	Jane Goldman	Jonathan Ross
Roseanne Barr	Tom Arnold	Dulcie Gray	Michael Dennison
Majel Barrett	Gene Roddenberry	Sarah Greene	Mike Smith
Ann Bell	Robert Lang	Cheryl Hall	Robert Lindsay
Honor Blackman	Maurice Kaufmann	Sheila Hancock	John Thaw
Isla Blair	Julian Glover	Valentina Harris	Bob Harris
Connie Booth	John Cleese	Keeley Hawes	Matthew Macfadyen
Barbara Bosson	Steven Bochco	Melanie Hill	Sean Bean
Fern Britton	Phil Vickery	Amanda Holden	Les Dennis
Janet Brown	Peter Butterworth	Hattie Jacques	John Le Mesurier
Judy Carne	Burt Reynolds	Madhur Jaffrey	Saeed Jaffrey
Pauline Collins	John Alderton	Susan Jameson	James Bolam
Joan Collins	Anthony Newley	Yootha Joyce	Glynn Edwards
Fanny Cradock	Johnny Cradock	Lesley Judd	Derek Fowlds
Gemma Craven	Frazer Hines	Barbara Kelly	Bernard Braden
Abigail Cruttenden	Sean Bean	Alex Kingston	Ralph Fiennes
Sinead Cusack	Jeremy Irons	Belinda Lang	Hugh Fraser
Judi Dench	Michael Williams	Phyllida Law	Eric Thompson
Sandra Dickinson	Peter Davison	Rula Lenska	Dennis Waterman
Michele Dotrice	Edward Woodward	Maureen Lipman	Jack Rosenthal
Dale Evans	Roy Rogers	Sue Lloyd	Ronald Allen
Mia Farrow	Frank Sinatra,	Judy Loe	Richard Beckinsale
	André Previn	Joanna Lumley	Jeremy Lloyd
Farrah Fawcett	Lee Majors	Debbie McGee	Paul Daniels
Judy Finnigan	Richard Madeley	Cathy McGowan	Hywel Bennett
Lucy Fleming	Simon Williams	Ruth Madoc	Philip Madoc

Lesley Manville	Gary Oldman	Prunella Scales	Timothy West
Jean Marsh	Jon Pertwee	Dinah Sheridan	Jimmy Hanley
Anna Massey	Jeremy Brett	Maggie Smith	Robert Stephens
Sharon Maughan	Trevor Eve	Alison Steadman	Mike Leigh
Madelaine Newton	Kevin Whately	Sheila Steafel	Harry H Corbett
Sue Nicholls	Mark Eden	Shirley Stelfox	Don Henderson
Coleen Nolan	Shane Richie	Pamela Stephenson	Nicholas Ball,
Wendy Padbury	Melvyn Hayes		Billy Connolly
Rhea Perlman	Danny De Vito	Miriam Stoppard	Tom Stoppard
Maggie Philbin	Keith Chegwin	Susan Stranks	Robin Ray
Siân Phillips	Peter O'Toole	Una Stubbs	Peter Gilmore,
Patricia Phoenix	Tony Booth		Nicky Henson
Billie Piper	Chris Evans	Mollie Sugden	William Moore
Caroline Quentin	Paul Merton	Josephine Tewson	Leonard Rossiter
Louie Ramsay	George Baker	Emma Thompson	Kenneth Branagh
Esther Rantzen	Desmond Wilcox	Angela Thorne	Peter Penry-Jones
Anthea Redfern	Bruce Forsyth	Lalla Ward	Tom Baker
Amanda Redman	Robert Glenister	Denise Welch	Tim Healy
Angharad Rees	Christopher Cazenove	Billie Whitelaw	Peter Vaughan
Amy Robbins	Robert Daws	Penelope Wilton	Ian Holm
Jennifer Saunders	Adrian Edmondson	Victoria Wood	Geoffrey Durham
Julia Sawalha	Alan Davies	Helen Worth	Michael Angelis

....

The Mystery Movies

The NBC Mystery Movie (simply Mystery Movie in the UK), which ran 1971–7, was the umbrella title for screenings of different detective series, namely:

SERIES (STAR/S)
Amy Prentiss (Jessica Walter)
Banacek (George Peppard)
Columbo (Peter Falk)
Cool Million (James Farentino)
Faraday & Company (Dan Dailey, James Naughton)
Hec Ramsey (Richard Boone)
Lanigan's Rabbi (Art Carney, Bruce Solomon)
Madigan (Richard Widmark)
McCloud (Dennis Weaver)
McCoy (Tony Curtis)
McMillan and Wife (Rock Hudson, Susan Saint James)
Quincy, ME (Jack Klugman)
The Snoop Sisters (Helen Hayes, Mildred Natwick)
Tenafly (James McEachin)

Some Working Titles for Successful Series

SERIES	WORKING TITLE
Airwolf	Blackwolf
Bottom	Your Bottom
Brookside	Meadowcroft
Budgie	Loser
Coronation Street	Florizel Street
Crossroads	The Midland Road
The Dick Van Dyke Show	Head of the Family
Drop the Dead Donkey	Dead Belgians Don't Count
Dynasty	Oil
EastEnders	East 8, London Pride
Emergency – Ward 10	Calling Nurse Roberts
The Flintstones	The Flagstones
Friends	Across the Hall, Six of One, Friends Like Us, Insomnia Café
The Goodies	Super-Chaps Three
Leave It to Beaver	Wally and Beaver
Lost in Space	Space Family Robinson
The Man from UNCLE	Solo
Neighbours	One-Way Street
Only Fools and Horses	Readies
The Outer Limits	Please Stand By, Beyond Control
Rentaghost	Second Chance
Rising Damp	The Banana Box, Rooksby
Scooby-Doo, Where Are You?	Mysteries Five
Seinfeld	The Seinfeld Chronicles
Upstairs, Downstairs	Behind the Green Baize Door, Below Stairs

The Day the Running Stopped

August 29 1967 has become known in TV land as 'The Day the Running Stopped'. This was the date of the original US transmission of the last episode of the massively popular drama series The Fugitive. Actor David Janssen made his bow as Richard Kimble in 1963 and for four seasons portrayed the runaway doctor who had been wrongly convicted for the murder of his wife and was now being pursued by relentless police officer Lieutenant Gerard. More than 70 per cent of American viewers tuned in for that rare event, a proper conclusion for a drama series, where Kimble finally tracked down the 'One-Armed Man' he suspected of being his wife's killer. The episode was transmitted one day later in the UK.

Why Emmy?

The annual Emmy awards are handed out by the National Academy of Television Arts (NATAS) and its associate bodies, so why aren't they called Nats? The name Emmy was apparently coined by Harry Lubcke, president of the Academy at the time of the first ceremony in 1949. He thought it a witty play on the word 'immy', which was a trade nickname for a piece of television equipment called an image orthicon tube. That's an engineer's sense of humour for you.

Notable TV Pop Shows

PROGRAMME	CHANNEL/DATES	MAIN HOST(S)
Cool for Cats	ITV 1956–61	Kent Walton
Six-Five Special	BBC 1957–8	Pete Murray, Jo Douglas
Oh Boy!	ITV 1958–9	Tony Hall, Jimmy Henny
Drumbeat	BBC 1959	Gus Goodwin, Trevor Peacock
Juke Box Jury	BBC 1 1959–67, 1979, 1989–90	David Jacobs, Noel Edmonds, Jools Holland
Thank Your Lucky Stars	ITV 1961–6	Keith Fordyce, Brian Matthew
Ready, Steady, Go!	ITV 1963–6	Keith Fordyce, Cathy McGowan
Top of the Pops	BBC 1/2 1964–	Numerous
The Beat Room	BBC 2 1964–5	Pat Campbell
Gadzooks! It's All Happening	BBC 2 1965	Alan David, Christine Holmes
Colour Me Pop	BBC 2 1968–9	No host
Lift Off	ITV 1969–74	Ayshea Brough, Wally Whyton
Old Grey Whistle Test	BBC 2 1971–88	Bob Harris, Anne Nightingale
Supersonic	ITV 1975–7	No host
So it Goes	ITV 1976–7	Tony Wilson, Clive James
All You Need Is Love	ITV 1977	No host (documentary)
Get It Together	ITV 1977–81	Roy North
Rock Goes to College	BBC 2 1978–81	Bob Harris
Pop Quiz	BBC 1981–4	Mike Read
The Tube	Channel 4 1982–7	Jools Holland, Paula Yates
Later with Jools Holland	BBC 2 1992–	Jools Holland
The White Room	BBC 2 1995–6	Mark Radcliffe
CD:UK	ITV 1998–	Ant and Dec, Cat Deeley
Popstars	ITV 2001–2	Davina McCall
Pop Idol	ITV 2001–2	Ant and Dec

A Register of TV Doctors

DOCTOR	**Ben Casey**
SERIES	Ben Casey
STAR	Vince Edwards
CREATOR	James E Moser
COLLEAGUE	David Zorba
PRACTICE	County General Hospital

DOCTOR	**David Cheriton**
SERIES	The Royal
STAR	Julian Ovenden
CREATOR	Yorkshire TV
COLLEAGUE	Gordon Ormerod
PRACTICE	St Aidan's Royal Free Hospital

DOCTOR	**Andrew Collin**
SERIES	Cardiac Arrest
STAR	Andrew Lancel
CREATOR	John MacUre
COLLEAGUE	Claire Maitland
PRACTICE	Crippen Ward

DOCTOR	**Stephen Daker**
SERIES	A Very Peculiar Practice
STAR	Peter Davison
CREATOR	Andrew Davies
COLLEAGUES	Bob Buzzard, Rose Marie
PRACTICE	Lowlands University

DOCTOR	**Paul Dangerfield**
SERIES	Dangerfield
STAR	Nigel Le Vaillant
CREATOR	Don Shaw
COLLEAGUE	Joanna Stevens
PRACTICE	Dangerfield Health Centre

DOCTOR	**Alan Dawson**
SERIES	Emergency – Ward 10
STAR	Charles Tingwell
CREATOR	Tessa Diamond
COLLEAGUE	Chris Anderson
PRACTICE	Oxbridge General Hospital

DOCTOR	**John ('JD') Dorian**
SERIES	Scrubs
STAR	Zach Braff
CREATOR	Bill Lawrence
COLLEAGUES	Chris Turk, Elliott Reid
PRACTICE	Sacred Heart Hospital

DOCTOR	**Alan Finlay**
SERIES	Dr Finlay's Casebook
STAR	Bill Simpson
CREATOR	AJ Cronin
COLLEAGUES	Angus Cameron, Janet
PRACTICE	Arden House, Tannochbrae

DOCTOR	**Joel Fleischman**
SERIES	Northern Exposure
STAR	Rob Morrow
CREATORS	Joshua Brand, John Falsey
COLLEAGUE	Marilyn Whirlwind
PRACTICE	Cicely, Alaska

DOCTOR	**Jeffrey Geiger**
SERIES	Chicago Hope
STAR	Mandy Patinkin
CREATOR	David E Kelley
COLLEAGUE	Aaron Shutt
PRACTICE	Chicago Hope Hospital

DOCTOR	**Tom Gilder**
SERIES	Born and Bred
STAR	Michael French
CREATORS	Chris Chibnall, Nigel McCery
COLLEAGUE	Arthur Gilder
PRACTICE	Ormston

DOCTOR	**Beth Glover**
SERIES	Peak Practice
STAR	Amanda Burton
CREATOR	Lucy Gannon
COLLEAGUES	Jack Kerruish, Will Preston
PRACTICE	Cardale

DOCTOR	**Lawrence Golding**
SERIES	The Practice
STAR	John Fraser
CREATOR	Granada
COLLEAGUE	Judith Vincent
PRACTICE	Castlehulme Health Centre

DOCTOR	**Mark Greene**
SERIES	ER
STAR	Anthony Edwards
CREATOR	Michael Crichton
COLLEAGUES	Douglas Ross, Susan Lewis
PRACTICE	Cook County General Hospital

DOCTOR	**John Hardy**
SERIES	The Expert
STAR	Marius Goring
CREATORS	Gerard Glaister, NJ Crisp
COLLEAGUE	Jo Hardy
PRACTICE	Warwickshire

DOCTOR	**Douglas 'Doogie' Howser**
SERIES	Doogie Howser, MD
STAR	Neil Patrick Harris
CREATORS	Steven Bochco, David Kelley
COLLEAGUE	David Howser
PRACTICE	Eastman Medical Center

DOCTOR	**Geoffrey Hoyt**
SERIES	Medics
STAR	Tom Baker
CREATOR	Granada
COLLEAGUE	Ruth Parry
PRACTICE	Henry Park Hospital

DOCTOR	**Michael Jimson**
SERIES	Health and Efficiency
STAR	Gary Olsen
CREATOR	Andrew Marshall
COLLEAGUE	Kate Russell
PRACTICE	St James's General Hospital

DOCTOR	**James Kildare**
SERIES	Dr Kildare
STAR	Richard Chamberlain
CREATOR	Max Brand
COLLEAGUE	Leonard Gillespie
PRACTICE	Blair General Hospital

DOCTOR	**Robert Kingsford**
SERIES	Always and Everyone/ A&E
STAR	Martin Shaw
CREATOR	Granada
COLLEAGUE	Christine Fletcher
PRACTICE	St Victor's Hospital

DOCTOR	**Toby Latimer**
SERIES	Don't Wait Up
STAR	Tony Britton
CREATOR	George Layton
COLLEAGUE	Tom Latimer
PRACTICE	Harley Street

DOCTOR	**Iain McCallum**
SERIES	McCallum
STAR	John Hannah
CREATOR	Stuart Hepburn
COLLEAGUE	Angela Moloney
PRACTICE	St Patrick's Hospital

DOCTOR	**Brendan McGuire**
SERIES	Doctors
STAR	Christopher Timothy
CREATOR	BBC
COLLEAGUES	Steve Rawlings, Helen Thompson
PRACTICE	Riverside

DOCTOR	**Anton Meyer**
SERIES	Holby City
STAR	George Irving
CREATOR	BBC
COLLEAGUES	Nick Jordan, Kirstie Collins
PRACTICE	Holby City Hospital

DOCTOR	**William Parker Brown**	DOCTOR	**Barbara 'Baz' Samuels**
SERIES	General Hospital	SERIES	Casualty
STAR	Lewis Jones	STAR	Julia Watson
CREATOR	ATV	CREATORS	Jeremy Brock, Paul Unwin
COLLEAGUES	Matthew Armstrong, Neville Bywaters	COLLEAGUES	Charlie Fairhead, Ewart Plimmer
PRACTICE	Midland General Hospital	PRACTICE	Holby City Hospital

DOCTOR	**Benjamin 'Hawkeye' Pierce**	DOCTOR	**John Somers**
SERIES	M*A*S*H	SERIES	The Doctors
STAR	Alan Alda	STAR	John Barrie
CREATOR	Larry Gelbart	CREATOR	Donald Bull
COLLEAGUES	'Trapper John' McIntyre, BJ Hunnicutt	COLLEAGUES	Roger Hayman, Liz McNeal
PRACTICE	Korea	PRACTICE	North London

DOCTOR	**Quincy**	DOCTOR	**Caroline Todd**
SERIES	Quincy, ME	SERIES	Green Wing
STAR	Jack Klugman	STAR	Tamsin Greig
CREATORS	Glen A Larson, Lou Shaw	CREATOR	Victoria Pile
COLLEAGUE	Sam Fujiyama	COLLEAGUES	Guy Secretan, Dr McCartney
PRACTICE	Los Angeles	PRACTICE	Hospital Green Wing

DOCTOR	**Michaela Quinn**	DOCTOR	**Michael Upton**
SERIES	Dr Quinn: Medicine Woman	SERIES	Doctor in the House
STAR	Jane Seymour	STAR	Barry Evans
CREATOR	Beth Sullivan	CREATOR	Richard Gordon
COLLEAGUE	Byron Sully	COLLEAGUE	Duncan Waring
PRACTICE	Colorado Springs	PRACTICE	St Swithin's Hospital

DOCTOR	**Sam Ryan**	DOCTOR	**Marcus Welby**
SERIES	Silent Witness	SERIES	Marcus Welby, MD
STAR	Amanda Burton	STAR	Robert Young
CREATOR	Nigel McCrery	CREATOR	David Victor
COLLEAGUE	Tom Adams	COLLEAGUE	Steven Kiley
PRACTICE	Cambridge	PRACTICE	Santa Monica

DOCTOR	**Sheila Sabatini**	DOCTOR	**Donald Westphall**
SERIES	Surgical Spirit	SERIES	St Elsewhere
STAR	Nichola McAuliffe	STAR	Ed Flanders
CREATOR	Peter Learmouth	CREATORS	Joshua Brand, John Falsey
COLLEAGUE	Jonathan Haslam	COLLEAGUES	Mark Craig, Victor Ehrlich
PRACTICE	Gillies Hospital	PRACTICE	St Elegius Hospital

A Dastardly Inventor

To viewers in the UK, his name may not be familiar but his voice rings plenty of bells. Who can forget the malevolent scheming tones of Dick Dastardly in Wacky Races or the eccentricity of Tigger in the Winnie the Pooh movies? The voice belonged to the late Paul Winchell, one of America's top ventriloquists. But Winchell had other strings to his bow, too. He was a qualified doctor of acupuncture, worked as a medical hypnotist and was also an inspired inventor. Among his creations was the artificial heart, for which he held a patent, granted in the early 1960s. He also claimed to have been the first to develop a disposable razor and other inventions such as a flameless cigarette lighter, a portable defroster of blood plasma, an alphabet that can only be read in a mirror and battery-heated gloves.

First Night: ITV's Opening Schedule (22 September 1955)

7.15pm The Ceremony at Guildhall. John Connell watches the guests arrive; music from the Halle Orchestra under Sir John Barbirolli; inaugural speeches.

8.00 Channel 9. A variety show from ABC's television theatre, introduced by Jack Jackson. Featured artists include Shirley Abicair, Reg Dixon, Hughie Green, Billy Cotton, John Hanson and Harry Secombe.

8.40 Drama. Robert Morley introduces excerpts from The Importance of Being Earnest (Oscar Wilde), Baker's Dozen ('Saki') and Private Lives (Noël Coward), performed by stars like Dame Edith Evans, Sir John Gielgud, Alec Guinness and Margaret Leighton.

9.10 Professional Boxing. Jack Solomons presents Terence Murphy v Lew Lazar, a middleweight contest from Shoreditch Town Hall. Commentators Len Harvey and Tony Van den Burgh.

10.00 News and Newsreel

10.15 Gala Night at the Mayfair. Leslie Mitchell introduces guests attending the Opening Gala Night at London's Mayfair Hotel, plus a fashion show.

10.30 Star Cabaret. Music provided by Billy Ternant and his Orchestra.

10.50 Preview. A look ahead to some programmes to be featured on Independent Television in coming months.

11.00 Epilogue. The National Anthem and closedown.

Chewing Gum for the Eyes

'TV is chewing gum for the eyes.' - Architect Frank Lloyd Wright

Chat Show Hosts

HOST	PROGRAMME
Clive Anderson	Clive Anderson Talks Back, Clive Anderson All Talk
Michael Aspel	Aspel & Company
Danny Baker	The Danny Baker Show, Danny Baker After All
Derek Batey	Look Who's Talking
Gay Byrne	The Late Late Show
Johnny Carson	The Tonight Show
Dick Cavett	The Dick Cavett Show
Simon Dee	Dee Time
Russell Harty	Russell Harty Plus, Russell Harty
Gloria Hunniford	Gloria Live, Open House with Gloria Hunniford
Clive James	Saturday Night Clive
Jay Leno	The Tonight Show
David Letterman	Late Night with David Letterman
Graham Norton	So Graham Norton
Paul O'Grady	The Paul O'Grady Show
Michael Parkinson	Parkinson
Richard & Judy	This Morning, Richard & Judy
Gaby Roslin	The Gaby Roslin Show
Jonathan Ross	The Last Resort, Friday Night with Jonathan Ross
Frank Skinner	The Frank Skinner Show
Johnny Vaughan	The Johnny Vaughan Show
Harold Wilson	Friday Night ... Saturday Morning
Terry Wogan	Wogan

. . . .

Danny Baker's TV Heroes

In a series of ten-minute shorts aired between 1993 and 1995, Danny Baker affectionately lifted the lid on some of TV's greatest discoveries. These included:

Fanny Cradock	Johnny Morris
Election night presenters	David Nixon
Peter Glaze	Pinky and Perky
Noele Gordon	Oliver Postgate
Deryck Guyler	Peter Purves
Rolf Harris	Sooty
Bob Harris	The Top of the Pops audience
Spike Milligan	Barbara Woodhouse

Badges Worn by Key UNCLE Operatives

Mr Waverly 1

Illya Kuryakin 2

Napoleon Solo 11

Mark Slate 14

April Dancer 22

Some Famous People Who Read for Jackanory

Joss Ackland
Jenny Agutter
Jane Asher
Michael Barrymore
Lynda Bellingham
Alan Bennett
Hywel Bennett
Brian Blessed
James Bolam
Jeremy Brett
Richard Briers
Kathy Burke
George Cole
Tom Conti
Harry H Corbett
Ronnie Corbett
Wendy Craig
Bernard Cribbins
Rosalie Crutchley
Judi Dench
Maurice Denham
Roy Dotrice
Denholm Elliott
Julie Felix
Edward Fox
Dawn French
Hannah Gordon
Joyce Grenfell

Susan Hampshire
Sheila Hancock
Patricia Hayes
Bernard Hepton
Thora Hird
Michael Hordern
HRH The Prince of Wales
Jeremy Irons
Derek Jacobi
Hattie Jacques
David Jason
Michael Jayston
Stratford Johns
James Robertson Justice
Penelope Keith
Roy Kinnear
John Laurie
John Le Mesurier
Robert Lindsay
Maureen Lipman
Arthur Lowe
Joanna Lumley
Magnus Magnusson
Alfred Marks
Anna Massey
Geraldine McEwan
Ian McKellen
Paul Merton

Spike Milligan
Hayley Mills
Helen Mirren
Michael Palin
Jon Pertwee
Siân Phillips
Anthony Quayle
Ted Ray
Miranda Richardson
Patricia Routledge
William Rushton
Margaret Rutherford
Prunella Scales
Patrick Stewart
David Suchet
Molly Sugden
David Tomlinson
Patrick Troughton
Margaret Tyzack
Colin Welland
Kevin Whately
Billie Whitelaw
June Whitfield
Kenneth Williams
Michael Williams
Frank Windsor
Victoria Wood
Susannah York

Some Programmes with Titles Changed for UK Audiences

ORIGINAL TITLE	UK TITLE
Card Sharks	Play Your Cards Right*
Colargol	Barnaby
College Bowl	University Challenge*
Family Feud	Family Fortunes*
The Golden Girls	Brighton Belles*
Good Times	The Fosters*
Gunsmoke	Gun Law
Hollywood Squares	Celebrity Squares*
Ironside	A Man Called Ironside
Mad about You	Loved by You*
Married ... with Children	Married for Life*
Maude	Nobody's Perfect*
Prisoner	Prisoner: Cell Block H
Rock and Roll	Dancing in the Street
The $64,000 Question	The 64,000 Question*
The $10,000 Pyramid	The Pyramid Game*
Sugarfoot	Tenderfoot
Tales of Wells Fargo	Wells Fargo
Teenage Mutant Ninja Turtles	Teenage Mutant Hero Turtles
That '70s Show	Days Like These*
Tic Tac Dough	Criss Cross Quiz*
Top Cat	Boss Cat
Who's the Boss?	The Upper Hand*

* Titles adopted when re-created for UK television.

....

TV Characters With No Known First Names

CHARACTER	SERIES
Columbo	Columbo
Gilligan	Gilligan's Island
BJ Hunnicutt	M*A*S*H
MacGyver	MacGyver
Mr Big	Sex and the City
Mulberry	Mulberry
Murdoch	The A-Team
Quincy	Quincy, ME
Spenser	Spenser: for Hire

Note: The first name of Inspector Morse was left undeclared until, in the 1997 story Death Is Now My Neighbour, it was revealed to be Endeavour.

Eurovision Facts and Figures

FIRST WINNER	Lys Assia (Switzerland) 1956, Refrain
UK WINNERS	Sandie Shaw 1967, Puppet on a String
	Lulu (joint) 1969, Boom Bang-a-Bang
	Brotherhood of Man 1976, Save Your Kisses for Me
	Bucks Fizz 1981, Making Your Mind Up
	Katrina and the Waves 1997, Love Shine a Light
FIRST 'NUL POINTS'	Austria, Belgium, Netherland, Spain, all 1962
MOST NOTABLE 'NUL POINTS'*	Jahn Teigen (Norway) 1978, Mil Etter Mil
FIRST UK 'NUL POINTS'	Jemini 2003, Cry Baby
YEARS UK DIDN'T ENTER	1956, 1958
UK HOSTING VENUES	1960 Royal Festival Hall, London (host: Katie Boyle)
	1963 BBC Television Centre, London (host: Katie Boyle)
	1968 Royal Albert Hall, London (host: Katie Boyle)
	1972 Usher Hall, Edinburgh (host: Moira Shearer)
	1974 The Dome, Brighton (host: Katie Boyle)
	1977 Wembley Conference Centre (host: Angela Rippon)
	1982 Harrogate Conference Centre (host: Jan Leeming)
	1998 National Indoor Arena, Birmingham (host: Ulrika Jonsson)

* Early scoring systems made it relatively easy to score zero, but by the time Jahn Teigen achieved this feat the scoring system had been revamped with many more points available.

....

'Spectrum' Officers

Captain Scarlet and his colourful colleagues.

OFFICER CODE NAME	REAL IDENTITY
Captain Scarlet	Paul Metcalfe
Captain Blue	Adam Svenson
Captain Brown	Not revealed
Captain Grey	Bradley Holden
Captain Magenta	Patrick Donaghue
Captain Ochre	Richard Fraser
Colonel White	Charles Gray
Dr Fawn	Edward Wilkie
Lieutenant Green	Seymour Griffiths

Captain Black (Conrad Turner) was a Spectrum agent until being converted to the cause of Spectrum's enemies, the Mysterons. Spectrum agents were supported in action by the Angels team of female fighter pilots, individually known as Destiny (Juliette Pontoin), Harmony (Chan Kwan), Melody (Magnolia Jones), Rhapsody (Dianne Sims), and Symphony (Karen Wainwright).

The 100 Greatest Kids' TV Shows

As selected by viewers for the Channel 4 programme broadcast on 27 August 2001.

1　The Simpsons
2　The Muppet Show
3　Dangermouse
4　Bagpuss
5　Grange Hill
6　Mr Benn
7　Rainbow
8　Scooby-Doo, Where are You?
9　Doctor Who
10　He-Man and Masters of the Universe
11　The Magic Roundabout
12　The Clangers
13　Wallace and Gromit
14　Rentaghost
15　Maid Marian and Her Merry Men
16　Tom and Jerry
17　The Wombles
18　The Flintstones
19　Hong Kong Phooey
20　Worzel Gummidge
21　Knightmare
22　Trumpton
23　Postman Pat
24　Thunderbirds
25　Jim'll Fix It
26　Thomas the Tank Engine and Friends
27　Roobarb and Custard
28　Jamie and the Magic Torch
29　SM:TV Live
30　Sesame Street
31　The Basil Brush Show
32　Boss/Top Cat
33　Blue Peter
34　Byker Grove
35　Banana Splits
36　The Sooty Show

37 Chorlton and the Wheelies
38 Roland Rat
39 The Adventure Game
40 Why Don't You ... ?
41 Tiswas
42 Battle of the Planets
43 Play School
44 Batman
45 Captain Pugwash
46 Press Gang
47 Crackerjack
48 Fingerbobs
49 The Tomorrow People
50 Multi-Coloured Swap Shop
51 Captain Scarlet and the Mysterons
52 The Herbs
53 Timmy Mallett's Wide Awake Club
54 Animal Magic
55 Pipkins
56 The Wind in the Willows
57 Flower Pot Men
58 Metal Mickey
59 Pob's Programme
60 The Adventures of Black Beauty
61 Andy Pandy
62 Lassie
63 John Craven's Newsround
64 The Famous Five
65 How!
66 Here Come the Double Deckers
67 The Snowman
68 Record Breakers
69 Mary, Mungo and Midge
70 Jackanory
71 Bob the Builder
72 Michael Bentine's Potty Time
73 Pokemon
74 Skippy
75 Noggin the Nog

CURIOUS FACT

Vision On artist Tony Hart was the designer of the Blue Peter ship logo

....

Radio on TV (Fictitious Radio Stations)

RADIO STATION	PROGRAMME
Brixton Broadcasting Corporation	The Lenny Henry Show
Chorley FM	Peter Kay's Phoenix Nights
KACL	Frasier
KBBL	The Simpsons
KBHR	Northern Exposure
Radio Fab FM	Harry Enfield's Television Programme
Radio Newtown	The Kit Curran Radio Show
Radio Norwich	I'm Alan Partridge
Radio West	Shoestring
WBCW	Dawson's Creek
WKRP	WKRP in Cincinnati

The Gladiators

ITV's Gladiators (1992–8) pitched members of the public into a series of strength- and stamina-sapping challenges staged at Birmingham's National Indoor Arena. Their opponents were a team of super-athletes, body-builders and muscular wrestlers, who squeezed into colourful leotards and performed under the following evocative pseudonyms:

Female	PSEUDONYM	REAL NAME
	Amazon	Sharron Davies
	Falcon	Bernadette Hunt
	Flame	Kimbra Standish
	Fox	Tammy Marie Baker
	Gold	Lize van der Walt
	Jet	Diane Youdale Mayhew
	Laser	Tina Andrew
	Lightning	Kim Betts
	Nightshade	Judy Simpson
	Panther	Helen O'Reilly
	Phoenix	Sandy Young
	Rebel	Jennifer Stoute
	Rio	Jane Omorogbe
	Rocket	Pauline Richards
	Scorpio	Nikki Diamond
	Siren	Alison Paton
	Vogue	Suzanne Cox
	Zodiac	Kate Staples

Male	PSEUDONYM	REAL NAME
	Ace	Warren Furman
	Cobra	Michael Willson
	Diesel	Darren Crawford
	Hawk	Aleks Georgijev
	Hunter	James Crossley
	Khan	Radosav Nekic
	Raider	Carlton Headley
	Rhino	Mark Smith
	Saracen	Mike Lewis
	Shadow	Jefferson King
	Trojan	Mark Griffin
	Vulcan	John Seru
	Warrior	Michael Ahearne
	Wolf	Michael van Wijk

Villains Encountered in Batman

VILLAIN	ACTOR(S)
The Archer	Art Carney
The Black Widow	Tallulah Bankhead
The Bookworm	Roddy McDowall
Catwoman	Julie Newmar, Lee Meriwether, Eartha Kitt
The Clock King	Walter Slezak
Colonel Gumm	Roger C Carmel
Dr Cassandra Spellcraft	Ida Lupino
Egghead	Vincent Price
False Face	Malachi Throne
Fingers	Liberace
The Joker	Cesar Romero
King Tut	Victor Buono
Lady Penelope Peasoup	Glynis Johns
Lola Lasagna	Ethel Merman
Lord Ffogg	Rudy Vallee
Louie the Lilac	Milton Berle
Ma Parker	Shelley Winters
The Mad Hatter	David Wayne
Marsha, the Queen of Diamonds	Carolyn Jones
Minerva	Zsa Zsa Gabor
The Minstrel	Van Johnson
Mr Freeze	George Sanders, Otto Preminger, Eli Wallach
Nora Clavicle	Barbara Rush
Olga	Anne Baxter
The Penguin	Burgess Meredith
The Puzzler	Maurice Evans
The Riddler	Frank Gorshin, John Astin
The Sandman	Michael Rennie
Shame	Cliff Robertson
The Siren	Joan Collins
Zelda the Great	Anne Baxter

. . . .

The Ultimate Insult

It is rather sad to report that the 'father of television', John Logie Baird, was not even invited to the opening ceremony when regular high-definition broadcasting started formally on 2 November 1936. Undaunted by this snub, the great man arrived at Alexandra Palace hoping to be allowed in, only to find that there was no place reserved for him among the higher echelons of the BBC and the Government enjoying the event.

Ventriloquists and Their Dummies

VENTRILOQUIST	DUMMY(IES)
Ray Alan	Mikki the Martian, Lord Charles, Tich and Quackers, Ali Cat
Peter Brough	Archie Andrews
Roger De Courcey	Nookie Bear
Terry Hall	Lenny the Lion
Keith Harris	Orville, Cuddles
Shari Lewis	Lamb Chop, Charley Horse, Hush Puppy
Ronn Lucas	Scorch the Dragon
Jimmy Tamley	Knuckles the Biker, Lightning Les, Grandad
Paul Winchell	Jerry Mahoney, Knucklehead Smiff

....

Ten Memorable Blue Peter 'Makes'

ITEM	COMPONENTS
Advent crown	Wire coathangers, flame-proof tinsel, candles, ribbons, baubles
Animal Hospital set	Cardboard box, paint, yoghurt tub, washing-up liquid bottles, cardboard tube, matchboxes
Dolls' hammock	Shoebox, wire coathangers, ceiling tiles (for a lawn)
Father Christmas decoration	Newspaper, brown paper, red crepe paper, cotton wool
Luxury cat's bed	Washing-up bowl, foam, waterproof material, elastic
Pencil case	Washing-up liquid bottle, cardboard, paint, a cork
Puppet theatre	Washing powder boxes, simple light fittings, magazine pictures for sets, figures from Christmas cards for cast
Table football game	Cardboard box, washing powder boxes, garden canes, clothes pegs, numbers from an old calendar, stiff card, table-tennis ball
Tracy Island model	Cardboard box, cereal packet, washing powder box, matchboxes, newspaper, drinking straw, washing-up liquid bottles
Winter bird cake	Unsalted chopped nuts, millet, maize, sunflower seeds, currants, bird seed, biscuit crumbs, fat

Note: The construction of these items may also require the use of 'sticky tape' and 'sticky-backed plastic' – no trade names, please.

Christmas Day Big Film Premieres

The era of the big BBC1 Christmas Day movie didn't begin until the mid-1970s. Previously viewers were treated to a selection of old, worthy and often-screened films, such as Rebecca (a 1940 film, shown in 1961), The Gold Rush (1925, shown in 1963) and Bridge on the River Kwai (1957, shown in 1974). Here are the premieres from 1975 onwards. Although some films would have been old, it was their first airing on UK TV.

1975	The Wizard of Oz, Butch Cassidy and the Sundance Kid
1976	Oliver, Airport
1977	Funny Girl
1978	The Sound of Music
1979	The Sting
1980	International Velvet, Death on the Nile
1981	In Search of the Castaways, Loophole
1982	20,000 Leagues under the Sea, Airport 1975
1983	Treasure Island, Better Late than Never
1984	Mary Poppins
1985	Absence of Malice
1986	Annie, Educating Rita
1987	Indiana Jones and the Temple of Doom
1988	Back to the Future, Silverado
1989	Crocodile Dundee, Clockwise
1990	ET, Baby Boom
1991	Batman, Coming to America
1992	Indiana Jones and the Last Crusade, Shirley Valentine
1993	Back to the Future Part III, Ghost
1994	Robin Hood: Prince of Thieves
1995	Hook, Indecent Proposal
1996	Jurassic Park
1997	The Flintstones, The Mask
1998	Babe
1999	Jumanji
2000	Titanic
2001	Toy Story
2002	Chicken Run
2003	Stuart Little
2004	102 Dalmatians, Harry Potter and the Philosopher's Stone

Some Notable Alumni of Cambridge Footlights

Douglas Adams	Hugh Dennis	Rory McGrath
Clive Anderson	David Frost	Joe Melia
David Baddiel	Stephen Fry	Jonathan Miller
Morwenna Banks	Graeme Garden	Jimmy Mulville
Humphrey Barclay	Bamber Gascoigne	Bill Oddie
Sacha Baron Cohen	Mel Giedroyc	Sue Perkins
Robert Bathurst	Germaine Greer	Steve Punt
John Bird	Nick Hancock	Frederic Raphael
Eleanor Bron	Eric Idle	Jan Ravens
Tim Brooke-Taylor	Clive James	Griff Rhys Jones
Graham Chapman	Hugh Laurie	Tony Slattery
John Cleese	John Lloyd	Emma Thompson
Peter Cook	Jonathan Lynn	Sandi Toksvig
Julie Covington	Miriam Margolyes	Bob Wellings

....

The Pythons

John Cleese   Eric Idle

Michael Palin   Terry Jones   Terry Gilliam

....

TV Dinners

Question: Take 520,000 lbs of surplus turkey and the creative mind of a salesman and what do you get? Answer: The TV Dinner. Back in 1953 US food company Swanson's found itself with far too much turkey than it knew how to handle. The management, brothers Clarke and Gilbert Swanson, turned to its workforce for ideas and it was salesman Gerry Thomas who, it is said, came up with the goods after experiencing an early form of airline meal on a recent trip. With the television boom sounding all across America, he spotted the potential for a quick and easy meal that could be comfortably eaten while diners remained glued to the small screen. He designed a three-compartment metal tray that could simply be transferred from freezer to oven and his bosses gave it a whirl. Five thousand sample dinners were prepared and proved so successful that just over a year later a staggering 25 million had been sold. New varieties were introduced but turkey, as it happened, proved to be the most popular, retailing at $1.29 a pack. Swanson's TV Dinners switched the aluminium tray for plastic in 1986, so that the meal could be microwaved, but the metal tray can still be found – as part of an exhibit at the Smithsonian Institution in Washington, DC. Gerry Thomas has also been honoured, with a star on Hollywood's Walk of Fame.

M*A*S*H Facts

The only actor from the original movie to appear in the TV series was Gary Burghoff, reprising his role of Radar O'Reilly.

In all, 251 episodes were produced, aired over 11 years.

Before joining M*A*S*H, Jamie Farr, who played Maxwell Klinger, was working as a game show writer.

Despite being part of the series from its inception (excepting the pilot episode), William Christopher, who played Father Mulcahy, was only paid day rates and was not given a contract until year 6.

Radar's real name is Walter. He gets his nickname from the uncanny way he can predict incoming wounded and other people's thoughts.

Alan Alda is the only person to have won Emmy awards for acting, writing and directing – all achieved in episodes of M*A*S*H.

The short scene in which the death of Colonel Henry Blake is announced came as a surprise even to the actors. Some like Jamie Farr and Loretta Swit, who had finished filming, were called back on set especially for this shoot. The stars were only given their scripts moments before the cameras started turning, so their shock was genuine.

William Christopher missed most of one season through illness. He was suffering from hepatitis, which was later written into the storyline of one episode.

Before being cast as Colonel Potter, Harry Morgan had guest-starred in one episode, taking the part of Major General Bartford Hillman Steele. It could be said, therefore, that his return was really a demotion.

David Ogden Stiers, who played Charles Winchester, starred in the pilot episode of Charlie's Angels.

When M*A*S*H was broadcast in the UK the canned laughter used in America was not considered necessary.

Jamie Farr had actually served with the US Army in Korea.

As well as two sequel series, Trapper John MD and After MASH, there was also a series pilot called Walter, starring Gary Burghoff, but this was not developed further.

Seventy-seven per cent of all Americans watching TV on the evening of 19 September 1983 were glued to the final, two-and-a-half-hour episode, Goodbye, Farewell and Amen.

In total, M*A*S*H was nominated for 97 Emmy awards, winning 14 times.

The BBC's Great Railway Journeys of the World

1980 SERIES

Ludovic Kennedy (journalist)	New York–Los Angeles
Michael Frayn (playwright)	Sydney–Perth
Brian Thompson (playwright)	Bombay–Cochin
Michael Palin (comedian)	London–Kyle of Lochalsh
Michael Wood (historian)	Cape Town–Victoria Falls
Miles Kington (journalist)	Lima–La Paz
Eric Robson (broadcaster)	Paris–Budapest

1994 SERIES

Clive Anderson (chat show host)	Hong Kong–Ulan Bator
Natalia Makarova (ballerina)	St Petersburg–Tashkent
Rian Malan (author)	Cape Town–Bophutatswana
Michael Palin (comedian)	Derry–Kerry
Lisa St Aubin (novelist-poet)	Santos–Santa Cruz
Mark Tully (journalist)	Karachi–Khyber Pass

1996 SERIES

Victoria Wood (comedian)	Crewe–Crewe (via northern Britain)
Alexei Sayle (comedian)	Aleppo–Aqaba
Henry Louis Gates Jr (educationist)	Great Zimbabwe–Kilimatinde
Buck Henry (screenwriter-actor)	High Andes–Patagonia
Benedict Allen (explorer)	Mombasa–Mountains of the Moon
Ben Okri (novelist)	London–Arcadia
Chris Bonington (mountaineer)	Halifax–Porteau Cove

1999 SERIES

Ian Hislop (satirist)	India: East–West
Michael Portillo (politician)	Granada–Salamanca
Fergal Keane (journalist)	Tokyo–Kagoshima
Rick Stein (chef)	Los Mochis–Veracruz
Nick Hancock (comedian)	Guantanamo–Pinar Del Rio
Danny Glover (actor)	St Louis–Dogon Country
Stephen Tompkinson (actor)	Singapore–Bangkok

....

First Sky Package

On its launch on 5 February 1989, Sky Television's first package consisted of just four channels:

Sky Channel   Eurosport   Sky News   Sky Movies

The Hair Bear Bunch

Hair Bear   Bubi Bear   Square Bear

X Facts

Remember the little boy's voice declaring 'I made this' at the end of The X-Files? The voice belonged to Nathan Couturier, son of the programme's sound editor, Thierry Couturier. The programme was produced by the Ten Thirteen company, named after founder Chris Carter's birthdate (13 October).

The 'Doctor' Comedy Series

Doctor in the House
Doctor at Large
Doctor in Charge
Doctor at Sea
Doctor on the Go
Doctor Down Under
Doctor at the Top

Who Shot JR?

One of the most demanded questions of 1980 was 'Who Shot JR?' The Dallas supersoap had reached its zenith at this time, with millions of viewers all across the world addicted to the antics of the oil-rich Ewing family. When an unknown assailant fired a gun at the family's notorious bully-boy, JR (John Ross) Ewing, at the end of one series, the world was kept waiting until the start of the next to discover the culprit. There were plenty of options – JR was not the most popular man in Texas – and to conceal the truth the studio filmed alternative solutions. It was ultimately revealed that the attacker was Kristin Shepard, the sister-in-law JR had made pregnant.

S Club 7

Jo (O'Meara)
Bradley (McIntosh)
Rachel (Stevens)
Tina (Barrett)
Jon (Lee)
Hannah (Spearritt)
Paul (Cattermole)

US TV Networks

Although, regionally, television had been broadcast since the 1930s in the USA, national television only took off after World War II. It wasn't until 1951 that the whole of the US was 'networked', with major broadcasters supplying their programmes by cable to a 'network' of smaller, affiliated TV stations across the country for transmission locally. The four network broadcasters that monopolised US TV until the cable revolution of the 1980s were:

NBC   DuMont (closed 1956)   ABC   CBS

15 Steps Towards Becoming a Millionaire

The prize levels in Who Wants to be a Millionaire?:

£100

£200

£300

£500

£1,000 (guaranteed level)

£2,000 (no lose gamble)

£4,000

£8,000

£16,000

£32,000 (second guaranteed level)

£64,000 (no lose gamble)

£125,000

£250,000

£500,000

£1 million

The Divisions of UNCLE

The United Network Command for Law and Enforcement, the secret agency featured in The Man from UNCLE, is divided into eight sections with overlapping areas of control:

1   Policy and Operations
2   Operations and Enforcement
3   Enforcement and Intelligence
4   Intelligence and Communications
5   Communications and Security
6   Security and Personnel
7   Propaganda and Finance
8   Camouflage and Deception

Chronology of US TV Programmes

YEAR	PROGRAMME (DATE OF FIRST US BROADCAST)
1948	The Ed Sullivan Show (20 June)
1949	Hopalong Cassidy (24 June)
	The Lone Ranger (15 September)
1950	The George Burns and Gracie Allen Show (12 October)
	The Jack Benny Show (28 October)
1951	Amos 'n' Andy (28 June)
	I Love Lucy (15 October)
	The Roy Rogers Show (30 December)
1952	Dragnet (3 January)
1954	Lassie (12 September)
1955	Gunsmoke (10 September)
	The Phil Silvers Show (20 September)
	The Honeymooners (1 October)
1957	Have Gun Will Travel (14 September)
	Wagon Train (18 September)
	Perry Mason (21 September)
	Maverick (22 September)
1959	Rawhide (9 January)
	Bonanza (12 September)
	The Twilight Zone (2 October)
	The Untouchables (15 October)
1960	The Flintstones (30 September)
	The Andy Griffith Show (3 October)
1961	Top Cat (27 September)
	Dr Kildare (28 September)
	Mister Ed (1 October)
	Ben Casey (2 October)
	The Dick Van Dyke Show (3 October)
1962	The Virginian (19 September)
	The Beverly Hillbillies (26 September)
1963	The Fugitive (17 September)
1964	Peyton Place (15 September)
	Bewitched (17 September)
	The Addams Family (18 September)
	The Man from UNCLE (22 September)
	The Munsters (24 September)

1965	Lost in Space (15 September)
	Get Smart (18 September)
1966	Daktari (11 January)
	Batman (12 January)
	Star Trek (8 September)
	The Monkees (12 September)
	Mission: Impossible (17 September)
1967	Ironside (14 September)
1968	Rowan and Martin's Laugh-In (22 January)
	Wacky Races (14 September)
	Hawaii Five-O (26 September)
1969	The Pink Panther Show (6 September)
	Scooby-Doo, Where Are You? (13 September)
	Sesame Street (10 November)
1970	The Mary Tyler Moore Show (19 September)
1971	All in the Family (12 January)
	Cannon (14 September)
1972	The Waltons (14 September)
	M*A*S*H (17 September)
	Kung Fu (14 October)
1973	Kojak (24 October)
1974	Happy Days (15 January)
	The Six Million Dollar Man (18 January)
	Little House on the Prairie (11 September)
	The Rockford Files (13 September)
1975	Starsky and Hutch (3 September)
1976	Rich Man, Poor Man (1 February)
	Charlie's Angels (22 September)
1977	Roots (23 January)
	Soap (13 September)
	The Love Boat (24 September)
1978	Dallas (2 April)
	Taxi (12 September)
1979	The Dukes of Hazzard (26 January)
1980	Magnum, PI (11 December)
1981	Dynasty (12 January)
	Hill Street Blues (15 January)
	The Fall Guy (4 November)
	Falcon Crest (4 December)

CURIOUS FACT

Actors Danny De Vito and Rhea Perlman (Carla in Cheers) were married during a lunchbreak while recording the comedy series Taxi

Chronology of US TV Programmes

YEAR	PROGRAMME (DATE OF FIRST US BROADCAST)
1982	Late Night with David Letterman (2 February)
	Cagney and Lacey (25 March)
	Family Ties (22 September)
	Knight Rider (26 September)
	Cheers (30 September)
1983	The A-Team (23 January)
1984	Miami Vice (16 September)
	The Cosby Show (20 September)
	Murder, She Wrote (30 September)
1985	Moonlighting (3 March)
	The Golden Girls (14 September)
1986	LA Law (3 October)
1988	Roseanne (18 October)
	Murphy Brown (14 November)
1989	Baywatch (22 September)
	The Simpsons (17 December)
1990	Twin Peaks (8 April)
	Seinfeld (31 May)
	Northern Exposure (12 July)
	Law and Order (13 September)
1991	Home Improvement (17 September)
1993	The X-Files (10 September)
	Frasier (16 September)
	NYPD Blue (21 September)
1994	ER (19 September)
	Friends (22 September)
1995	Murder One (19 September)
1996	Everybody Loves Raymond (13 September)
1997	Buffy the Vampire Slayer (10 March)
	Ally McBeal (8 September)
1998	Sex and the City (6 June)
	Will and Grace (21 September)
1999	The Sopranos (10 January)
	The West Wing (22 September)
2000	Malcolm in the Middle (9 January)
	CSI: Crime Scene Investigation (6 October)
2001	24 (6 November)
2002	The Osbournes (5 March)

Actors Starring as Sherlock Holmes on TV

ACTOR	DRAMA
Tom Baker	The Hound of the Baskervilles (1982)
Jeremy Brett	The Adventures of Sherlock Holmes (1984–5), The Return of Sherlock Holmes (1986–8), The Casebook of Sherlock Holmes (1991), The Memoirs of Sherlock Holmes (1994)
Peter Cushing	Sherlock Holmes (1968)
James D'Arcy	Case of Evil (2002)
Rupert Everett	Sherlock Holmes and the Case of the Silk Stocking (2004)
Matt Frewer	Various stories (2000–2)
Stewart Granger	The Hound of the Baskervilles (1972)
Louis Hector	The Three Garridebs (1937)
Guy Henry	Young Sherlock – the Mystery of the Manor House (1982)
Charlton Heston	The Crucifer of Blood (1991)
Anthony Higgins	1994 Baker Street: Sherlock Holmes Returns (1993)
Ronald Howard	Sherlock Holmes (1954–5)
Frank Langella	Sherlock Holmes (1981)
Christopher Lee	Sherlock Holmes and the Leading Lady (1991), Incident at Victoria Falls (1991)
John Longden	The Man with the Twisted Lip (1951)
Roger Moore	Sherlock Holmes in New York (1976)
Roger Ostime	The Baker Street Boys (1983)
Michael Pennington	The Return of Sherlock Holmes (1987)
Christopher Plummer	Silver Blaze (1977)
Richard Roxborough	Hound of the Baskervilles (2002)
Alan Wheatley	Sherlock Holmes (1951)
Geoffrey Whitehead	Sherlock Holmes and Doctor Watson (1980)
Douglas Wilmer	Sherlock Holmes (1965)
Edward Woodward	Hands of a Murderer (1990)

....

The First Question on Mastermind

'Picasso's Guernica was a protest about the bombing by Spanish planes of a village. In what year did the event take place that inspired the painting?'

ANSWER: 1937   **DATE**: Monday, 11 September 1972

The same question was used as the final question of the last series of Mastermind's original run in 1997.

Detectives' Quirks

DETECTIVE	QUIRKS
Jim Bergerac	Gammy leg, reformed alcoholic
George Bulman	Fingerless gloves, nasal inhaler, plastic bag
Albert Campion	Aristocrat, horn-rimmed glasses
Frank Cannon	Grossly overweight, bon viveur
Columbo	Grubby raincoat, cigar
Jonathan Creek	Windmill home, duffel coat, maker of magic tricks
Sonny Crockett	Stubbled chin, houseboat home, pet alligator
Adam Dalgliesh	Windmill home, poet
Christopher Foyle	Female driver, good whisky
Sherlock Holmes	Pipe, violin, deerstalker hat
Marty Hopkirk	A ghost
Ken Hutchinson (Hutch)	Health foods, striped car
Robert Ironside	Wheelchair-bound
Jason King	Novelist, beautiful girls
Theo Kojak	Shaven head, lollipop, fancy waistcoats
Mike Longstreet	Blind, with guide dog
Sam McCloud	Cowboy in the city
Monk	Phobias about everything
Inspector Morse	Real ale, crosswords, Wagnerian opera
Harry Orwell	Beach house, whisky, public transport
Mark Saber	One arm
Eddie Shoestring	Radio presenter, scruffy, heavy drinker, good artist
Dave Starsky	Chunky cardigans, striped car
Paul Temple	Novelist, exceptionally wealthy
Piet Van der Valk	Dutch
Inspector Wexford	Literary quotations, good cooking
Lord Peter Wimsey	Bon viveur toff

....

A Strange and Unknown World

'You have put something in my room which will never let me forget how strange is this world – and how unknown.'

– British Prime Minister Ramsay MacDonald on being given an exhibition of television by John Logie Baird in 1930

Some Famous University Challenge Alumni

All the following took part in the high-brow quiz while undergraduates:

David Aaronovitch (journalist)
Sebastian Faulkes (novelist)
Julian Fellowes (actor/writer)
Stephen Fry (actor/comedian)
Clive James (writer/presenter)
Miriam Margolyes (actor)
David Mellor (politician)
Malcolm Rifkind (politician)
John Simpson (journalist)

The Rainbow Puppets

Moony	George
Sunshine	Bungle
Zippy	Cleo

A Bird You Must Not Miss

The theme music for the children's magazine programme Magpie was credited on soundtrack recordings as being by 'The Murgatroyd Band'. This was a pseudonym (based on the name of the programme's fat magpie mascot) for former chart toppers The Spencer Davis Group who, by the time of the recording in 1968, had lost their lead singer, Steve Winwood. The lyrics were based on an old rhyme:

'One for sorrow, Two for joy, Three for a girl and Four for a boy,
Five for silver, Six for Gold, Seven is a secret never to be told.
Eight's a wish and Nine a kiss, Ten is a bird you must not miss'.

The programme offered ten corresponding badges to viewers who wrote in, achieved something remarkable or appeared on the programme.

Charity Begins

FUND-RAISING PROGRAMME	DATE FIRST BROADCAST
Children in Need	21 November 1980*
Live Aid	13 July 1985
Comic Relief	5 February 1988
ITV Telethon	29–30 May 1988**
Sport Relief	13 July 2002

* On radio since 1927
** First Telethon in London region took place on 2–3 October 1980

Spin-offs and Sequels

PROGRAMME	SPIN-OFF/SEQUEL
A for Andromeda	The Andromeda Breakthrough
Absolutely	Mr Don and Mr George
All in the Family	Archie Bunker's Place
And Mother Makes Three	And Mother Makes Five
Are You Being Served?	Grace and Favour
The Army Game	Bootsie and Snudge
Around the World in 80 Days	Pole to Pole, Full Circle, Sahara with Michael Palin, Himalaya with Michael Palin
Babylon 5	Crusade
Barney Miller	Fish
Battlestar Galactica	Galactica 1980
Baywatch	Baywatch Nights
The Beavis and Butt-head Show	Daria
The Beiderbecke Affair	The Beiderbecke Tapes, The Beiderbecke Connection
Beverly Hills 90210	Melrose Place
Bewitched	Tabitha
The Bill	Burnside, MIT
The Black Stuff	Boys from the Blackstuff
Blue Peter	Go with Noakes, Val Meets the VIPs, Duncan Dares
Bootsie and Snudge	Foreign Affairs
Bouquet of Barbed Wire	Another Bouquet
Bourbon Street Beat	Surfside Six
Brookside	Damon and Debbie
Brothers in Law	Mr Justice Duncannon
Budgie	Charles Endell Esquire
Buffy the Vampire Slayer	Angel
Burke's Law	Honey West
Camberwick Green	Trumpton, Chigley
Canned Carrott	The Detectives
Cannon	Barnaby Jones
Casualty	Holby City
Cheers	Frasier
Cheyenne	Bronco
Columbo	Mrs Columbo
Coronation Street	Pardon the Expression

The Cosby Show	A Different World
Crane	Orlando
CSI: Crime Scene Investigation	CSI: Miami, CSI: NY
Dallas	Knots Landing, Dallas: The Early Years
Dangermouse	Count Duckula
The Day Today	Knowing Me, Knowing You with Alan Partridge, I'm Alan Partridge
Department S	Jason King
Doctor Who	K9 and Company
The Doctors	Owen MD
Dynasty	Dynasty II: The Colbys
EastEnders	Civvy Street
Educating Marmalade	Danger – Marmalade at Work
Emergency – Ward 10	Call Oxbridge 2000
Emu's World	Grotbags
The Fall and Rise of Reginald Perrin	The Legacy of Reginald Perrin
The Fast Show	Ted and Ralph, Swiss Toni, Grass
The Fellows	Spindoe
The Fenn Street Gang	Bowler
Fingerbobs	Fingermouse
The Flintstones	Pebbles and Bamm Bamm
Friends	Joey
Gazette	Hadleigh
The Gentle Touch	CATS Eyes
Ghost Squad	GS5
The Glittering Prizes	Oxbridge Blues
The Golden Girls	The Golden Palace, Empty Nest
Gone to the Dogs	Gone to Seed
Grange Hill	Tucker's Luck
Happy Days	Laverne and Shirley, Mork and Mindy, Joanie Loves Chachi
He-Man and the Masters of the Universe	She-Ra: Princess of Power
Heartbeat	The Royal
The Herbs	The Adventures of Parsley
Hercules: The Legendary Journeys	Xena: Warrior Princess
Hill Street Blues	Beverly Hills Buntz
Holding the Fort	Relative Strangers
House of Cards	To Play the King, The Final Cut
It's Dark Outside	Mr Rose
Jake and the Fatman	Diagnosis Murder
Last of the Summer Wine	First of the Summer Wine

Spin-offs and Sequels

PROGRAMME	SPIN-OFF/SEQUEL
Late Night Line Up	Film Night, Colour Me Pop
Law and Order	Law and Order: Criminal Intent, Special Victims Unit
The Likely Lads	Whatever Happened to the Likely Lads?
Little House on the Prairie	Little House: a New Beginning
Love, American Style	Happy Days
M*A*S*H	Trapper John, MD, After M*A*S*H
A Man Called Ironside	Amy Prentiss
Man about the House	George and Mildred, Robin's Nest
Man of the World	The Sentimental Agent
The Man in Room 17	The Fellows
The Man from UNCLE	The Girl from UNCLE
Marion and Geoff	A Small Summer Party, The Keith Barret Show
The Mary Tyler Moore Show	Lou Grant, Phyllis, Rhoda
Murder, She Wrote	The Law and Harry McGraw
Naked Video	Rab C Nesbitt, The Baldy Man
Nationwide	Watchdog
No Hiding Place	Echo Four-Two
No, Honestly	Yes, Honestly
Now Look Here ...	The Prince of Denmark
The Odd Man	It's Dark Outside
Oh, Brother!	Oh, Father!
Oh No! It's Selwyn Froggitt	Selwyn
On the Buses	Don't Drink the Water
Pardon the Expression	Turn Out the Lights
Pebble Mill at One	Saturday Night at the Mill, Pebble Mill Showcase, Pebble Mill on Sunday
Petticoat Junction	Green Acres
Picture Book	Bizzy Lizzy
The Plane Makers	The Power Game
Please Sir!	The Fenn Street Gang
The Pogles	Pogles' Wood
Police Story	Police Woman
Porridge	Going Straight
The Practice	Boston Legal
Rainbow	Rod, Jane and Freddy
Rich Man, Poor Man	Rich Man, Poor Man: Book II, Beggarman, Thief

The Rifleman	Law of the Plainsman
Rockliffe's Babies	Rockliffe's Folly
Romany Jones	Yus My Dear
Roots	Roots: the Next Generations
Rutland Weekend Television	The Rutles
The Saint	Return of the Saint
Secret Army	Kessler
The Secret Diary of Adrian Mole, Aged 13¾	The Growing Pains of Adrian Mole, Adrian Mole: the Cappuccino Years
Shadow Squad	Skyport
The Shillingbury Tales	Cuffy
A Show Called Fred	Son of Fred
The Six Million Dollar Man	The Bionic Woman
Smuggler	Adventurer
Soap	Benson
Softly, Softly	Barlow At Large, Barlow, Second Verdict
Strangers	Bulman
The Superstars	The Superteams
Take Three Girls	Take Three Women
That's Life	The Big Time, In at the Deep End
Till Death Us Do Part	In Sickness and in Health
Tinker, Tailor, Soldier, Spy	Smiley's People
Tiswas	OTT
The Tracey Ullman Show	The Simpsons
Up Pompeii!	Whoops Baghdad!
Up the Elephant and Round the Castle	Home James
The Upchat Line	The Upchat Connection
Upstairs, Downstairs	Thomas and Sarah
The Virginian	The Men from Shiloh
Wacky Races	The Perils of Penelope Pitstop, Dastardly and Muttley in Their Flying Machines
Widows	She's Out
The Winds of War	War and Remembrance
A Woman of Substance	Hold That Dream
The XYY Man	Strangers
Yes, Minister	Yes, Prime Minister
Z Cars	Softly, Softly

For Star Trek, see separate list.

Eighteen English Towns

Architecture was given a new sheen when Alec Clifton-Taylor extolled the virtues of the buildings of Six English Towns for BBC 2 in 1978. He followed up the series with Six More English Towns in 1981, and Another Six English Towns in 1984.

SIX ENGLISH TOWNS

Chichester   Richmond (Yorkshire)   Tewkesbury
Stamford   Totnes   Ludlow

SIX MORE ENGLISH TOWNS

Warwick   Berwick-upon-Tweed   Saffron Walden
Lewes   Bradford-on-Avon   Beverley

ANOTHER SIX ENGLISH TOWNS

Cirencester   Whitby   Bury St Edmunds
Devizes   Sandwich   Durham

The Crew of the Black Pig

Captain Pugwash
Master Mate
Barnabas
Willy
Tom the cabin boy

Elder Child and Lively Youngster

'Side by side, the known and the unknown: the famous elder child and the lively youngster.'

– Rt. Hon. Charles Hill, MP, Postmaster General, comparing the BBC and its new rival in a speech to mark the opening night of ITV in 1955

The Six Wives of Henry VIII

In the acclaimed BBC production starring Keith Michell, King Henry VIII's wives were played by:

Annette Crosbie (Catherine of Aragon)
Dorothy Tutin (Anne Boleyn)
Anne Stallybrass (Jane Seymour)
Elvi Hale (Anne of Cleves)
Angela Pleasence (Catherine Howard)
Rosalie Crutchley (Catherine Parr)

TV Characters' Middle Names

CHARACTER	SERIES
Adam Llewellyn De Vere Adamant	Adam Adamant Lives!
Wednesday Thursday Addams	The Addams Family
René François Artois	'Allo 'Allo
Edith Melba Artois	'Allo 'Allo
Mike Vernon Baldwin	Coronation Street
Josiah Edward Bartlet	The West Wing
Chandler Muriel Bing	Friends
Woody Tiberius Boyd	Cheers
Alan Beresford B'Stard	The New Statesman
John Truman Carter	ER
George Louis Costanza	Seinfeld
John 'Jack' Harold Duckworth	Coronation Street
Fred Handel Elliott	Coronation Street
Len Franklin Fairclough	Coronation Street
Bob Andrew Scarborough Ferris	The Likely Lads
Norman Stanley Fletcher	Porridge
Ross Eustace Geller	Friends
Elizabeth 'Bet' Theresa Gilroy	Coronation Street
Rachel Karen Green	Friends
Anthony Aloysius Hancock	Hancock's Half Hour
James Tiberius Kirk	Star Trek
Thomas Sullivan Magnum	Magnum, PI
Ally Marie McBeal	Ally McBeal
Eddie Wolfgang Munster	The Munsters
Hilda Alice Ogden	Coronation Street
Ashley Sibellius Peacock	Coronation Street
Reginald Iolanthe Perrin	The Fall and Rise of Reginald Perrin
Benjamin Franklin Pierce	M*A*S*H
Deirdre Anne Barlow	Coronation Street
William Thomas Riker	Star Trek: the Next Generation
Arnold Judas Rimmer	Red Dwarf
Alfred Sidney Roberts	Coronation Street
Homer Jay Simpson	The Simpsons
Albert Ladysmith Steptoe	Steptoe and Son
John 'Jack' Jacob Sugden	Emmerdale
Buffy Anne Summers	Buffy the Vampire Slayer
Joey Marcello/Francis Tribbiani	Friends
Rodney Charlton Trotter	Only Fools and Horses
Derek Bernard Wilton	Coronation Street
Charles Emerson Winchester	M*A*S*H
Toby Zachary Ziegler	The West Wing

A New Low

'Television has raised writing to a new low.'

– Sam Goldwyn, film producer

....

Actors Who Have Played British Kings and Queens on TV

MONARCH	ACTOR	PROGRAMME
Elizabeth II	Prunella Scales	A Question of Attribution (1992)
	Anne Stallybrass	Diana: Her True Story (1993)
George VI	Lyndon Brook	Churchill and the Generals (1979)
	Owen Holder	Mountbatten (1986)
	James Wilby	Bertie and Elizabeth (2002)
	Anthony Andrews	Cambridge Spies (2003)
Edward VIII	Richard Chamberlain	Portrait: the Woman I Love (1972)
	Ian Ogilvy	Walk with Destiny (1974)
	Edward Fox	Edward and Mrs Simpson (1978)
	Charles Edwards	Bertie and Elizabeth (2002)
George V	Marius Goring	Edward and Mrs Simpson (1978)
	Alan Bates	Bertie and Elizabeth (2002)
	Tom Hollander	The Lost Prince (2003)
Edward VII	Thorley Walters	The Edwardians (1973)
	Timothy West	Edward the Seventh (1975)
	Denis Lill	Lillie (1978)
	Michael Gambon	The Lost Prince (2003)
Victoria	Patricia Routledge	Victoria Regina (1964)
	Annette Crosbie	Edward the Seventh (1975)
	Rosemary Leach	Disraeli (1978)
	Sheila Reed	Lillie (1978)
	Miriam Margolyes	Blackadder's Christmas Carol (1978)
	Margaret Heale	Rhodes (1996)
	Victoria Hamilton	Victoria and Albert (2001)
	Prunella Scales	Station Jim (2001)
		Looking for Victoria (2003)
	Janine Duvitski	The Young Visiters (2003)
Charles II	James Villiers	The First Churchills (1969)
	Simon Treves	By the Sword Divided (1985)
	Nathaniel Parker	The Private Life of Samuel Pepys (2003)
	Rupert Everett	Charles II – the Power and the Passion (2003)
	Julian Wadham	Wren – the Man Who Built Britain (2004)

Charles I	Jeremy Clyde	By the Sword Divided (1983)
	Stephen Fry	Blackadder: the Cavalier Years (1988)
	Martin Turner	Charles II – the Power and the Passion (2003)
James I	Robert Carlyle	Gunpowder, Treason and Plot (2004)
Elizabeth I	Jean Kent	Sir Francis Drake (1961–2)
	Gemma Jones	Kenilworth (1967)
	Glenda Jackson	Elizabeth R (1971)
	Charlotte Cornwell	Drake's Venture (1980)
	Miranda Richardson	Blackadder II (1986)
	Catherine McCormack	Gunpowder, Treason and Plot (2004)
Henry VIII	Keith Michell	The Six Wives of Henry VIII (1970)
		The Prince and the Pauper (1996)
	Brian Blessed	The Nearly Complete and Utter History of Everything (2000)
	Alan Bates	The Prince and the Pauper (2000)
	Chris Larkin	The Six Wives of Henry VIII (2001)
	Ray Winstone	Henry VIII (2003)
Henry VII	John Woodnutt	The Six Wives of Henry VIII (1970)
	James Maxwell	Shadow of the Tower (1972)
	Joss Ackland	Henry VIII (2003)
Richard III	Paul Daneman	An Age of Kings (1960)
	Ian Holm	The War of the Roses (1965)
Richard I	Bruce Seton	Ivanhoe (1958)
	Dermot Walsh	Richard the Lionheart (1962–3)
	Julian Glover	Doctor Who (1965)
	Michael J Jackson	The Legend of Robin Hood (1975)
	Michael Byrne	The Devil's Crown (1978)
	Rory Edwards	Ivanhoe (1997)

....

Nicknames of Some TV Stars

Joan Bakewell	Thinking Man's Crumpet
Lucille Ball	The First Lady of Television
Milton Berle	Mr Television
Dick Clark	The World's Oldest Teenager
Perry Como	The Singing Barber
Freddie Davies	Parrot Face
Richard Dimbleby	Bumble
Alan Freeman	Fluff
Graham Kerr	The Galloping Gourmet
Richard Murdoch	Stinker
Ed Sullivan	The Great Stone Face
Jess Yates	The Bishop

Prominent TV Chefs

CHEF	MAJOR PROGRAMME
Michael Barry	Food and Drink
Mary Berry	Mary Berry's Ultimate Cakes
Susan Brooks	This Morning
Sarah Brown	Vegetarian Kitchen
Ross Burden	Ready, Steady, Cook
Antonio Carluccio	Antonio Carluccio's Northern Italian Feast
Robert Carrier	Food, Wine and Friends
Glynn Christian	Breakfast Time
Fanny Cradock	Kitchen Magic
Clarissa Dickson-Wright	Two Fat Ladies
Hugh Fearnley-Whittingstall	Escape to River Cottage
Keith Floyd	Floyd on Fish
Sophie Grigson	Grow Your Greens, Eat Your Greens
Philip Harben	Man in the Kitchen
Ainsley Harriott	Ainsley's Barbecue Bible
Valentina Harris	Italian Regional Cookery
Ken Hom	Ken Hom's Chinese Cookery
Madhur Jaffrey	Indian Cookery
Graham Kerr	Entertaining with Kerr: the Galloping Gourmet
Nigella Lawson	Nigella Bites
James Martin	Simply Fish
Nick Nairn	Wild Harvest with Nick Nairn
Jamie Oliver	The Naked Chef
Jennifer Paterson	Two Fat Ladies
Gordon Ramsay	Ramsay's Kitchen Nightmares
Gary Rhodes	Rhodes around Britain
Zena Skinner	Ask Zena Skinner
Nigel Slater	Real Food
Dorothy Sleightholme	Farmhouse Kitchen
Delia Smith	Delia Smith's Cookery Course
Rick Stein	Rick Stein's Taste of the Sea
Brian Turner	Out to Lunch
Phil Vickery	Ready, Steady, Cook
Lesley Waters	Can't Cook, Won't Cook
Kevin Woodford	Can't Cook, Won't Cook
Antony Worrall Thompson	Food and Drink

Prime Time

Prime time is the term used by US broadcasters for the time of day when audiences are at their highest (and therefore of greatest interest to advertisers), namely 7.30–11pm. In the UK the term 'peak time' tends to be used and broadly covers the hours 7–10.30pm.

National Lottery Statistics

DATE OF FIRST DRAW	19 November 1994
FIRST PRESENTER	Noel Edmonds
FIRST ON-THE-ROAD VENUE	Rhondda Heritage Park, Mid Glamorgan (26 November 1994)
FIRST WINNING NUMBERS	30, 3, 5, 44, 14, 22; bonus ball 10
NAMES OF ORIGINAL MACHINES	Lancelot, Arthur, Guinevere, Merlin, Gallahad, Vyvyan
NAMES OF LATER MACHINES	Amethyst, Garnet, Moonstone, Opal, Pearl, Topaz

Ally Pally

The first home of the BBC's television service was in the eastern section of Alexandra Palace, a large Victorian edifice in North London which had opened in 1873 but was then re-built after a fire two years later. When the building was being equipped for the start of television broadcasts, two sets of studios and control rooms had to be constructed to house the two systems under trial. The two systems operated on alternate weeks. The first, a mechanical system pioneered by John Logie Baird, was eventually rejected in February 1937 on grounds of quality and practicality, leaving the second, an electronic system produced by Marconi-EMI to lay down the groundwork for future television developments. Ally Pally remained in use with the BBC until 1981. From 1956 it was used solely for news broadcasts, before adopting its final role as a production centre for Open University programming.

The UK's Best-selling TV Listings Magazines

	MAGAZINE	COPIES SOLD
1	What's on TV	1,587,251
2	Radio Times	1,104,501
3	TV Choice	1,102,989
4	TV Times	473,788
5	TV Quick	337,149
6	TV and Satellite Week	210,953

Figures correct to end 2004. Source: ABC

Pre-School Pals

Fimbles	Florrie, Fimbo, Pom
The Storymakers	Milton Wordsworth, Byron Wordsworth, Shelley Wordsworth, Webster Wordsworth, Rosetti Wordsworth, Blake Wordsworth
Teletubbies	Tinky Winky, Dipsy, Laa-laa, Po
Tots TV	Tom, Tiny, Tilly
Tweenies	Jake, Fizz, Bella, Milo

....

Blue Peter Annual Appeals

YEAR	COLLECTABLE	CAUSE
1962–3	Toys	Christmas presents
1964	Silver paper	Guide dogs
1965	Wool	Tractor for Uganda
1966	Paperback books	Lifeboats
1967	Stamps	Home for the homeless
1968	Wool	Hospital truck for Biafra
1969	Model cars	Senior citizens' bus
1970	Cutlery	Holiday caravans for deprived children
1971	Socks and pillowcases	Children's dormitory in Kenya
1972	Thimbles and metal	Senior citizens' day centre
1973	Stamps	Aid for Ethiopia
1974	Buttons, badges, buckles	Guide dog
1975	Rags	Riding for people with disabilities
1976	Stamps	Medical aid for Lebanon
1977	Keys and cars	Equipment for hearing-impaired children
1978	Stamps and coins	Medi-bikes for Tanzania
1979	Bring and buy	Cambodia
1980	Bring and buy	Equipment for people with disabilities
1981	Stamps	Clean water for Java
1982	Treasure hunt	Hospital equipment
1983	Bring and buy	Shelter for flood victims
1984	Stamps and postcards	Aid for Ethiopia; UK lifeboats
1985	Keys and coins	Equipment for hearing-impaired children
1986	Bring and buy	Eye care in Africa
1987	Rags	Riding for people with disabilities
1988	Bring and buy	Kampuchea
1989	Aluminium cans	Baby unit equipment
1990	Bring and buy	Aid for Romanian orphans
1991	Aluminium cans	Equipment for elderly people

1992	Bring and buy	Eye care in Africa
1993	Coins, jewellery, cars	Lifeboats
1994	Bring and buy	Well water for India
1995	Paper	Electric wheelchairs
1996	Bring and buy	Leprosy care in Brazil
1997	Bring and buy	Cystic fibrosis equipment
1998	Foil and cans	Mozambique schools
1999	Bring and buy	Baby unit equipment
2000	Stamps	Health centres in the Andes
2001	Bring and buy	Transport for senior citizens
2002	Bring and buy	Safe water for Africa
2003	Bring and buy	Clubs for children with learning disabilities
2004	Clothes	Re-uniting families in Angola

....

Who Wants to be a Millionaire? Facts about a Quiz Phenomenon

In the UK there have been four winners of the £1 million top prize:
Judith Keppel, a garden designer, on 20 November 2000
David Edwards, a teacher, on 21 April 2001
Robert Brydges, a banker, on 29 September 2001
Pat Gibson, a software developer, on 24 April 2004

A fifth winner, former army major Charles Ingram, was later disqualified for cheating and found guilty of attempting to defraud the show in a subsequent trial.

The terms 'Ask The Audience', '50:50' and 'Phone a Friend' have all been trademarked by production company Celador.

Duncan Bickley holds the record for the most money lost on the show in the UK. In October 2000, he decided to answer the £500,000 question, but gave the wrong answer, leaving with £32,000 but losing £218,000 at the same time.

Kenya, in 2002, was the 100th country to take the programme. To date, 107 countries have their own versions, including China, India, Russia, Japan, Malaysia, the Philippines and Kazakhstan.

The first person to win the top European prize of 1 million Euros was Gerhard Krammer, a contestant on the German version, on 18 October 2002.

John Carpenter, the first US winner in November 1999, used the Phone a Friend lifeline on the $1 million question just to tell his dad that he knew the right answer and was going to become a millionaire.

A Who Wants to be a Millionaire? Live roadshow was launched in summer 2005, with hosts Eamonn Holmes, Les Dennis and Paul Ross.

Real Names of TV Personalities

STAR	REAL NAME
Russ Abbot	Russ Roberts
Alan Alda	Alfonso D'Abruzzo
Dave Allen	David Tynan O'Mahony
Desi Arnaz	Desiderio Alberto Arnaz y de Acha
James Arness	James Aurness
Beatrice Arthur	Bernice Frankel
Bobby Ball	Robert Harper
Glynis Barber	Glynis van der Reit
Amanda Barrie	Shirley Ann Broadbent
Gene Barry	Eugene Klass
Michael Barrymore	Michael Parker
Lennie Bennett	Michael Berry
Jack Benny	Benjamin Kubelsky
Milton Berle	Mendel Berlinger
Cilla Black	Priscilla White
Lionel Blair	Henry Lionel Ogus
Jim Bowen	James Whittaker
Katie Boyle	Caterina Irene Elena Maria Imperiali di Francavilla
Jeremy Brett	Jeremy Huggins
Dora Bryan	Dora Broadbent
Rob Brydon	Robert Brydon Jones
George Burns	Nathan Birnbaum
Max Bygraves	Walter Bygraves
Marti Caine	Lynne Shepherd
Tommy Cannon	Thomas Derbyshire
David Carradine	John Arthur Carradine
Jasper Carrott	Robert Davis
Chuckle Brothers	Paul and Barry Elliott
Maurice Colbourne	Roger Middleton
Robbie Coltrane	Anthony McMillan
Perry Como	Pierino Como
Chuck Connors	Kevin Connors
William Conrad	William Cann
Fanny Cradock	Phyllis Cradock
Michael Craig	Michael Gregson
Michael Crawford	Michael Dumble Smith
Jimmy Cricket	James Mulgrew
Tony Curtis	Bernard Schwartz
Paul Daniels	Newton Edward Daniels
James Darren	James Ercolani

Peter Davison	Peter Moffet
Bobby Davro	Robert Nankeville
Elizabeth Dawn	Sylvia Butterfield
Les Dennis	Leslie Heseltine
Angie Dickinson	Angeline Brown
Sandra Dickinson	Sandra Searles
Diana Dors	Diana Fluck
Charlie Drake	Charles Springall
Pete Duel	Pete Dueul
Buddy Ebsen	Christian Rudolf Ebsen
Vince Edwards	Vincento Eduardo Zoine
Kenny Everett	Maurice Cole
Adam Faith	Terence Nelhams
Barbara Flynn	Barbara McMurray
Steve Forrest	William Forrest Andrews
Bruce Forsyth	Bruce Forsyth-Johnson
John Forsythe	John Freund
James Garner	James Baumgarner
Dustin Gee	Gerald Harrison
Lew Grade	Louis Winogradsky
Richard E Grant	Richard Esterhuysen
Peter Graves	Peter Aurness
Larry Grayson	William White
Jeremy Hawk	Cedric Lange
Jack Hedley	Jack Hawkins
Benny Hill	Alfred Hawthorne Hill
Harry Hill	Matthew Hall
Ian Holm	Ian Holm Cuthbert
Robert Horton	Mead Howard Horton
Rock Hudson	Roy Scherer
Hattie Jacques	Josephina Edwina Jacques
David Janssen	David Meyer
David Jason	David White
Michael Jayston	Michael James
Jimmy Jewell	James Marsh
Miriam Karlin	Miriam Samuels
Boris Karloff	William Pratt
Howard Keel	Harry Leek
Larry King	Lawrence Zeiger
Danny La Rue	Daniel Patrick Carroll
Cheryl Ladd	Cheryl Stoppelmoor
Mark Lamarr	Mark Jones
Michael Landon	Eugene Orowitz

CURIOUS FACT

Jonathan Creek
is really
a place
in Kentucky,
USA

Real Names of TV Personalities

STAR	REAL NAME
Belinda Lang	Belinda Lange
Eddie Large	Eddie McGinnis
Josie Lawrence	Wendy Lawrence
John Le Mesurier	John Elton Halliley
Rula Lenska	Roza Maria Lubienska
Shari Lewis	Shari Hurwitz
Liberace	Wladziu Valentino Liberace
Robert Lindsay	Robert Stevenson
Syd Little	Cyril Mead
Margaret Lockwood	Margaret Mary Lockwood Day
Louise Lombard	Louise Perkins
Jack Lord	John Joseph Ryan
Magnus Magnusson	Magnus Sigursteinnson
Lee Majors	Harvey Lee Yeary II
Patrick Malahide	Patrick Duggan
Karl Malden	Karl Mladen Sekulovich
Sharon Maughan	Sharon Mughan
Bill Maynard	Walter Williams
Sylvester McCoy	James Kent-Smith
Geraldine McEwan	Geraldine McKeown
Leo McKern	Reginald McKern
Avid Merrion	Leigh Francis
Paul Merton	Paul Martin
William Mervyn	William Mervyn Pickwoad
Spike Milligan	Terence Milligan
Helen Mirren	Ilynea Lydia Mironoff
Warren Mitchell	Warren Misell
Clayton Moore	Jack Carlton Moore
Eric Morecambe	Eric Bartholomew
Harry Morgan	Harry Bratsburg
Arthur Mullard	Arthur Mullord
Jimmy Nail	James Bradford
Paul Nicholas	Paul Beuselinck
Sue Nicholls	Susan Harmer-Nicholls
Dandy Nichols	Daisy Nichols
Graham Norton	Graham Walker
Bill Owen	Bill Rowbotham
Nicola Pagett	Nicola Scott
Lynne Perry	Jean Dudley
Conrad Phillips	Conrad Philip Havord
Patricia Phoenix	Patricia Pilkington
Stefanie Powers	Stefania Federkiewicz

Ted Ray	Charles Olden
Jemma Redgrave	Jemima Redgrave
George Reeves	George Brewer
Vic Reeves	Jim Moir
Duncan Renaldo	Renaldo Duncan
Debbie Reynolds	Mary Frances Reynolds
Anneka Rice	Annie Rice
Stan Richards	Stan Richardson
Shane Richie	Shane Roche
Roy Rogers	Leonard Slye
Susan Saint James	Susan Miller
Telly Savalas	Aristotle Savalas
Prunella Scales	Prunella Illingworth
John Sessions	John Marshall
Jane Seymour	Joyce Frankenberg
Martin Sheen	Ramon Estevez
Phil Silvers	Philip Silversmith
John Simpson	John Fidler-Simpson
Frank Skinner	Chris Collins
David Soul	David Solberg
Kathy Staff	Minnie Higginbottom
Barbara Stanwyck	Ruby Stevens
Freddie Starr	Freddie Fowell
Craig Stevens	Gail Shikles
Mark Strong	Marco Salussolia
William Tarmey	William Piddington
Gwen Taylor	Gwen Allsop
Terry-Thomas	Thomas Terry Hoar Stevens
Frank Thornton	Frank Thornton Ball
Denise Van Outen	Denise Outen
Peter Vaughan	Peter Ohm
Johnny Vegas	Michael Pennington
Clint Walker	Norman Eugene Walker
Max Wall	Maxwell Lorimer
Ruby Wax	Ruby Wachs
Colin Welland	Colin Williams
Richard Wilson	Iain Wilson
Barbara Windsor	Barbara-Ann Deeks
Mike and Bernie Winters	Mike and Bernie Weinstein
Harry Worth	Harry Illingsworth
Jane Wyman	Sarah Jane Faulks
Patrick Wymark	Patrick Cheeseman
Susannah York	Susannah Fletcher

CURIOUS FACT

Cold Feet star
Fay Ripley's
aunt is 1960s
'death disc'
singer Twinkle

Mr Benn Out of the Closet

In the Watch with Mother animation Mr Benn, the title character ventures into the changing room of a fancy dress shop and emerges in a new persona, ready to embark on an exciting adventure. In episode order, these are the identities he assumes:

Red Knight	Diver
Hunter	Cowboy
Cook	Wizard
Caveman	Clown
Balloonist	Spaceman
Zoo-Keeper	Pirate

There was also an episode called The Magic Carpet, in which Mr Benn discovers a genie.

....

The Indoor League

Yorkshire Television's 1970s pub games series, hosted by Fred Trueman, featured competitive tournaments in the following 'sports':

Arm wrestling
Bar billiards
Darts
Pool
Shove-ha'penny
Table football
Table skittles

....

Sacred Sunday

For the first 18 months of its time on air, the BBC didn't broadcast on a Sunday. With just a few exceptions the Sabbath was kept clear of TV intrusion until April 1938.

....

Topics on the Bullseye Category Board

Food*	Britain
Words	Places
Books	Sport
Spelling	Showbiz
History	Affairs

* Later replaced by Pot Luck and then Faces.

Countdown's Top Dictionary Corner Guests

	CELEBRITY	VISITS
1	Gyles Brandreth	279
2	Richard Stilgoe	235
3	Nigel Rees	184
4	Philip Franks	162
5	Geoffrey Durham	160
6	Jan Harvey	134
7	Martin Jarvis	127
8	Bill Tidy	117
9	Richard Digance	101
10	Tom O'Connor	97
11	Tim Rice	94
12	Ned Sherrin	87
13	Barry Cryer	65
14	Keith Barron	62
14	David Jacobs	62
14	Simon Williams	62
17	Eve Pollard	60
18	Rick Wakeman	53
19	Denis Norden	52
20	Kenneth Williams	48

Figures correct to 1 July 2005

....

The Main Hosts of Crackerjack

Eamonn Andrews   Leslie Crowther
Michael Aspel   Ed Stewart   Stu Francis

....

The TV Licence: How Charges Have Increased

A sample of annual prices since the licence was introduced in 1946:

1946	£2	1979	£34
1954	£3	1981	£46
1957	£4	1985	£58
1965	£5	1990	£71
1968	£10*	1995	£86.50
1971	£12	2000	£104
1975	£18	2003	£116
1977	£21	2005	£126.50

* New price for colour television.
Black and white television licences remain cheaper (1968 price: £5; 2005 price: £42).

Too Much Choice?

'57 Channels (and Nothin' On)' – Bruce Springsteen song title

....

The Pipkins

Angus McHare
Hartley Hare
Moony the Badger
Octavia Ostrich
Pig
Pigeon
Topov the Monkey
Tortoise
Uncle Hare

....

Here is the Nose

In Bewitched, Samantha's twiddling nose, with which she cast her spells, was not a camera trick. It was just something that star Elizabeth Montgomery could do that not many people can manage (try it!).

....

Winners of Mastermind

THE MAGNUS MAGNUSSON YEARS:

1972	Nancy Wilkinson	1985	Ian Meadows
1973	Patricia Owen	1986	Jennifer Keaveney
1974	Elizabeth Horrocks	1987	Jeremy Bradbrooke
1975	John Hart	1988	David Beamish
1976	Roger Prichard	1989	Mary Elizabeth Raw
1977	Sir David Hunt	1990	David Edwards
1978	Rosemary James	1991	Stephen Allen
1979	Philip Jenkins	1992	Steve Williams
1980	Fred Housego	1993	Gavin Fuller
1981	Leslie Grout	1994	Dr George Davidson
1982	No contest	1995	Kevin Ashman
1983	Christopher Hughes	1996	Richard Sturch
1984	Margaret Harris	1997	Anne Ashurst

THE JOHN HUMPHRYS YEARS:

2003	Andy Page	2004	Shaun Wallace

In 2001 Discovery Channel broadcast a version of the programme with Clive Anderson as the presenter. The winner was Michael Penrice.

Celebrated American News Anchors

ANCHOR	CHANNEL	PROGRAMME
David Brinkley	NBC	The Huntley-Brinkley Report (1956–70)
Tom Brokaw	NBC	NBC Nightly News (1982–2004)
Walter Cronkite	CBS	CBS Evening News (1962–81)
Chet Huntley	NBC	The Huntley-Brinkley Report (1956–70)
Peter Jennings	ABC	World News Tonight (1983–)
Ted Koppel	ABC	Nightline (1980–)
Dan Rather	CBS	CBS Evening News (1981–2005)
Harry Reasoner	ABC	ABC Evening News (1970–8)

....

The Rugrats

Charles 'Chuckie' Finster Jr
Tommy Pickles
Phil DeVille
Lillian 'Lil' DeVille
Dylan 'Dil' Pickles
Kimi Wantabe-Finster
Susie Carmichael
Angelica Pickles

....

An Unlikely Celebrity

For two months in 1982 Ian McDonald was one of the most famous
people in Britain. Few people had heard of him before, and few, it seems,
have heard of him since. McDonald was the bespectacled, sober-suited
press officer from the Ministry of Defence who provided daily updates
on the progress of the Falklands campaign. His civil service deadpan
delivery imparted gravitas to his televised briefings and suggested
political independence. With the acknowledgement that television is a
powerful ally during times of war, recent conflicts in the Balkans, Gulf and
elsewhere have brought ministers more into the spotlight, leaving
the likes of Mr McDonald quietly in the backroom.

....

The Wallace and Gromit Films

A Grand Day Out (1989)
The Wrong Trousers (1993)
A Close Shave (1995)
The Curse of the Wererabbit (2005)

The characters have also appeared in a series of ten short films produced under
the umbrella title of Cracking Contraptions for Internet viewing.

TV Programmes Inspired by Films

PROGRAMME	FILM
The Adventures of Rin-Tin-Tin	The Man from Hell's River* (1922)
The Adventures of Tugboat Annie	Tugboat Annie* (1933)
Airwolf	Blue Thunder (1983)
Alias Smith and Jones	Butch Cassidy and the Sundance Kid (1969)
Alien Nation	Alien Nation (1988)
All Creatures Great and Small	All Creatures Great and Small* (1974)
Anna and the King	Anna and the King of Siam (1946)
Baby Boom	Baby Boom (1987)
Bagdad Cafe	Bagdad Cafe (1987)
Bewitched	I Married a Witch (1942)
The Big Easy	The Big Easy (1987)
Billy Liar	Billy Liar (1963)
Blue Thunder	Blue Thunder (1983)
Buffy the Vampire Slayer	Buffy the Vampire Slayer (1992)
Cheyenne	Cheyenne (1947)
The Cisco Kid	The Caballero's Way* (1914)
Colditz	The Colditz Story (1955)
Cowboy in Africa	Africa – Texas Style! (1967)
Daktari	Clarence the Cross-Eyed Lion (1965)
Dirty Dancing	Dirty Dancing (1987)
Dixon of Dock Green	The Blue Lamp (1950)
Doctor in the House	Doctor in the House* (1954)
Dr Kildare	Internes Can't Take Money* (1937)
Fame	Fame (1980)
Flamingo Road	Flamingo Road (1949)
Flipper	Flipper (1963)
The Four Just Men	The Four Just Men (1939)
The Four Seasons	The Four Seasons (1981)
Freebie and the Bean	Freebie and the Bean (1974)
Gentle Ben	Gentle Giant (1967)
The Ghost and Mrs Muir	The Ghost and Mrs Muir (1947)
Gideon's Way	Gideon's Day (1958)
Gidget	Gidget (1959)
Going My Way	Going My Way (1944)
Hannay	The Thirty-Nine Steps (1978)
Hart to Hart	The Thin Man* (1934)
Harry and the Hendersons	Bigfoot and the Hendersons (1987)
Highlander	Highlander (1986)
Hopalong Cassidy	Hop-A-Long Cassidy* (1935)
Hotel	Hotel (1967)

In the Heat of the Night	In the Heat of the Night (1967)
Lassie	Lassie Come Home* (1943)
The Life and Times of Grizzly Adams	The Life and Times of Grizzly Adams (1974)
Logan's Run	Logan's Run (1976)
Man at the Top	Room at the Top (1959)
M*A*S*H	M*A*S*H (1970)
McClain's Law	Big Jim McLain (1952)
McCloud	Coogan's Bluff (1968)
McMillan and Wife	The Thin Man* (1934)
Mickey Spillane's Mike Hammer	I, the Jury (1953)
Mr Ed	Francis* (1950)
My Friend Flicka	My Friend Flicka* (1943)
Naked City	The Naked City (1948)
The New Adventures of Charlie Chan	Behind that Curtain* (1929)
9 to 5	Nine to Five (1980)
No Time for Sergeants	No Time for Sergeants (1958)
The Odd Couple	The Odd Couple (1968)
Parenthood	Parenthood (1989)
Petrocelli	The Lawyer (1970)
Peyton Place	Peyton Place* (1957)
The Pink Panther Show	The Pink Panther* (1963)
Planet of the Apes	Planet of the Apes* (1968)
Private Benjamin	Private Benjamin (1980)
Quiller	The Quiller Memorandum (1966)
The Saint	The Saint in New York* (1938)
Serpico	Serpico (1973)
Shaft	Shaft (1971)
Shane	Shane (1953)
Snowy River: the McGregor Saga	The Man from Snowy River* (1982)
Stargate SG-1	Stargate (1994)
Tarzan	Tarzan of the Apes* (1918)
The Thin Man	The Thin Man* (1934)
Topper	Topper* (1937)
The Virginian	The Virginian (1914)
Voyage to the Bottom of the Sea	Voyage to the Bottom of the Sea (1961)
The Wackiest Ship in the Army	The Wackiest Ship in the Army (1960)
Wacky Races	The Great Race (1965)
The Waltons	Spencer's Mountain (1963)
The Wilde Alliance	The Thin Man* (1934)
The Young Indiana Jones Chronicles	Raiders of the Lost Ark* (1981)
Zorro	The Mark of Zorro* (1920)

* The first in a series of films starring the same characters.

Antagonisms

'Seeing a murder on television can help work off one's antagonisms. And if you haven't any antagonisms, the commercials will give you some.' - Alfred Hitchcock

Some Entertainers Discovered by Opportunity Knocks

Russ Abbot (with The Black Abbots)
Pam Ayres
The Bachelors
Stan Boardman
Candlewick Green
Cannon and Ball
Frank Carson
Bobby Crush
Paul Daniels
Freddie Davies
Les Dawson
Bernie Flint
Stuart Gillies
Ken Goodwin
Mary Hopkin
Bonnie Langford
Little and Large
Paul Melba
Middle of the Road (as Los Caracas)
Millican and Nesbitt
Tony Monopoly
Gerry Monroe
New World
Tom O'Connor
Paper Lace
Peters and Lee
The Real Thing
Neil Reid
Freddie Starr
Lena Zavaroni

Some Entertainers Discovered by New Faces

Michael Barrymore
Patti Boulaye
Malandra Burrows
(as Malandra Newman)
Marti Caine
Jim Davidson
Roger De Courcey
Les Dennis
Aiden J Harvey
Lenny Henry
Our Kid
Showaddywaddy
Sweet Sensation
Roy Walker
Gary Wilmot
Victoria Wood

The Banana Splits

Fleegle, a dog
Bingo, a gorilla
Drooper, a lion
Snorky, an elephant

US Versions of UK Programmes

UK PROGRAMME	US VERSION
Agony	The Lucy Arnaz Show
Are You Being Served?	Beane's of Boston
Ballykissangel	Hope Island
Billy Liar	Billy
Birds of a Feather	Stand by Your Man
Changing Rooms	Trading Spaces
Dad's Army	Rear Guard
The Fall and Rise of Reginald Perrin	Reggie
Fawlty Towers	Amanda's, Payne
For the Love of Ada	A Touch of Grace
George and Mildred	The Ropers
The Grimleys	The Grubbs
Home to Roost	You Again?
It's a Knockout	Almost Anything Goes
Keep It in the Family	Too Close for Comfort
Man about the House	Three's Company
Mind Your Language	What a Country!
Miss Jones and Son	Miss Winslow and Son
Nearest and Dearest	Thicker than Water
Not the Nine O'Clock News	Not Necessarily the News
On the Buses	Lotsa Luck
One Foot in the Grave	Cosby
Open All Hours	Open All Night
Pig in the Middle	Oh Madeline
Please Sir!	Welcome Back, Kotter
Pop Idol	American Idol
Porridge	On the Rocks
Rising Damp	27 Joy Street
Robin's Nest	Three's a Crowd
The Royle Family	The Furst Family
Scrapheap Challenge	Junkyard Wars
Steptoe and Son	Sanford and Son
This Life	First Years
Till Death Us Do Part	All in the Family
Tom, Dick and Harriet	Foot in the Door
Tripper's Day	Check It Out
Two's Company	The Two of Us
Upstairs, Downstairs	Beacon Hill

Commercial Break

The amount of advertising a commercial channel is allowed to broadcast in the UK is controlled by the regulatory body, Ofcom. Under its authority, advertising on ITV, Channel 4 and Five is restricted to an average of seven minutes in an hour, with a maximum of 12 minutes allowed in any single hour (eight minutes per hour maximum during the peak hours of 7–9am and 6–11pm). Other digital/cable channels are permitted an average of nine minutes per hour. Teleshopping channels follow different rules.

The Rutles

Eric Idle's spin-off from Rutland Weekend Television featured the Beatle-like 'Prefab Four' Rutles, whose members were:

Dirk McQuickly (Eric Idle)
Ron Nasty (Neil Innes)
Stig O'Hara (Rikki Fataar)
Barry Wom* (John Halsey)

* Barrington Womble (full name)

TV Ships and Boats

SERIES	VESSEL
The Adventures of Tugboat Annie	Narcissus
The Buccaneers	Sultana
Captain Pugwash	Black Pig
Gilligan's Island	Minnow
Glencannon	Inchcliffe Castle
Hornblower	HMS Justinian, HMS Indefatigable
Howards' Way	Barracuda
The Love Boat	Pacific Princess
McHale's Navy	PT73
Miami Vice	St Vitus' Dance
Noah and Nelly	SkylArk
The Onedin Line	Charlotte Rhodes
Rosie and Jim	Ragdoll
Sea Hunt	Argonaut
Sir Francis Drake	Golden Hind
The Sky Larks	HMS Aerial
Tales of Para Handy	Vital Spark
Voyage to the Bottom of the Sea	Seaview
The Wackiest Ship in the Army	Kiwi
Warship	HMS Hero

TV-AM's Famous Five Founder/Presenters

Anna Ford   David Frost
Robert Kee   Michael Parkinson   Angela Rippon

Blue Remembered Actors

Dennis Potter's 1979 Play for Today cast the following adult actors in the roles of wartime schoolchildren:

Colin Welland
Michael Elphick
Robin Ellis
John Bird
Helen Mirren
Janine Duvitski
Colin Jeavons

The Many Wives of Patrick

In Patrick Cargill's comedy series The Many Wives of Patrick (1976–8) his character Patrick Woodville had been married six times. His interfering wives were:

Elizabeth   Nancy   Josephine
Laura   Betsy   Helen

First Sitting for Breakfast

Although the BBC launched Britain's first national breakfast television programmes on 17 January 1983 (pipping TV-am's Good Morning Britain by two weeks), breakfast television was actually available in one part of the UK nearly six years earlier. Yorkshire Television presented Good Morning Calendar – a version of its evening news magazine – as a short-term experiment from 28 March 1977.

Top of the Pops Original Hosts

The four regular presenters of Top of the Pops during its first three years on air were:

Jimmy Savile   Pete Murray   David Jacobs   Alan Freeman

Television the Sincere

'Imitation is the sincerest form of television.'

– Fred Allen, US comedian

Some Programme Sponsors

Series	Sponsor(s)
Ally McBeal	BeMe.com
Ant & Dec's Saturday Night Takeaway	Imperial Leather, KFC
Big Brother	Talk Talk
The Bill	Co-operative Bank/CIS
Cold Feet	Cockburn's Port
Coronation Street	Cadbury's
Emmerdale	Heinz
Footballers' Wives	Softlips
Frasier	Equitable Life
Friends	Nescafé, Jacobs Creek
Heartbeat	Cadbury's Hot Chocolate
Hell's Kitchen	Tio Pepe
Hollyoaks	Nescafé
I'm a Celebrity ...	First Choice
Inspector Morse	Beamish Stout
ITV Mystery Dramas	Leerdammer Cheese
ITV Weather	Powergen
LK Today	Dove soap
Parkinson	Prudential
Peak Practice	Crookes E45 moisturiser
A Place in the Sun	Tropicana
Popstars	T&T drinks
Popstars: the Rivals	McDonald's
Ramsay's Kitchen Nightmares	Anadin
Rosemary & Thyme	Lindemans
The Royal	Voltarol
Sex and the City	Bailey's Irish Cream
The Simpsons	Domino's Pizzas
The South Bank Show	Barclays Private Banking
Teachers	Toyota
This Morning	Pedigree
Who Wants to Be a Millionaire?	Jacob's Crackers, The Sun, Alliance and Leicester, Learn Direct, Network Q
Wish You Were Here?	The Post Office
The X Factor	Nokia
You've Been Framed	Felix

The 19 Faces of Jim

In 1961 comedian Jimmy Edwards starred in The Seven Faces of Jim, in which each 'face'/episode covered a different topic. A follow up, Six More Faces of Jim, was broadcast in 1962, with a third helping, More Faces of Jim, airing in 1963.

THE SEVEN FACES OF JIM

Devotion   Genius   Power
Dedication   Duty   Guilt   Enthusiasm

SIX MORE FACES OF JIM

Fatherhood   Renunciation   Wisdom
Perseverance   Loyalty   Tradition

MORE FACES OF JIM

Amnesia   Growing up   Spreadeagling
Upbringing   Espionage   Empire

Gone to the Dogs

American actor Don Messick specialised in providing voices for cartoon animals, especially dogs that included:

Astro (The Jetsons)
Bandit (Jonny Quest)
Chu Chu (Amazing Chan and the Chan Clan)
Muttley (Wacky Races)
Pupstar (Space Kidettes)
Scooby-Doo (Scooby Doo Where Are You?)

A Familiar Face

The most viewed person in UK television history is Carole Hersee. Her face first appeared in 1967 when she posed as the 'test card girl', playing noughts and crosses on a blackboard, accompanied by a rag doll. Carole was the daughter of BBC engineer and test card designer George Hersee, and the card she illustrated was known as Test Card F.

Fictitious Countries Targeted in Mission: Impossible

Camagua	Marnsburg
Elkabar	San Cristobal
Ghalea	Santa Costa
Jamada	Santales
Kuala Rokat	Svardia
Lombuanda	Valeria

The Secret Agent Dossier

AGENT	**Steve Austin**
SERIES	The Six Million Dollar Man
STAR	Lee Majors
CREATOR	Henri Simoun
COLLEAGUE	Oscar Goldman
AGENCY	OSI

AGENT	**Jack Bauer**
SERIES	24
STAR	Kiefer Sutherland
CREATORS	Joel Surnow, Robert Cochran
COLLEAGUE	Tony Almeida
AGENCY	CTU

AGENT	**William Bodie**
SERIES	The Professionals
STAR	Lewis Collins
CREATOR	Brian Clemens
COLLEAGUE	Ray Doyle
AGENCY	CI5

AGENT	**Neil Burnside**
SERIES	The Sandbaggers
STAR	Roy Marsden
CREATOR	Ian MacKintosh
COLLEAGUE	C
AGENCY	SIF

AGENT	**David Callan**
SERIES	Callan
STAR	Edward Woodward
CREATOR	James Mitchell
COLLEAGUES	Hunter, Lonely
AGENCY	British Intelligence

AGENT	**Sam Casey**
SERIES	Gemini Man
STAR	Ben Murphy
CREATOR	Universal
COLLEAGUE	Leonard Driscoll
AGENCY	INTERSECT

AGENT	**April Dancer**
SERIES	The Girl from UNCLE
STAR	Stefanie Powers
CREATORS	Norman Felton, Sam Rolfe
COLLEAGUE	Mark Slate
AGENCY	UNCLE

AGENT	**James Dempsey**
SERIES	Dempsey and Makepeace
STAR	Michael Brandon
CREATOR	Tony Wharmby
COLLEAGUE	Harriet Makepeace
AGENCY	SI10

AGENT	**John Drake**
SERIES	Danger Man
STAR	Patrick McGoohan
CREATOR	Ralph Smart
COLLEAGUE	Hobbs
AGENCY	NATO/MI9

AGENT	**Maggie Forbes**
SERIES	CATS Eyes
STAR	Jill Gascoine
CREATOR	Terence Feely
COLLEAGUES	Pru Standfast, Fred Smith
AGENCY	CATS

AGENT	**Jason King**
SERIES	Department S
STAR	Peter Wyngarde
CREATORS	Monty Berman, Dennis Spooner
COLLEAGUES	Stewart Sullivan, Annabelle Hurst
AGENCY	Department S

AGENT	**MacGyver**
SERIES	MacGyver
STAR	Richard Dean Anderson
CREATOR	Lee David Zlotoff
COLLEAGUE	Peter Thornton
AGENCY	Phoenix Foundation

AGENT	**Joe McClaine**
SERIES	Joe 90
STAR	Len Jones: voice
CREATORS	Gerry Anderson, Sylvia Anderson
COLLEAGUE	Shane Weston
AGENCY	WIN

AGENT	Sharon McCready		AGENT	Maxwell Smart
SERIES	The Champions		SERIES	Get Smart
STAR	Alexandra Bastedo		STAR	Don Adams
CREATORS	Monty Berman,		CREATORS	Mel Brooks,
	Dennis Spooner			Buck Henry
COLLEAGUES	Craig Stirling,		COLLEAGUE	Agent 99
	Richard Barrett		AGENCY	CONTROL
AGENCY	Nemesis			
			AGENT	Napoleon Solo
AGENT	John Mannering		SERIES	The Man from
SERIES	The Baron			UNCLE
STAR	Steve Forrest		STAR	Robert Vaughn
CREATOR	John Creasey		CREATORS	Norman Felton,
COLLEAGUE	Cordelia Winfield			Sam Rolfe
AGENCY	British Intelligence		COLLEAGUE	Illya Kuryakin
			AGENCY	UNCLE
AGENT	Jim Phelps			
SERIES	Mission: Impossible		AGENT	Jaime Sommers
STAR	Peter Graves		SERIES	The Bionic Woman
CREATOR	Bruce Geller		STAR	Lindsay Wagner
COLLEAGUES	Cinnamon Carter,		CREATOR	Kenneth Johnson
	Rollin Hand		COLLEAGUE	Oscar Goldman
AGENCY	IMF		AGENCY	OSI
AGENT	Tom Quinn		AGENT	Edward Straker
SERIES	Spooks		SERIES	UFO
STAR	Matthew Macfadyen		STAR	Ed Bishop
CREATOR	BBC		CREATORS	Gerry Anderson,
COLLEAGUES	Zoë Reynolds,			Sylvia Anderson
	Danny Hunter		COLLEAGUE	Alec Freeman
AGENCY	MI5		AGENCY	SHADO
AGENT	Captain Scarlet		AGENT	Father Stanley Unwin
SERIES	Captain Scarlet and		SERIES	The Secret Service
	the Mysterons		STAR	Stanley Unwin
STAR	Francis Matthews: voice		CREATORS	Gerry Anderson,
CREATORS	Gerry Anderson,			Sylvia Anderson
	Sylvia Anderson		COLLEAGUE	Matthew Harding
COLLEAGUE	Captain Blue		AGENCY	BISHOP
AGENCY	Spectrum			
			AGENT	Dr Daniel Westin
			SERIES	The Invisible Man
AGENT	Spider Scott		STAR	David McCallum
SERIES	The XYY Man		CREATOR	Universal
STAR	Stephen Yardley		COLLEAGUE	Walter Carlson
CREATOR	Kenneth Royce		AGENCY	KLAE Corporation
COLLEAGUE	Fairfax			
AGENCY	British Intelligence			

*For an explanation of agency names, see lists of TV acronyms.

TV's Eponymous Families

FAMILY	**The Adams Family**
PARENTS	Gomez, Morticia
CHILDREN	Wednesday, Pugsley
RESIDENCE	Cemetary Ridge
PETS	Aristotle (octopus)

FAMILY	**The Appleyards**
PARENTS	Dad, Mum
CHILDREN	John, Janet, Tommy, Margaret
RESIDENCE	Home Counties
PETS	n/a

FAMILY	**The Brady Bunch**
PARENTS	Mike, Carol
CHILDREN	Greg, Peter, Bobby, Marcia, Jan, Cindy
RESIDENCE	Los Angeles
PET	Tiger (dog)

FAMILY	**The Flintstones**
PARENTS	Fred, Wilma
CHILD	Pebbles
RESIDENCE	Bedrock
PET	Dino (dinosaur)

FAMILY	**The Grimleys**
PARENTS	Janet, Baz
CHILDREN	Gordon, Darren, Lisa
RESIDENCE	Dudley
PETS	n/a

FAMILY	**The Grove Family**
PARENTS	Bob, Gladys
CHILDREN	Pat, Jack, Daphne, Lennie
RESIDENCE	Hendon
PETS	n/a

FAMILY	**The Jetsons**
PARENTS	George, Jane
CHILDREN	Judy, Elroy
RESIDENCE	Space City
PET	Astro (dog)

FAMILY	**The Munsters**
PARENTS	Herman, Lily
CHILDREN	Eddie, Marilyn (niece)
RESIDENCE	Mockingbird Heights
PET	Spot (dragon)

FAMILY	**The Osbournes**
PARENTS	Ozzy, Sharon
CHILDREN	Kelly, Jack
RESIDENCE	Beverly Hills
PETS	Lola, Minnie, Maggie, Martini, Baby, Lulu, Pipi (dogs), Puss (cat)

FAMILY	**The Partridge Family**
PARENT	Shirley
CHILDREN	Keith, Laurie, Danny, Christopher, Tracy
RESIDENCE	San Pueblo
PET	Simone (dog)

FAMILY	**The Royle Family**
PARENTS	Jim, Barbara
CHILDREN	Denise, Anthony
RESIDENCE	Manchester
PETS	n/a

FAMILY	**The Simpsons**
PARENTS	Homer, Marge
CHILDREN	Bart, Lisa, Maggie
RESIDENCE	Springfield
PETS	Santa's Litle Helper (dog), Snowball (cat)

FAMILY	**The Sopranos**
PARENTS	Tony, Carmela
CHILDREN	Meadow, Anthony
RESIDENCE	New Jersey
PET	Pie-Oh-My (racehorse)

FAMILY	**The Waltons**
PARENTS	John, Olivia
CHILDREN	John Boy, Mary Ellen, Jason, Erin, Jim-Bob, Ben, Elizabeth
RESIDENCE	Walton's Mountain
PET	Reckless (dog)

FAMILY	**The Woodentops**
PARENTS	Daddy, Mummy
CHILDREN	Jenny, Willy, Baby
RESIDENCE	n/a
PETS	Spotty (dog), Buttercup (cow)

Daily Soap Arrives

The arrival of ITV in 1955 also saw the arrival of Britain's first daily soap opera. In 15-minute instalments, Sixpenny Corner related events in the lives of newlyweds Bill and Sally Norton, drawing in also their friends, close relatives and customers at the garage they ran in the fictional town of Springwood. The series, which ran for less than a year, was co-created by Hazel Adair, who later co-created the more durable Crossroads.

....

Watch with Mother/See Saw Programmes

Watch with Mother, a 15-minute, Monday–Friday lunchtime strand was first broadcast in 1953. In 1980 the name was changed to See Saw. These were the component programmes:

PROGRAMME	YEAR*	PROGRAMME	YEAR*
The Adventures of Spot	1987	Joe	1966
Along the River	1970	King Rollo	1980
Along the Seashore	1970	Little Misses	1983
Along the Trail	1972	Mary, Mungo and Midge	1969
Andy Pandy	1953	Mop and Smiff	1985
Animal Fair	1986	Mr Benn	1971
Bagpuss	1974	The Mr Men	1974
Barnaby	1973	On the Farm	1970
Bertha	1985	Over the Moon	1978
Bizzy Lizzy**	1967	Picture Book	1955
Bod	1975	Pie in the Sky	1986
Bric-a-Brac	1980	Pigeon Street	1981
Camberwick Green	1966	Pinny's House	1986
Chigley	1969	Playboard	1976
Chock-a-Block	1981	Pogle's Wood	1966
Fingerbobs	1972	Postman Pat	1981
Fingermouse	1985	Rag, Tag and Bobtail	1953
Fireman Sam	1987	Ragtime	1973
Flower Pot Men	1953	Ring-a-Ding	1973
The Flumps	1977	Rubovia	1976
Gran	1983	Stop – Go!	1981
Heads and Tails	1977	Tales of the Riverbank	1963
The Herbs	1968	Teddy Edward	1973
Hokey-Cokey	1983	Thomas	1975
How Do You Do!	1977	Trumpton	1967
In the Town	1973	The Woodentops	1955

Note: Little Misses usually shared the 15-minute slot with The Mr Men, and Ring-a-Ding and Teddy Edward also shared a slot.

* Year of first broadcast as a Watch with Mother/See Saw component; some programmes were broadcast individually earlier.

** First seen as part of Picture Book.

The 100 Greatest TV Characters

As selected by viewers for the Channel 4 programme broadcast on 5–6 May 2001.

1   Homer Simpson (The Simpsons)
2   Basil Fawlty (Fawlty Towers)
3   Blackadder (Blackadder)
4   Del Boy Trotter (Only Fools and Horses)
5   Father Dougal McGuire (Father Ted)
6   The Doctor (Doctor Who)
7   Alan Partridge (I'm Alan Partridge)
8   Ali G (Da Ali G Show)
9   Victor Meldrew (One Foot in the Grave)
10 Dr Niles Crane (Frasier)
11 Jim Royle (The Royle Family)
12 BA Baracus (The A-Team)
13 The Fonz (Happy Days)
14 Rick (The Young Ones)
15 Kevin the Teenager (Harry Enfield and Chums)
16 Tubbs (The League of Gentlemen)
17 Alan B'Stard (The New Statesman)
18 Columbo (Columbo)
19 Ted and Ralph (The Fast Show)
20 Patsy Stone (Absolutely Fabulous)
21 Captain Mainwaring (Dad's Army)
22 Frank Spencer (Some Mothers Do 'Ave 'Em)
23 Mr Spock (Star Trek)
24 Rigsby (Rising Damp)
25 Ally McBeal (Ally McBeal)
26 Norman Stanley Fletcher (Porridge)
27 Number 6 (The Prisoner)
28 Dennis Pennis (Anyone for Pennis)
29 Miss Piggy (The Muppet Show)
30 Inspector Morse (Inspector Morse)
31 Sir Humphrey Appleby (Yes, Minister)
32 Ernie Bilko (The Phil Silvers Show)
33 Emma Peel (The Avengers)
34 Compo Simmonite (Last of the Summer Wine)
35 Hawkeye Pierce (M*A*S*H)
36 Fitz (Cracker)

37 Arthur Daley (Minder)
38 JR Ewing (Dallas)
39 Albert Steptoe (Steptoe and Son)
40 Rab C Nesbitt (Rab C Nesbitt)
41 Stuart Jones (Queer as Folk)
42 Jack Frost (A Touch of Frost)
43 Arnold Jackson (Diff'rent Strokes)
44 Margot Leadbetter (The Good Life)
45 Huggy Bear (Starsky and Hutch)
46 Dot Cotton (EastEnders)
47 Beth Jordache (Brookside)
48 Desmond Ambrose (Desmond's)
49 Alf Garnett (Till Death Us Do Part)
50 Anna Forbes (This Life)
51 Hancock (Hancock's Half Hour)
52 Hyacinth Bucket (Keeping up Appearances)
53 Mrs Overall (Victoria Wood – as Seen on TV)
54 Mrs Merton (The Mrs Merton Show)
55 Oz Osbourne (Auf Wiedersehen, Pet)
56 Kojak (Kojak)
57 Yosser Hughes (Boys from the Blackstuff)
58 Terry Collier (The Likely Lads)
59 Dame Edna Everage (The Dame Edna Experience)
60 Wolfie Smith (Citizen Smith)
61 Charlene Robinson (Neighbours)
62 Claudius (I, Claudius)
63 Mr Humphries (Are You Being Served?)
64 Max Headroom (Max Headroom)
65 Francis Urquhart (House of Cards)
66 Hilda Ogden (Coronation Street)
67 Dorien Green (Birds of a Feather)
68 Pete (Not Only ... But Also ...)
69 Jack Regan (The Sweeney)
70 Jimmy Corkhill (Brookside)
71 Napoleon Solo (The Man from UNCLE)
72 Loadsamoney (Saturday Live)
73 Lurcio (Up Pompeii!)
74 Jack Duckworth (Coronation Street)
75 Den and Angie Watts (EastEnders)

CURIOUS FACT

In the very last episode of the original series of Perry Mason, creator Erle Stanley Gardner guest-starred as the judge

76	Beverley (Abigail's Party)
77	Simon Templar (The Saint)
78	Jane Tennison (Prime Suspect)
79	Bet Lynch (Coronation Street)
80	Sid Abbott (Bless This House)
81	Kim Tate (Emmerdale)
82	Quentin Crisp (The Naked Civil Servant)
83	Lucy Ricardo (I Love Lucy)
84	Darius Jedbergh (Edge of Darkness)
85	Mildred Roper (Man about the House)
86	Jason King (Department S)
87	Jill Munroe (Charlie's Angels)
88	Delbert Wilkins (The Lenny Henry Show)
89	Philip Marlowe (The Singing Detective)
90	Michael Murray (GBH)
91	Mr Hudson (Upstairs, Downstairs)
92	Benny Hawkins (Crossroads)
93	Keith Pratt (Nuts in May)
94	Charlie Barlow (Z Cars)
95	Hari Kumar (The Jewel in the Crown)
96	Reggie Perrin (The Fall and Rise of Reginald Perrin)
97	Peter Manson (Bouquet of Barbed Wire)
98	Buffy (Buffy the Vampire Slayer)
99	Brian Potter (Peter Kay's Phoenix Nights)
100	Budgie (Budgie)

....

Famous Names to Have Appeared in Coronation Street

Michael Ball
Richard Beckinsale
Honor Blackman
Ray Brooks
Michael Elphick
HRH The Prince of Wales
Roy Hudd
Davy Jones
Peter Kay
Ben Kingsley
Maureen Lipman
Joanna Lumley

Ian McKellen
Bill Maynard
Peter Noone
Leonard Sachs
Prunella Scales
Paul Shane
Martin Shaw
Mollie Sugden
Max Wall
Joanne Whalley
Paula Wilcox
Norman Wisdom

Doctor Who's Greatest Adversaries

ENEMY	NO. OF STORIES
The Master	21
The Daleks	19
The Cybermen	10
Davros	5
The Black Guardian	4
The Ice Warriors	4
The Sontarans	4
The Autons	3
Borusa	3
The Yeti	3

The Original Novelists Behind Successful TV Series

SERIES	NOVELIST
All Creatures Great and Small	James Herriot
Chocky	John Wyndham
The Darling Buds of May	HE Bates
The Demon Headmaster	Gillian Cross
The Fall and Rise of Reginald Perrin	David Nobbs
Follyfoot	Monica Dickens
Frank Stubbs Promotes	Simon Nye
The Invisible Man	HG Wells
The Irish RM	Somerville and Ross
Ivanhoe	Sir Walter Scott
Just William	Richmal Crompton
Lizzie Dripping	Helen Cresswell
Men Behaving Badly	Simon Nye
Monarch of the Glen	Compton McKenzie
Paddington	Michael Bond
Poldark	Winston Graham
Quiller	Adam Hall
The Racing Game	Dick Francis
Raffles	EW Hornung
The Saint	Leslie Charteris
The Scarlet Pimpernel	Baroness Orczy
The Secret Diary of Adrian Mole, Aged 13¾	Sue Townsend
Sharpe	Bernard Cornwell
The Wombles	Elisabeth Beresford

See also The Detectives' Casefile, A Register of TV Doctors and The Secret Agent Dossier.

Back to School

SCHOOL	PROGRAMME
Bamfylde	To Serve Them All My Days
Barton Wood	three seven eleven
Bayside High	Saved by the Bell
Burgrove	AJ Wentworth, BA
Chiselbury	Whack-o!
Clinton Elementary	The Brady Bunch
Fenn Street Secondary Modern	Please Sir!
Filmore Junior High	The Brady Bunch
Galfast High	Chalk
Greyfriars	Billy Bunter of Greyfriars School
Hope Park	Hope and Glory
Jefferson High	Happy Days
John Buchanan High	Welcome Back, Kotter
Little Dipper	The Jetsons
Mansion	Bonjour La Classe
Middlefield Academy	Running the Halls
Monroe High	Head of the Class
Norbridge High	Press Gang
Oxford Lane	A Bunch of Fives
Robert F Kennedy Junior High	The Wonder Years
Rocket Academy	Julia Jekyll and Harriet Hyde
Rugby	Tom Brown's Schooldays
School of the Arts	Fame
Springfield Elementary	The Simpsons
Summerdown Comprehensive	Teachers
Sunnydale High	Buffy the Vampire Slayer
West Beverly Hills High	Beverly Hills 90210
Westdale High	The Brady Bunch
William McKinley High	The Wonder Years

....

The Krypton Factor Challenges

Mental Agility (taxing puzzles)
Physical Ability (assault course)
Observation (spotting film details/identification parade)
Intelligence (constructing 3D items)
Response (aircraft simulator skills)
General Knowledge (quick fire questions)

Note: major changes were made for the final series.

Stars Who Have Sung the Theme Songs to Their Own Series

STAR(S)	SERIES
Ronnie Barker	Going Straight
Nick Berry	Heartbeat
The Brady Bunch	The Brady Bunch
Michelle Collins	Sunburn
Peter Davison	Campion
Judi Dench	A Fine Romance
David Essex	The River
Kelsey Grammer	Frasier
Karl Howman	Mulberry
The Monkees	The Monkees
Jimmy Nail	Crocodile Shoes
Paul Nicholas	Just Good Friends
The Partridge Family	The Partridge Family
Su Pollard	Oh Doctor Beeching!
Carroll O'Connor and Jean Stapleton	All in the Family
Pauline Quirke and Linda Robson	Birds of a Feather
Paul Shane	Hi-De-Hi!
Michael Starke	The Royal
David Threlfall and John Simm	Men of the World
Dennis Waterman	Minder, On the Up, Stay Lucky
Emma Wray	Watching

....

Political Power

September 26 1960 was the day politicians really began to take television seriously. That was the date of the first broadcast debate between the two candidates for the White House, Richard Nixon for the Republicans and John Kennedy for the Democrats. Kennedy could have been made for the television era, his handsome, youthful, naturally-tanned looks worked well on the small screen. The same could not be said for Nixon, whose sullen and shifty appearance was not helped by a recent spell in hospital, a refusal to wear make up and an unfortunate five o'clock shaving shadow. In polls taken immediately after the debate, Nixon – previously considered one of the most effective politicians when it came to television – took the honours among those who had listened on the radio, but Kennedy was overwhelming winner among the TV audience. As his subsequent winning margin in the presidential elections turned out to be wafer thin, it seems that television may well have decided the race. Since that day, politicians across the world have learned to treat this great magnifier of mannerisms with the utmost respect.

Gerry Anderson's Puppet Series

The Adventures of Twizzle* (1957–8)
Torchy, the Battery Boy* (1960)
Four Feather Falls (1960)
Supercar (1961–2)
Fireball XL5 (1962–3)
Stingray (1964–5)
Thunderbirds (1965–6)
Captain Scarlet and the Mysterons (1967–8)
Joe 90 (1968–9)
The Secret Service (1969)
Terrahawks (1983–6)
Dick Spanner PI (1985)
Lavender Castle (1999)

* Director only; other series as creator/producer and occasional director.

Directors-General of the BBC

DIRECTOR-GENERAL	TERM	REASON FOR LEAVING
John Reith	1927–38	Resigned to become Chairman of Imperial Airways
Frederick Ogilvie	1938–42	Resigned during wartime difficulties
Robert Foot	1942–4*	Resigned to become Chairman of the Mining Association
Cecil Graves	1942–3*	Resigned through ill health
William Haley	1944–52	Resigned to become Editor of The Times
Ian Jacob	1952–9	Resigned to make way for 'groomed' successor
Hugh Carleton Greene	1960–9	Resigned because of marital problems
Charles Curran	1969–77	Resigned to become MD of Visnews
Ian Trethowan	1977–82	Resigned and served on other media boards
Alasdair Milne	1982–7	Forced to resign after conflict with the board
Michael Checkland	1987–93	Resigned after criticising BBC Chairman
John Birt	1993–2000	Resigned to join House of Lords
Greg Dyke	2000–4	Resigned after criticism of the BBC in the Hutton Inquiry
Mark Thompson	2004–	

* Joint Directors-General

Some Tricky Mastermind Specialist Subjects

The British Chemical Industry
British Church Architecture
The Buddhist sage Niciren
Drama in Athens, 500–388 BC
Famous British Poisoners
The History and Genealogy of European Royalty
The History of Singapore, 1819–1969
The Indian Tribes of North America, 1550–1900
The Life-Cycle and Habits of the Honey-bee
Personalities in Russian History and the Arts
The Spanish Anarchist Movement, 1908–74
Spanish and South American Ethnology

Note: one less expansive subject was offered in the 2003 season: The Harry Potter Films (there were only two at the time).

....

Transatlantic Exchange

On 11 July 1962 Richard Dimbleby excitedly introduced the first ever live television pictures to Britain by satellite from across the Atlantic. The pictures were supplied courtesy of Telstar I, a telecommunications satellite that, because it did not orbit the Earth at the same speed the planet was revolving, was only able to supply images for 18 minutes in every two-and-a-half-hour orbit. 'Geostationery' satellites, which matched the Earth's speed, were introduced later, notably through Early Bird in 1965, making trans-world pictures permanently available. However, if Telstar brought the first satellite TV pictures from America to the UK, the UK was at least able to respond musically. The space-age instrumental track called 'Telstar', produced by Joe Meek and performed by The Tornados, became the first US Number 1 hit for a UK group.

....

TV Soccer Dramas

SERIES	TEAM
Dream Team (Sky 1 1997–)	Harchester United
Footballers' Wives (ITV 2002–)	Earl's Park
Hero to Zero (BBC 1 2000)	Hope Rangers
Jossy's Giants (BBC 1 1986–7)	Glipton Grasshoppers
Playing the Field (BBC 1 1998–2002)	Castlefield Blues
Striker (BBC 1 1975–6)	Brenton Boys
The Manageress (Channel 4 1989–90)	Team not named
United! (BBC 1 1965–7)	Brentwich United

Famous TV Spacecraft

VESSEL	PROGRAMME
Britannia Seven	Come Back Mrs Noah
Enterprise	Star Trek
Fireball XL5	Fireball XL5
Galactica	Battlestar Galactica
Galasphere 347	Space Patrol
Heart of Gold	Hitch-hiker's Guide to the Galaxy
Jupiter II	Lost in Space
Liberator	Blake's 7
Phoenix	Battle of the Planets
Ranger III	Buck Rogers in the 25th Century
Red Dwarf	Red Dwarf
Scorpio	Blake's 7
Spindrift	Land of the Giants
Starbug	Red Dwarf
Tardis	Doctor Who
Thunderbird 3	Thunderbirds
Voyager	Galloping Galaxies/Star Trek: Voyager

....

The Major TV Awards

AWARD	WHEN HELD	FIRST YEAR	DONOR/VOTERS
Emmys	September	1949	Academy of Television Arts and Sciences/National Academy of Television Arts and Sciences/ International Academy of Television Arts and Sciences
BAFTAs	April	1954*	British Academy of Film and Television Arts
Golden Globes	January	1955**	Hollywood Foreign Press Association
The Golden Rose	May	1961	International juries of media professionals
Royal Television Society Awards	February	1969	Royal Television Society
Broadcasting Press Guild Awards	April	1974	Writers about television
British Comedy Awards	December	1990	Comedy industry professionals
National Television Awards	October	1995	Viewers
British Soap Awards	May	1999	Viewers

* As the Guild of Television Producers and Directors.
** Year television first included; awards actually date back to 1943.

Principal Officers of the USS Enterprise in Star Trek

Captain James T Kirk	Captain
Mr Spock	First Officer
Dr Leonard McCoy	Chief Medical Officer
Mr Sulu	Chief Navigator
Lieutenant Uhura	Head of Communications
Engineer Montgomery Scott	Chief Engineer
Christine Chapel	Nurse
Ensign Pavel Chekov	Assistant Navigator

Principal Officers of the USS Enterprise in Star Trek: the Next Generation

Captain Jean-Luc Picard	Captain
Commander William T Riker	First Officer
Lieutenant Geordi La Forge	Helmsman/Chief Engineer
Lieutenant Worf	Klingon Officer/Chief of Security
Lieutenant Tasha Yar	Chief of Security
Dr Beverly Crusher	Chief Medical Officer
Deanna Troi	Counsellor
Lieutenant Commander Data	Android
Wesley Crusher	Apprentice Helmsman

Thomas the Tank Engine and Friends

NO.	NAME	TYPE	COLOUR
1	Thomas	tank engine	blue
2	Edward	tank engine	blue
3	Henry	tank engine	green
4	Gordon	express engine	blue
5	James	mixed traffic engine	red
6	Percy	saddle tank	green
7	Toby	tram engine	brown
8	Montague ('Duck')	GWR tank engine	green
9	Donald	Scottish engine	black
10	Douglas	Scottish engine	black
11	Oliver	GWR engine	green

Alongside these initial 'star' engines works Daisy, a green diesel, and later additions include Boco, Diesel, Bill, Ben, Peter Sam, Sir Handel, Skarloey, Stepney, Duke ('Granpuff'), Rusty, Rheneas, Mavis and Duncan. Thomas's carriages are Annie and Clarabel and also part of the action are Bertie the bus, Terence the tractor, Trevor the traction engine and Harold the helicopter.

Morecambe and Wise 'Dame' Performers

The 1977 Morecambe and Wise Christmas special featured a team of newsreaders, sports presenters and film critics performing (complete with unlikely acrobatic cartwheels and somersaults) 'There Is Nothing Like a Dame' from the musical South Pacific. They were:

Michael Aspel
Richard Baker
Frank Bough
Philip Jenkinson
Barry Norman
Eddie Waring
Richard Whitmore
Peter Woods

The Big Read

In 2003 the BBC organised a national poll of the UK's best-loved book. The 21 shortlisted candidates (in final finishing order) and the celebrities who championed their cause were as follows:

	BOOK	CELEBRITY
1	The Lord of the Rings, by JRR Tolkien	Ray Mears
2	Pride and Prejudice, by Jane Austen	Meera Syal
3	His Dark Materials, by Philip Pullman	Benedict Allen
4	The Hitchhiker's Guide to the Galaxy, by Douglas Adams	Sanjeev Bhaskar
5	Harry Potter and the Goblet of Fire, by JK Rowling	Fay Ripley
6	To Kill a Mockingbird, by Harper Lee	John Humphrys
7	Winnie the Pooh, by AA Milne	Phill Jupitus
8	Nineteen Eighty-Four, by George Orwell	Jo Brand
9	The Lion, the Witch and the Wardrobe, by CS Lewis	Ronni Ancona
10	Jane Eyre, by Charlotte Brontë	Lorraine Kelly
11	Catch-22, by Joseph Heller	John Sergeant
12	Wuthering Heights, by Emily Brontë	Alastair McGowan
13	Birdsong, by Sebastian Faulks	William Hague
14	Rebecca, by Daphne du Maurier	Alan Titchmarsh
15	The Catcher in the Rye, by JD Salinger	Ruby Wax
16	The Wind in the Willows, by Kenneth Grahame	Bill Oddie
17	Great Expectations, by Charles Dickens	David Dimbleby
18	Little Women, by Louisa May Alcott	Sandi Toksvig
19	Captain Corelli's Mandolin, by Louis de Bernieres	Clare Short
20	War and Peace, by Leo Tolstoy	Simon Schama
21	Gone with the Wind, by Margaret Mitchell	Arabella Weir

Longest Running UK TV Series for Children

SERIES	NO. OF YEARS	BROADCAST HISTORY
Blue Peter	47+	BBC 1 1958–
Newsround	33+	BBC 1 1972–
Jackanory	31	BBC 1/BBC 2 1965–96
Crackerjack	29	BBC 1 1955–84
Record Breakers	29	BBC 1 1972–2001
Grange Hill	27+	BBC 1 1978–
Watch with Mother*	27	BBC 1 1953–80
Play School	24	BBC 2 1964–88
The Sooty Show**	24	ITV 1968–92
Rainbow***	23	ITV 1972–95
Why Don't You...?	22	BBC 1 1973–95
Animal Magic	21	BBC 1 1962–83
Chucklevision	18+	BBC 1 1987–
Byker Grove	16+	BBC 1 1989–
Art Attack	15+	ITV 1990–
How 2	15+	ITV 1990–
How!	15	ITV 1966–81

* An umbrella title for a collection of programmes, including many repeats.
** Sooty has remained on television in other programmes since this series ended.
*** Revamped as Rainbow Days (1996–7)

....

Anyone Seen an Emmy?

Everyone knows what an Oscar looks like, but who can recognise TV's equivalent, an Emmy? The gold-plated statuette takes the form of a winged lady holding aloft an atom, thus representing a merger of the arts and sciences. Each statuette weighs $4^{3}/_{4}$ lbs and stands 16 inches tall.

....

The Grand Knockout Tournament

In 1987 four members of the Royal Family took part in a special, celebrity-packed charity edition of the game show It's a Knockout, presented from Alton Towers by Stuart Hall, Les Dawson and Su Pollard. These were the designated good causes of the teams they captained:

TEAM CAPTAIN	CAUSE
HRH The Prince Edward	The Duke of Edinburgh's International Project 87
HRH The Princess Anne	Save the Children
HRH The Duke of York	World Wildlife Fund
HRH The Duchess of York	International Year of Shelter for the Homeless 1987

BBC Sports Personality of the Year

YEAR	PERSONALITY	TEAM	OVERSEAS PERSONALITY
1954	Chris Chataway (athletics)		
1955	Gordon Pirie (athletics)		
1956	Jim Laker (cricket)		
1957	Dai Rees (golf)		
1958	Ian Black (swimming)		
1959	John Surtees (motor racing)		
1960	David Broome (show jumping)	Cooper Racing (motor racing)	Herb Elliot (athletics)
1961	Stirling Moss (motor racing)	Tottenham Hotspur FC (football)	Valerie Brumel (athletics)
1962	Anita Lonsbrough (swimming)	BRM (motor racing)	Donald Jackson (ice skating)
1963	Dorothy Hyman (athletics)	West Indies (cricket)	Jacques Anquetil (cycling)
1964	Mary Rand (athletics)	England Youth (football)	Abebe Bikila (athletics)
1965	Tommy Simpson (cycling)	West Ham United FC (football)	Ron Clarke (athletics), Gary Player (golf)
1966	Bobby Moore (football)	England World Cup (football)	Eusebio (football), Gary Sobers (cricket)
1967	Henry Cooper (boxing)	Celtic FC (football)	George Moore (horse racing)
1968	David Hemery (athletics)	Manchester United FC (football)	Protopopov and Belovsova (ice skating)
1969	Ann Jones (tennis)	Women's 4 x 400m relay (athletics), Ryder Cup (golf)	Rod Laver (tennis)
1970	Henry Cooper (boxing)	Nijinksy team (horse racing)	Pele (football)
1971	HRH The Princess Anne (equestrianism)	British Lions (rugby union)	Lee Trevino (golf)
1972	Mary Peters (athletics)	Olympic 3-Day Event (equestrianism)	Olga Korbut (gymnastics)
1973	Jackie Stewart (motor racing)	Sunderland FC (football)	Muhammad Ali (boxing)
1974	Brendan Foster (athletics)	British Lions (rugby union)	Muhammad Ali (boxing)

1975	David Steele (cricket)	Men's swimming team	Arthur Ashe (tennis)
1976	John Curry (ice skating)	Modern Pentathlon team	Nadia Comaneci (gymnastics)
1977	Virginia Wade (tennis)	Liverpool FC (football)	Nicki Lauda (motor racing)
1978	Steve Ovett (athletics)	Davis and Whiteman Cup teams (tennis)	Muhammad Ali (boxing)
1979	Sebastian Coe (athletics)	British Showjumping team	Bjorn Borg (tennis)
1980	Robin Cousins (ice skating)	England (rugby union)	Jack Nicklaus (golf)
1981	Ian Botham (cricket)	Bob Champion and Aldaniti (horse racing)	Chris Evert (tennis)
1982	Daley Thompson (athletics)	Torvill and Dean (ice dancing)	Jimmy Connors (tennis)
1983	Steve Cram (athletics)	Torvill and Dean (ice dancing)	Carl Lewis (athletics)
1984	Torvill and Dean (ice dancing)	British Showjumping team	Bjorn Borg (tennis)
1985	Barry McGuigan (boxing)	Ryder Cup team (golf)	Boris Becker (tennis)
1986	Nigel Mansell (motor racing)	Liverpool FC (football)	Greg Norman (golf)
1987	Fatima Whitbread (athletics)	Ryder Cup team (golf)	Martina Navratilova (tennis)
1988	Steve Davis (snooker)	British Hockey team	Steffi Graf (tennis)
1989	Nick Faldo (golf)	Men's Athletics squad	Mike Tyson (boxing)
1990	Paul Gascoigne (football)	Scotland (rugby union)	Mal Meninga (rugby league)
1991	Liz McColgan (athletics)	England (rugby union), Men's 4 x 400 m Relay (athletics)	Mike Powell (athletics)
1992	Nigel Mansell (motor racing)	British Pairs (rowing)	Andre Agassi (tennis)
1993	Linford Christie (athletics)	England (rugby union)	Greg Norman (golf)
1994	Damon Hill (motor racing)	Wigan (rugby league)	Brian Lara (cricket)
1995	Jonathan Edwards (athletics)	European Ryder Cup (golf)	Jonah Lomu (rugby union)

BBC Sports Personality of the Year

YEAR	PERSONALITY	TEAM	OVERSEAS PERSONALITY
1996	Damon Hill (motor racing)	British Olympic Pair (rowing), Men's 4 x 400 m Relay (athletics)	Evander Holyfield (boxing), Michael Johnson (athletics)
1997	Greg Rusedski (tennis)	British Lions (rugby union)	Martina Hingis (tennis)
1998	Michael Owen (football)	Manchester United FC (football)	Mark O'Meara (golf)
1999	Lennox Lewis (boxing)	Manchester United FC (football)	Maurice Greene (athletics)
2000	Steve Redgrave (rowing)	British Olympic and Paralympic athletes	Tiger Woods (golf)
2001	David Beckham (football)	Liverpool FC (football)	Goran Ivanisevic (tennis)
2002	Paula Radcliffe (athletics)	European Ryder Cup (golf)	Ronaldo (football)
2003	Jonny Wilkinson (rugby union)	England World Cup (rugby union)	Lance Armstrong (cycling)
2004	Kelly Holmes (athletics)	Britain's Olympic Coxless Four (rowing)	Roger Federer (tennis)

Since 1999 additional awards have been made:

YEAR	NEWCOMER/YOUNG PERSONALITY	COACH	HELEN ROLLASON AWARD*
1999	Dean Macey (athletics)	Sir Alex Ferguson (football)	Jenny Pitman (horse racing)
2000	Jenson Button (motor racing)	Jurgen Grobler (rowing)	Tanni Grey-Thompson (athletics)
2001	Amy Spencer (athletics)	Sven-Goran Eriksson (football)	Ellen MacArthur (sailing)
2002	Wayne Rooney (football)	Arsene Wenger (football)	Jane Tomlinson (athletics)
2003	Kate Haywood (swimming)	Clive Woodward (rugby union)	Michael Watson (boxing)
2004	Andrew Murray (tennis)	Arsene Wenger (football)	Kirsty Howard (charity work)

* For outstanding courage and achievement in the face of adversity.

SPORTS PERSONALITY OF THE CENTURY (MILLENNIUM PROGRAMME, 1999)
Muhammad Ali (boxing)

YEAR	LIFETIME ACHIEVEMENT	UNSUNG HERO
2001	Sir Alex Ferguson (football)	
2002	George Best (football)	
2003	Martina Navratilova (tennis)	Nobby Woodcock (football)
2004	Ian Botham (cricket)	Abdullah Ben-Kmyayal (football)

GOLDEN AWARDS (50TH PROGRAMME, 2003)

Golden Personality: Sir Steve Redgrave (rowing)
Golden Team: England World Cup (football)

....

The Full Names of Comedy Double Acts

Alexander ARMSTRONG and Ben MILLER
David BADDIEL and Frank SKINNER
George BURNS and Gracie ALLEN
Tommy CANNON and Bobby BALL
Richard CHEECH Marin and Thomas CHONG
Peter COOK and Dudley MOORE
Les DENNIS and Dustin GEE
Richard 'DICK' McCourt and DOMinic Wood
Michael FLANDERS and Donald SWANN
Dawn FRENCH and Jennifer SAUNDERS
Stephen FRY and Hugh LAURIE
Gareth HALE and Norman PACE
Dr Evadne HINGE and Dame Hilda BRACKET
Mike HOPE and Albie KEEN
Moray HUNTER and Jack DOCHERTY
Jimmy JEWEL and Ben WARRIS
Stewart LEE and Richard HERRING
LENNIE Bennett and JERRY Stevens
Syd LITTLE and Eddie LARGE
MEL Giedroyc and SUE Perkins
Eric MORECAMBE and Ernie WISE
Rob NEWMAN and David BADDIEL
PENN Jillette and Raymond TELLER
Steve PUNT and Hugh DENNIS
Vic REEVES and Bob MORTIMER
Dan ROWAN and Dick MARTIN
Terry SCOTT and Bill MAYNARD
Mel SMITH and Griff Rhys JONES

Some Notable Theme Song Performers

PERFORMER	PROGRAMME
Charles Aznavour	Seven Faces of Woman
David Bowie and Erdal Kizilcay	The Buddah of Suburbia
Elkie Brooks	A Very Peculiar Practice
Chas and Dave	In Sickness and in Health
Tony Christie	The Protectors
Clannad	Harry's Game, Robin of Sherwood
Eric Clapton and Michael Kamen	Edge of Darkness
Billy Connolly	Supergran
Elvis Costello and Richard Harvey	GBH
Julie Covington	Executive Stress
Peter Davison	Button Moon
Dexy's Midnight Runners	Brush Strokes
Dido	Roswell
Ian Dury	The Secret Diary of Adrian Mole, Aged 13¾
Adrian Edmondson and Julie Driscoll	Absolutely Fabulous
Georgie Fame	El CID
Jose Feliciano	Chico and the Man
Bud Flanagan	Dad's Army
Eric Idle	One Foot in the Grave
Waylon Jennings	The Dukes of Hazzard
Jack Jones	The Love Boat
Kathy Kirby	Adam Adamant Lives!
Frankie Laine	Rawhide
Brian May	Frank Stubbs Promotes
Paul McCartney and Wings	Zoo Gang, Crossroads
Bob Monkhouse and Paul Shane	You Rang, M'Lord?
Oasis	The Royle Family
Cliff Richard	Trainer
The Scaffold	The Liver Birds
John Sebastian	Welcome Back, Kotter
Peter Skellern	Me and My Girl
Dusty Springfield	The Six Million Dollar Man

Are You Well Viewed?

'If you read a lot of books you are considered well read. But if you watch a lot of TV, you're not considered well viewed.' - Lily Tomlin

Original Coronation Street Cast

Characters who appeared in the first seven episodes of Coronation Street from its debut on 9 December 1960 to the end of that year.

CHARACTER	ACTOR
David Barlow	Alan Rothwell
Frank Barlow	Frank Pemberton
Ida Barlow	Noel Dyson
Kenneth Barlow	William Roache
Minnie Caldwell	Margot Bryant
Linda Cheveski	Anne Cunningham
Ivan Cheveski	Ernst Walder
Susan Cunningham	Patricia Shakesby
Christine Hardman	Christine Hargreaves
May Hardman	Joan Heath
Esther Hayes	Daphne Oxenford
Harry Hewitt	Ivan Beavis
Lucille Hewitt	Jennifer Moss
Elsie Lappin	Maudie Edwards
Florrie Lindley	Betty Alberge
Vera Lomax	Ruth Holden
Martha Longhurst	Lynne Carol
Concepta Riley	Doreen Keogh
Ena Sharples	Violet Carson
Leonard Swindley	Arthur Lowe
Elsie Tanner	Patricia Phoenix
Dennis Tanner	Philip Lowrie
Albert Tatlock	Jack Howarth
Jack Walker	Arthur Leslie
Annie Walker	Doris Speed

....

First Night: BBC2's Opening Schedule (20 April 1964)*

7.20pm Line-up. With John Stone and Denis Tuohy.

7.30 The Alberts Channel Too. Comic take on the opening of a new television network.

8.00 Kiss Me Kate by Cole Porter. Starring Patricia Morrison and Howard Keel.

9.35 Arkady Raikin. Showcase for the Soviet Union's top comedian.

10.20 Off with a Bang. Celebratory firework display from Southend pier.

10.35 Newsroom

11.00 Closedown

* Schedule did not happen. A power cut wiped out the evening's broadcasting.

Who Invented Television?

The established answer to this old quiz chestnut is Scotsman John Logie Baird, but the truth is that Baird was not the first person to experiment with television. Baird, to his credit, did develop the concept so that images like the human face were recognisable for the first time, but his primitive, mechanical scanning system, while trialled by the BBC, was not eventually adopted. Instead, the corporation opted for an electronic system based on the cathode ray tube, and the future of television lay not in Baird's hands. However, Baird was always an important figure, constantly pushing at the boundaries of television science and experimenting with such concepts as colour television and even video discs decades before they came into use.

....

Adventure Teams

TEAM	MEMBERS
The A-Team	Hannibal Smith, Howling Mad Murdock, BA Barracus, Faceman (Templeton Peck)
The Angels (Captain Scarlet)	Harmony, Destiny, Rhapsody, Melody, Symphony
The Avengers	Dr David Keel, John Steed, Martin King, Venus Smith, Cathy Gale, Emma Peel, Tara King
Charlie's Angels	Sabrina Duncan, Jill Monroe, Kelly Garrett, Kris Munroe, Tiffany Welles, Julie Rogers
The Double Deckers (Here Come the Double Deckers)	Scooper, Billie, Brains, Doughnut, Spring, Sticks, Tiger
The Famous Five	Julian, Dick, Anne, George (Georgina), Timothy (dog)
The Fantastic Four	Mr Fantastic (Reed Richards), Invisible Girl (Sue Richards), The Thing (Ben Grimm), The Human Torch (Johnny Storm)
The Forest Rangers	Chub, Peter, Mike, Ted, Johnny, Zeke, Timmy, Gaby, Kathy, Danny
The Four Just Men	Ben Manfred, Tim Collier, Jeff Ryder, Ricco Poccari
Freewheelers	Bill, Terry, Chris, Nick, Mike, Max, Sue, Steve, Jill, Eva, Dave
G-Force (Battle of the Planets)	Mark Venture, Princess, Jason, Keyop, Tiny
The Impossibles (Frankenstein Jr)	Multi Man, Fluid Man, Coil Man

International Rescue (Thunderbirds)	Scott Tracy (Thunderbird 1),
	Virgil Tracy (Thunderbird 2),
	Alan Tracy (Thunderbird 3),
	Gordon Tracy (Thunderbird 4),
	Alan Tracy (Thunderbird 5)
Josie and the Pussycats	Josie, Valerie, Melody
Mighty Morphin Power Rangers	Kimberly (Pink Ranger),
	Billy (Blue Ranger), Zack (Black Ranger),
	Jason (Red Ranger), Trini (Yellow Ranger),
	Tommy (Green/White Ranger),
	Rocky (Red Ranger), Aisha (Yellow Ranger),
	Adam (Black Ranger), Kat (Pink Ranger)
The New Avengers	John Steed, Purdey, Mike Gambit
The Persuaders	Lord Brett Sinclair, Danny Wilde
The Powerpuff Girls	Blossom, Bubbles, Buttercup
The Protectors	Harry Rule, Contessa di Contini, Paul Buchet
The Ratcatchers	Peregrine Smith, Brig. Davidson,
	Richard Hurst
Space Kidettes	Scooter, Snoopy, Jenny, Countdown
Teenage Mutant Ninja Turtles	Leonardo, Michelangelo, Donatello, Raphael
The Telebugs	Chip, Samantha, Bug
Terrahawks	Dr Tiger Ninestein, Capt. Mary Falconer,
	Capt. Kate Kestrel, Lt Hiro, Lt Hawkeye
The Three Musketeers	Porthos, Athos, Aramis (plus D'Artagnan)
Thundercats	Lion-O, Tygra, Cheetara, Panthro, Snarf,
	Wilykat, Wilykit
The Tomorrow People	John, Carol, Kenny, Stephen, Elizabeth, Tyso,
	Mike, Hsui Tai, Andrew
The Tomorrow People (remake)	Adam, Megabyte, Lisa, Kevin, Ami

....

Real People Who Became Cartoon TV Stars

Abbot and Costello
The Beatles
The Harlem Globetrotters
The Jackson Five (The Jackson 5ive)
Laurel and Hardy
Jerry Lewis (Will the Real Jerry Lewis Please Sit Down?)
The Osmonds
The Three Stooges (The New Three Stooges)

Notable British TV Plays

PLAY	**Abigail's Party**
WRITER	Mike Leigh
DIRECTOR	Mike Leigh
ANTHOLOGY	Play for Today
YEAR	1977

PLAY	**And Did Those Feet?**
WRITER	David Mercer
DIRECTOR	Don Taylor
ANTHOLOGY	The Wednesday Play
YEAR	1965

PLAY	**Another Sunday and Sweet FA**
WRITER	Jack Rosenthal
DIRECTOR	Michael Apted
ANTHOLOGY	Sunday Night Theatre
YEAR	1972

PLAY	**Bar Mitzvah Boy**
WRITER	Jack Rosenthal
DIRECTOR	Michael Tuchner
ANTHOLOGY	Play for Today
YEAR	1976

PLAY	**A Beast with Two Backs**
WRITER	Dennis Potter
DIRECTOR	Lionel Harris
ANTHOLOGY	The Wednesday Play
YEAR	1968

PLAY	**The Black Stuff**
WRITER	Alan Bleasdale
DIRECTOR	Jim Goddard
ANTHOLOGY	n/a
YEAR	1980

PLAY	**Blue Remembered Hills**
WRITER	Dennis Potter
DIRECTOR	Brian Gibson
ANTHOLOGY	Play for Today
YEAR	1979

PLAY	**Cathy Come Home**
WRITER	Jeremy Sandford
DIRECTOR	Ken Loach
ANTHOLOGY	The Wednesday Play
YEAR	1966

PLAY	**Caught on a Train**
WRITER	Stephen Poliakoff
DIRECTOR	Peter Duffell
ANTHOLOGY	Playhouse
YEAR	1980

PLAY	**A Day Out**
WRITER	Alan Bennett
DIRECTOR	Stephen Frears
ANTHOLOGY	n/a
YEAR	1972

PLAY	**Edna, the Inebriate Woman**
WRITER	Jeremy Sandford
DIRECTOR	Ted Kotcheff
ANTHOLOGY	Play for Today
YEAR	1971

PLAY	**An Englishman Abroad**
WRITER	Alan Bennett
DIRECTOR	John Schlesinger
ANTHOLOGY	n/a
YEAR	1983

PLAY	**The Evacuees**
WRITER	Jack Rosenthal
DIRECTOR	Alan Parker
ANTHOLOGY	n/a
YEAR	1975

PLAY	**Jamie, on a Flying Visit**
WRITER	Michael Frayn
DIRECTOR	Claude Whatham
ANTHOLOGY	The Wednesday Play
YEAR	1968

PLAY	**Kisses at Fifty**
WRITER	Colin Welland
DIRECTOR	Michael Apted
ANTHOLOGY	Play for Today
YEAR	1973

PLAY	**The Knowledge**
WRITER	Jack Rosenthal
DIRECTOR	Bob Brooks
ANTHOLOGY	n/a
YEAR	1979

PLAY	**Lena, O My Lena**
WRITER	Alun Owen
DIRECTOR	Ted Kotcheff
ANTHOLOGY	Armchair Theatre
YEAR	1960

PLAY	**The Lover**
WRITER	Harold Pinter
DIRECTOR	Joan Kemp-Welch
ANTHOLOGY	n/a
YEAR	1963

PLAY	**The Lump**
WRITER	Jim Allen
DIRECTOR	Jack Gold
ANTHOLOGY	The Wednesday Play
YEAR	1967

PLAY	**Man above Men**
WRITER	David Hare
DIRECTOR	Alan Clarke
ANTHOLOGY	Play for Today
YEAR	1973

PLAY	**A Night Out**
WRITER	Harold Pinter
DIRECTOR	Philip Saville
ANTHOLOGY	Armchair Theatre
YEAR	1960

PLAY	**No Trams to Lime Street**
WRITER	Alun Owen
DIRECTOR	Ted Kotcheff
ANTHOLOGY	Armchair Theatre
YEAR	1959

PLAY	**Nuts in May**
WRITER	Mike Leigh
DIRECTOR	Mike Leigh
ANTHOLOGY	Play for Today
YEAR	1976

PLAY	**Oi for England**
WRITER	Trevor Griffiths
DIRECTOR	Tony Smith
ANTHOLOGY	n/a
YEAR	1982

PLAY	**Penda's Fen**
WRITER	David Rudkin
DIRECTOR	Alan Clarke
ANTHOLOGY	Play for Today
YEAR	1974

PLAY	**The Rank and File**
WRITER	Jim Allen
DIRECTOR	Ken Loach
ANTHOLOGY	Play for Today
YEAR	1971

PLAY	**Ready When You Are Mr McGill**
WRITER	Jack Rosenthal
DIRECTOR	Mike Newell
ANTHOLOGY	Red Letter Day
YEAR	1976

PLAY	**The Road**
WRITER	Nigel Kneale
DIRECTOR	Christopher Morahan
ANTHOLOGY	First Night
YEAR	1963

PLAY	**Rumpole of the Bailey**
WRITER	John Mortimer
DIRECTOR	Robert Knights
ANTHOLOGY	Play for Today
YEAR	1975

PLAY	**Scum**
WRITER	Roy Minton
DIRECTOR	Alan Clarke
ANTHOLOGY	n/a
YEAR	1991 (made in 1977)

PLAY	**The Seekers (trilogy)**
WRITER	Ken Taylor
DIRECTOR	Alvin Rakoff
ANTHOLOGY	Theatre 625
YEAR	1964

PLAY	**A Soirée at Bossom's Hotel**
WRITER	Simon Raven
DIRECTOR	Gilchrist Calder
ANTHOLOGY	The Wednesday Play
YEAR	1966

PLAY	**Son of Man**
WRITER	Dennis Potter
DIRECTOR	Gareth Davies
ANTHOLOGY	The Wednesday Play
YEAR	1969

PLAY	**Spend, Spend, Spend**
WRITER	Jack Rosenthal
DIRECTOR	John Goldschmidt
ANTHOLOGY	Play for Today
YEAR	1977

PLAY	**Stand Up, Nigel Barton**
WRITER	Dennis Potter
DIRECTOR	Gareth Davies
ANTHOLOGY	The Wednesday Play
YEAR	1965

PLAY	**The Stone Tape**
WRITER	Nigel Kneale
DIRECTOR	Peter Sasdy
ANTHOLOGY	n/a
YEAR	1972

PLAY	**Stronger than the Sun**
WRITER	Stephen Poliakoff
DIRECTOR	Michael Apted
ANTHOLOGY	Play for Today
YEAR	1977

PLAY	**A Suitable Case for Treatment**
WRITER	David Mercer
DIRECTOR	Don Taylor
ANTHOLOGY	n/a
YEAR	1962

PLAY	**Talking to a Stranger**
WRITER	John Hopkins
DIRECTOR	Christopher Morahan
ANTHOLOGY	Theatre 625
YEAR	1966

PLAY	**United Kingdom**
WRITER	Jim Allen
DIRECTOR	Roland Joffe
ANTHOLOGY	Play for Today
YEAR	1981

PLAY	**Up the Junction**
WRITER	Nell Dunn
DIRECTOR	Ken Loach
ANTHOLOGY	The Wednesday Play
YEAR	1965

PLAY	**The Year of the Sex Olympics**
WRITER	Nigel Kneale
DIRECTOR	Michael Elliott
ANTHOLOGY	Theatre 625
YEAR	1968

Help Wanted

'Seeing by wireless. Inventor of apparatus wishes to hear from someone who will assist (not financially) in making working model.'

– Advertisement placed by John Logie Baird in The Times, 27 June 1923

Public Service National Television Broadcasters

AUSTRALIA	ABC (Australian Broadcasting Corporation)
	SBS (Special Broadcasting Service)
AUSTRIA	ORF (Österreichischer Rundfunk)
BELGIUM	RTBF (Radio Télévision Belge de la Communauté Française)
	VRT (Vlaamse Radio-en Televisieomroep)
	BRF (Belgischer Rundfunk der Deutschsprachigen Gemeinschaft)
CANADA	CBC (Canadian Broadcasting Corporation)
DENMARK	DR (Danmarks Radio)
FINLAND	YLE (Yleisradio)
FRANCE	France Télévision
GERMANY	ARD (Arbeitsgemeinschaft der öffentlich-rechtlichen Rundfunkanstalten der Bundesrepublik Deutschland)
	ZDF (Zweites Deutsches Fernsehen)
IRELAND	RTE (Radio Telefís Éireann)
ITALY	RAI (Radiotelevisione Italiana)
JAPAN	NHK (Nippon Hoso Kyokai)
NETHERLANDS	Omroep (Nederlandse Publieke Omroep)
NEW ZEALAND	TVNZ (Television New Zealand)
NORWAY	NRK (Norsk Rikskringkasting)
POLAND	KRRiT (Krajowa Rada Radiofonii i Telewizji)
PORTUGAL	RTP (Radiotelevisão Portuguesa)
RUSSIA	PTP (Russian Radiotelevision)
SOUTH AFRICA	SABC (South African Broadcasting Corporation)
SPAIN	RTVE (Radio Televisión Española)
SWEDEN	SVT (Sveriges Television)
SWITZERLAND	SBC (Swiss Broadcasting Corporation)
UK	BBC (British Broadcasting Corporation)
	Channel 4
	S4C (Sianel Pedwar Cymru)

More Than Just a Box in the Corner

'Television! Teacher, mother, secret lover.'

– Homer Simpson, The Simpsons

....

Comedy Playhouse Spin-offs

The following comedy series all began with pilot programmes shown as part of the BBC's Comedy Playhouse anthology (pilot episode title in brackets, if different):

All Gas and Gaiters (The Bishop Rides Again)

Are You Being Served?

As Good Cooks Go

B-And-B

Beggar My Neighbour

Brighton Belles*

The Gordon Peters Show (The Birthday)

Happy Ever After

Hudd

It's Awfully Bad for Your Eyes, Darling

Last of the Summer Wine

The Liver Birds

Me Mammy

Meet the Wife (The Bed)

Mr Big (The Big Job)

No Strings

Not in Front of the Children (House in a Tree)

Now Take My Wife (Just Harry and Me)

The Old Campaigner

The Reluctant Romeo (Room at the Bottom)

Steptoe and Son (The Offer)

The 10%ers*

That's Your Funeral (Last Tribute)

Thicker Than Water (The Family of Fred)

Till Death Us Do Part

Under and Over

The Vital Spark

The Walrus and the Carpenter

The Whitehall Worrier (The Mallard Imaginaire)

Wild, Wild Women

Wink to Me Only (View by Appointment)

* From an ITV revival of the concept with the same name.

The Worst Christmas Evening's Viewing?

This was ITV's festive line-up on Christmas Day 1982:

5.35 3-2-1

6.35 Game for a Laugh

7.25 Bruce Forsyth's Play Your Cards Right

7.55 Film: The Black Hole

9.50 Chas and Dave's Christmas Knees-Up

10.55 Cleo and John

....

Some Series That Changed Names

ORIGINAL NAME	NEW NAME
Alas Smith and Jones	Smith and Jones
All Quiet on the Preston Front	Preston Front
Always and Everyone	A&E
Band of Gold	Gold
Barlow at Large	Barlow
Children's Ward	The Ward
Emmerdale Farm	Emmerdale
Frank Stubbs Promotes	Frank Stubbs
Ghost Squad	GS5
The Growing Pains of PC Penrose	Rosie
Hancock's Half Hour	Hancock
Inigo Pipkin	Pipkins
The Kit Curran Radio Show	Kit Curran
Lollipop Loves Mr Mole	Lollipop
Mark Saber	Saber of London
Market in Honey Lane	Honey Lane
Mersey Beat	Merseybeat
Mogul	The Troubleshooters
Monty Python's Flying Circus	Monty Python
Old Grey Whistle Test	Whistle Test
Our Man at St Mark's	Our Man from St Mark's
Paradise Heights	The Eustace Brothers
Rainbow	Rainbow Days
Softly, Softly	Softly, Softly – Task Force
Sportsnight with Coleman	Sportsnight
Take the High Road	High Road
These Friends of Mine	Ellen
Toast of the Town	The Ed Sullivan Show
You'll Never Get Rich	The Phil Silvers Show

Syndication Names

Confusingly, older American series are sometimes known by more than one title. This is because the series was 'syndicated' – or sold for re-runs – while the original series was still running with new episodes in prime time. The syndicated title, as in the examples below, ensured that the public was aware that this was not a new episode.

ORIGINAL NAME	SYNDICATION NAME
The Andy Griffith Show	Andy of Mayberry
Bonanza	Ponderosa
Death Valley Days	Call of the West
Dragnet	Badge 714
Fury	Brave Stallion
Gunsmoke	Marshal Dillon
Hawaii Five-O	McGarrett
I Love Lucy	The Sunday Lucy Show, The Lucy Show
Lassie	Jeff's Collie, Timmy and Lassie
Mark Saber	Detective's Diary
The Phil Silvers Show	Sergeant Bilko
Private Secretary	Susie
The Rockford Files	Jim Rockford, Private Investigator
Wagon Train	Major Adams – Trailmaster

....

No Good Can Come of It

'Television? The word is half Latin and half Greek. No good can come of it.' - Attributed to CP Scott, Editor, The Guardian

....

In Praise of Gus Honeybun

One of UK TV's most fondly remembered puppets is Gus Honeybun – even though he only ever appeared in one of ITV's smallest regions. The rabbit first surfaced on Westward TV in 1961, when it was claimed that he was found on Dartmoor. His role throughout the 20 years that Westward was on air was mainly to chat to continuity announcers between children's programmes (initially, it is alleged, to a cover a dearth of advertising) and fool around while birthday greetings were read out, but he was also granted a programme of his own at one point. When TSW took over the Westward franchise in 1981, Gus remained part of the set up, clocking up a further 11 years of on-screen antics until TSW was itself ousted by Westcountry Television. His final appearance came on 31 December 1992 – TSW's last day on air – when he was seen returning at last to his burrow and his family.

The Superstars

Popular in the 1970s and revived in recent years, Superstars pits leading names from various sports against each other in a series of sporting contests. These are the UK series winners:

1973	David Hemery (athletics)
1974	John Conteh (boxing)
1975	No event
1976	David Hemery (athletics)
1977	Tim Crooks (rowing)
1978	Brian Jacks (judo)
1979	Brian Jacks (judo)
1980	No event
1981	Keith Fielding (rugby league)
1982	Brian Hooper (athletics)
1983	Brian Hooper (athletics)
1984	Gary Cook (athletics)
1985	Robin Brew (swimming)
2002	Austin Healey (rugby union)
2003	Du'aine Ladejo (athletics)/Zoe Baker (swimming) tied with Lesley McKenna (snowboarding)*
2004	No event
2005	Alain Baxter (skiing)/Zoe Baker (swimming)

* Female contest introduced from this year.

Live and Death

The perils of live television were highlighted on 30 November 1958 when actor Gareth Jones tragically collapsed and died while appearing in an Armchair Theatre play called Underground. The show must go on, however, and his fellow performers, who included Donald Houston and Andrew Cruickshank, finished the play by ad-libbing around his role.

Counting the Lines

The number of lines making up UK TV pictures has advanced thus:

SYSTEM	INAUGURATED
30-line	1920s (Baird trials)
405-line	2 November 1936 (BBC)
625-line	21 April 1964 (initially BBC 2)

US television uses a 525-line system.

Ranch Review

PROGRAMME	RANCH
The Big Valley	Barkley
Bonanza	Ponderosa
Dallas	Southfork
The Gene Autry Show	Melody
The High Chapparal	The High Chapparal
Hopalong Cassidy	Bar 20
The Rifleman	Dunlap
The Roy Rogers Show	The Double R Bar
The Virginian	Shiloh

TV Pick Ups

The demand for electricity is suppressed when major television programmes are being broadcast. However, as soon as the programme ends (or takes a break, such as half-time in football match), the National Grid experiences massive 'pick ups' as viewers turn on lights, switch on a kettle, etc. These are the programmes giving rise to the greatest pick ups since 1990.

	PROGRAMME	DATE	MW*
1	England v West Germany (World Cup 1990)	4 Jul 1990	2800
2	England v Brazil (World Cup 2002: half-time)	21 Jun 2002	2570
3	England v Nigeria (World Cup 2002: half-time)	12 Jun 2002	2340
4	EastEnders	5 Apr 2001	2290
5	The Darling Buds of May	28 Apr 1991	2200
5	The Darling Buds of May	12 May 1991	2200
7	England v Australia (Rugby World Cup Final: half-time)	22 Nov 2003	2110
8	Coronation Street	18 Apr 1994	2100
8	England v Argentina (World Cup 1998)	30 Jun 1998	2100
10	Coronation Street	7 Apr 2002	2010
11	Italy v Argentina (World Cup 1990)	3 July 1990	2000
11	Coronation Street	1 April 1991	2000
13	Coronation Street	20 April 1997	1960
14	EastEnders	5 April 1994	1900
14	Emmerdale	21 April 2002	1900

* Megawatts

Pilot Episodes of Drama Series

SERIES	PILOT EPISODE/FILM
Banacek	Detour to Nowhere
The Bill	Woodentop
Callan	A Magnum for Schneider
Columbo	Prescription Murder
Harry O	Smile Jenny You're Dead
Hec Ramsey	The Century Turns
Kojak	The Marcus Nelson Murders
Madigan	Brock's Last Case
McCloud	Who Killed Miss USA?
McMillan and Wife	Once Upon a Dead Man
The Sweeney	Regan
Taggart	Killer
The Waltons	The Homecoming

. . . .

Over and Out

On 19 March 1969 viewers in the Yorkshire Television area suddenly found themselves without a commercial TV service. The giant (1,265 ft) Emley Moor transmitter near Huddersfield had iced over and in strong winds the weight of the ice led to its dramatic collapse. Fortunately, no one was killed or seriously injured. The mast had been erected in 1964 to beef up the signal locally, taking over from a smaller (445 ft) transmitter that had been in place since 1956, when ITV arrived in the area. Normal service was resumed when a replacement mast was installed four days after the collapse. The mast was later permanently replaced by a new 1,083 ft concrete structure – the tallest in the UK.

. . . .

Commercial Identities

ACTOR	CHARACTER	COMMERCIAL
Terry Brooks	Milky Bar Kid	Nestlé's Milky Bar
Anna Chancellor	Gladys Althorpe	Boddingtons
Martin Fisk	lorry driver	Yorkie
John Hewer	Captain Birdseye	Birdseye Fish Fingers
Mary Holland	Katie	Oxo
Maureen Lipman	Beattie	British Telecom
Jenny Logan	vacuuming housewife	Shake 'N' Vac
Norman Lumsden	JR Hartley	Yellow Pages
Gary Myers	daredevil	Milk Tray
Gordon Rollings	Arkwright	John Smith's Bitter

The 100 Greatest Christmas Moments

As selected by viewers for the Channel 4 programme broadcast on 24 December 2004.

1   Band Aid: Do They Know It's Christmas?
2   Father Ted: A Christmassy Ted
3   The Snowman
4   The Office Christmas Specials
5   Only Fools and Horses: Christmas Specials
6   The Vicar of Dibley: Christmas Specials
7   Slade: Merry Xmas Everybody
8   Wallace and Gromit: A Close Shave
9   Blackadder's Christmas Carol
10   It's a Wonderful Life (film)
11   The Pogues featuring Kirsty MacColl: Fairytale of New York
12   The Simpsons: Christmas Specials
13   The Life of Brian (film)
14   Wizzard: I Wish It Could Be Christmas Everyday
15   EastEnders at Christmas
16   White Christmas (film)
17   Home Alone (film)
18   The Morecambe and Wise Show: Christmas Specials
19   French and Saunders: Christmas Specials
20   Knowing Me, Knowing Yule with Alan Partridge
21   South Park: Mr Hankey the Christmas Poo
22   The Royle Family at Christmas
23   The Chronicles of Narnia
24   Rising Damp: For the Man Who Has Everything
25   Stars In Their Eyes: Celebrity Christmas Specials
26   The Sound of Music (film)
27   John and Yoko: Happy Xmas (War Is Over)
28   One Foot in the Grave: Christmas Episodes
29   Robbie the Reindeer: Hooves of Fire
30   Ellen MacArthur: Sailing Through Heaven and Hell
31   The Osbournes: A Very Ozzy Christmas
32   The League Of Gentlemen: Christmas Special
33   Christmas on Coronation Street
34   Harry Enfield's Christmas Chums
35   Bing Crosby's Merrie Olde Christmas (duet with David Bowie)

CURIOUS FACT

Detectives Dalziel and Pascoe were first played on TV by comedians Hale and Pace

....

The Magic of Television

It's widely accepted that the world's first regular high-definition television service was launched by the BBC on 2 November 1936, but the corporation's first proper (non-test) broadcast came two and a half months earlier. For several days, from 26 August, the BBC transmitted a special programme to the Radiolympia exhibition in London. Its centrepiece, a music and dance variety showcase called Here's Looking at You, was introduced by Leslie Mitchell with the words: 'Good afternoon, ladies and gentlemen. It is with great pleasure that I introduce you to the magic of television'. It is reported that, far from just broadcasting to the exhibition itself, the transmitted signals were received in places as distant as the south coast and parts of the Midlands.

Cartoon Critters

CHARACTER (SERIES IF NOT SAME NAME)	TYPE OF ANIMAL
Alistair (Crystal Tipps and Alistair)	Dog
Astro (The Jetsons)	Dog
Bandit (Jonny Quest)	Dog
Batfink	Bat
Bengo (Blue Peter)	Dog
Boo Boo (Yogi Bear)	Bear
Bullwinkle (Rocky and His Friends)	Moose
Cecil (Beany and Cecil)	Sea serpent
Custard (Roobarb)	Cat
Dino (The Flintstones)	Dinosaur
Fleabag (The Oddball Couple)	Dog
Gertrude (Journey to the Center of the Earth)	Duck
Goober (Goober and the Ghost Chasers)	Dog
Hashimoto (The Hector Heathcote Show)	Mouse
Heckle and Jeckle	Magpies
Hong Kong Phooey	Dog
Jerry (Tom and Jerry)	Mouse
Julius (Wait Till Your Father Gets Home)	Dog
Midge (Mary, Mungo and Midge)	Mouse
Mr Jinx (The Huckleberry Hound Show)	Mice
Moschops	Dinosaur
Mungo (Mary, Mungo and Midge)	Dog
Muttley (Wacky Races)	Dog
Pixie and Dixie (The Huckleberry Hound Show)	Mice
Quick Draw McGraw	Horse
Reddy (The Ruff and Reddy Show)	Dog
Ren (The Ren & Stimpy Show)	Dog
Rocky (Rocky and His Friends)	Flying squirrel
Roobarb	Dog
Ruff (The Ruff and Reddy Show)	Cat
Scooby-Doo (Scooby-Doo, Where Are You?)	Dog
Scrappy-Doo (Scooby and Scrappy-Doo)	Dog
Sebastian (Josie and the Pussycats)	Cat
Sidney (The Hector Heathcote Show)	Elephant
Snagglepuss (Yogi Bear)	Lion
Spiffy (The Oddball Couple)	Cat
Squiddly Diddly (The Atom Ant/Secret Squirrel Show)	Octopus
Stimpy (The Ren & Stimpy Show)	Cat
Tom (Tom and Jerry)	Cat
Yakky Doodle (Yogi Bear)	Duck

ITV Regional News Programmes: a History

REGION (ITV COMPANY)	PROGRAMME (COMPANY IF NOT CLEAR)
North of Scotland (Grampian)	Grampian News North Tonight
Central Scotland (Scottish Television)	Dateline Scotland Today
The Borders (Border)	Lookaround
North-East England (Tyne Tees)	North East Roundabout North East Newsview Today at 6 Northern Life Tyne Tees Today (northern area)/ Network North (southern area) Tyne Tees News North East Tonight
North-West England (Granada)	Scene at 6.30 Six-O-One Granada Reports Granada Tonight
Yorkshire and Lincolnshire (Yorkshire)	Calendar
Midlands (ATV/Carlton/Central)	Midland Montage (ATV) ATV Today Central News (Central/Carlton)
East of England (Anglia)	About Anglia Anglia News Anglia News at Six
West of England (TWW/HTV)	TWW Reports Report West (HTV) HTV News
London (Thames/LWT/London News Network)	Today (Thames) Thames News 6 O'Clock Live (LWT) LWT News London Tonight (London News Network)
South and South-East England (Southern/TVS/Meridian)	Day by Day (Southern) Scene South East (Southern) Coast to Coast (TVS) Meridian Tonight

West Country (Westward/TSW/ Westcountry/Carlton)	Westward Diary
	Today South West (TSW)
	Today (TSW)
	TSW Today
	Westcountry Live (Westcountry/Carlton)
Wales (TWW/HTV)	TWW Reports
	Report Wales (HTV)
	Wales at Six (HTV)
	Wales Tonight (HTV)
	HTV News
Northern Ireland (Ulster)	UTV Reports
	Good Evening Ulster
	UTV Live at 6
Channel Islands (Channel)	Channel Reports

....

Origins of Programme Titles

PROGRAMME	ORIGIN
Catweazle	Word written on a country gate
Goodness Gracious Me	1960 Peter Sellers and Sophia Loren hit single
Heartbeat	Professions of the two lead characters: doctor and policeman
Jackanory	Rhyme: 'I'll tell you a story of Jackanory'
The League of Gentlemen	1960 Jack Hawkins movie
Old Grey Whistle Test	Tin Pan Alley saying: when the grey-haired doorman whistles your tune, you have a hit on your hands
Only Fools and Horses	Saying: 'Only fools and horses work'
Softly, Softly	Saying: 'Softly, softly, catchee monkey'
They Think It's All Over	Kenneth Wolstenholme World Cup Final commentary
Thunderbirds	Thunderbird US Air Force base
Two Pints of Lager and a Packet of Crisps	1980 hit for Splodgenessabounds

....

The Monkees

Davy (Jones)
Mickey (Dolenz)
Mike (Nesmith)
Peter (Tork)

TV Characters Often Mentioned But Never Seen

SERIES	CHARACTER
Are You Being Served?	Mrs Slocombe's pussy
Charlie's Angels	Charlie Townsend
Cheers	Vera Peterson
Columbo	Mrs Columbo*
Dad's Army	Elizabeth Mainwaring
Frasier	Maris Crane
I'm Alan Partridge	Carol Partridge
Keeping Up Appearances	Sheridan Bucket
Magnum, PI	Robin Masters
Minder	'Er indoors
Mork and Mindy	Orson
One Foot in the Grave	Mrs Swainey
Only Fools and Horses	Monkey Harris
Rhoda	Carlton, the doorman
Richard Diamond, Private Detective	Sam, the telephone operator
Sykes	Elsie Turnbull (Corky's wife)
The Royle Family	Beverly Macca
Twin Peaks	Diane, the secretary

* Later appeared in a spin-off series, Mrs Columbo.

Long and Winding Road

Although the long-running Midlands soap opera, Crossroads, took to the air in 1964, it was not fully networked by ITV until 1972. Even before this time it had already been cancelled by one region. Viewers in the Thames area found the plug pulled on Meg Richardson and her team in 1968. They protested, Thames gave way and Crossroads wound its way back to London, only with episodes six months behind the rest of the country until catching up in time for Meg's wedding to Hugh Mortimer in 1975.

Some UK Programmes Imported from the Continent

PROGRAMME	ORIGINAL
Crimewatch UK	Aktenzeichen XY Ungelost (West Germany)
Countdown	Des Chiffres et des Lettres (France)
Fort Boyard	Fort Boyard (France)
The Generation Game	Een van de Acht (Netherlands)
The Golden Shot	Der Goldener Schuss (West Germany)
Treasure Hunt	Chasse au Trésor (France)
3-2-1	Uno, Dos, Tres (Spain)

Destinations Seen on the 4077th M*A*S*H Signpost

Tokyo 259 miles
Burbank 5610 miles
Death Valley 6116 miles
Decatur 9412 miles
Seoul 34 miles
Coney Island 7033 miles
Indianapolis 6779 miles
San Francisco 5428 miles
Boston 8328 miles
Toledo 6133 miles

The Big Five

Before the consolidation of ITV into one entity, most of the programming to be networked – or screened nationally – was provided by one of five major (the wealthiest) franchise holders, leaving smaller contractors to contribute only a small part of the ITV national output. These giant companies also, in association with the IBA, for many years made decisions about which programmes should be networked. The 'Big Five' were:

Thames   LWT   Granada   ATV   Yorkshire

L!ve G!mm!cks

In order to capture viewers, the now-defunct* London cable TV station L!ve TV resorted to a series of gimmicks, most famous of which were:

News Bunny (in vision alongside the newsreader)
Topless darts
Weather in Norwegian

* Name now used for a digital TV channel.

Formulaic Episode Titles

FORMULA	SERIES	EXAMPLE
The ... Affair	The Man from UNCLE	The Green Opal Affair
The ... Beat	Madigan	The Manhattan Beat
The ... Case	International Detective	The Joplin Case
The Case of ...	Perry Mason	The Case of the Screaming Woman
The Night of ...	The Wild Wild West	The Night of the Human Trigger
The One with ...	Friends	The One with the Prom Video
Who Killed ... ?	Burke's Law	Who Killed What's His Name?

Some Fast Show Characters and Their Catchphrases

CHARACTER	CATCHPHRASE
Archie (pub nuisance)	Hardest game in the world
Arthur Atkinson (music hall entertainer)	How queer!
Chanel 9 Team (Continental TV channel)	Scorchio! Chrissie Waddle!
Cockney Chris (would-be thief)	I'm a little bit whoor, a little bit waay
Jesse (trailer-inhabiting eccentric)	This week I shall be mostly...
Johnny (amateur painter)	Black!
Kenneth and Kenneth (men's outfitters)	Suit you, sir!
Louis Balfour (jazz show host)	Nice!
Patrick Nice (middle-class liar)	Which was nice
Ron Manager (football pundit)	Jumpers for goalposts
Rowley Birkin QC (veteran barrister)	I was very, very drunk
Roy and Renee (husband and nagging wife)	What did I say, Roy?
Swiss Toni (car salesman)	Like making love to a beautiful woman
The 13th Duke of Wymborne (cad)	What were they thinking of?
Unlucky Alf (accident-prone codger)	Oh bugger!

Fingerbobs Creatures

The recurring finger puppet characters created by Yoffi (Rick Jones):

Fingermouse
Scampi
Flash (tortoise)
Gulliver (seagull)

The Goodies

Bill Oddie   Graeme Garden   Tim Brooke-Taylor

An Educational Device

'I find television very educating. Every time somebody turns on the set, I go into the other room and read a book.' - Groucho Marx

Nothing to Contemplate

In the 1960s US sitcom I Dream of Jeannie, nervous TV executives refused to allow actress Barbara Eden's navel to be seen by the camera. It was always hidden by her baggy trousers or obscured by make up.

Winners of University Challenge

1962–3	Leicester	1976	No contest
1963–4	No contest	1977	University College, Oxford
1964–5	New College, Oxford	1978	Durham
1966–7	Oriel College, Oxford	1979	Sidney Sussex College,
1968	Sussex		Cambridge
1969	Keele	1980	Bradford
1970	Sussex	1981	Merton College, Oxford
1971	Churchill College, Cambridge	1982	Queen's, Belfast
1972	Sidney Sussex College,	1983	St Andrews
	Cambridge	1984	Dundee
1973	University College, Oxford	1985	Open University
1974	Fitzwilliam College,	1986	Jesus College, Oxford
	Cambridge	1987	Keble College, Oxford
1975	Keble College, Oxford		

1994–5	Trinity College, Cambridge	2000–1	Imperial College, London
1995–6	Imperial College, London	2001–2	Somerville College, Oxford
1996–7	Magdalen College, Oxford	2002–3	Birkbeck College, London
1997–8	Magdalen College, Oxford	2003–4	Magdalen College, Oxford
1998–9	Open University	2004–5	Corpus Christi College,
1999–2000	Durham		Oxford

....

Soloists with The Black and White Minstrels

Dai Francis   Tony Mercer   John Boulter

....

The Wombles on TV

Bungo
Great Uncle Bulgaria
Madame Cholet
Orinoco
Tombermory
Tomsk
Wellington

A 1998 revival of this 1970s animation based on books by Elisabeth Beresford saw the introduction of four new Wombles:

Alderney   Obidos   Shanshi   Stepney

Character Catchphrases

CATCHPHRASE	CHARACTER
Aaaay!	Fonzie (Happy Days)
Ah do declare!	Cindy Bear (Yogi Bear)
All in the best possible taste	Cupid Stunt (The Kenny Everett Video Show)
And now for something completely different	Monty Python's Flying Circus
Bit of a cock up on the ... front	Jimmy (The Fall and Rise of Reginald Perrin)
Book 'em, Danno	Steve McGarrett (Hawaii Five-O)
Come the glorious day ...	Wolfie Smith (Citizen Smith)
Dagnabit!	Deputy Dawg
Did I ever tell you about Rosa Colletti?	Al Delvecchio (Happy Days)
Do you think that's wise, sir?	Sgt Wilson (Dad's Army)
Doh!	Homer Simpson (The Simpsons)
Don't have a cow, man	Bart Simpson (The Simpsons)
Don't panic!	Cpl Jones (Dad's Army)
Drat, drat and triple drat	Dick Dastardly (Wacky Races)
During the war ...	Uncle Albert (Only Fools and Horses)
Eat my shorts	Bart Simpson (The Simpsons)
Everybody out!	Paddy (The Rag Trade)
Exterminate!	Daleks (Doctor Who)
Feck! Drink! Girls!	Father Jack Hackett (Father Ted)
Freedom for Tooting!	Wolfie Smith (Citizen Smith)
Gissa job	Yosser Hughes (Boys from the Black Stuff)
Good moaning	Officer Crabtree ('Allo 'Allo)
Has he been?	Nellie Pledge (Nearest and Dearest)
Have you had your tea, Dave?	Barbara Royle (The Royle Family)
He who dares, wins	Del Boy Trotter (Only Fools and Horses)
Heavens to Murgatroyd	Snagglepuss (Yogi Bear)
Hold the bus!	The Banana Splits
I 'ate you, Butler	Insp. Blake (On the Buses)
I didn't get where I am today	CJ (The Fall and Rise of Reginald Perrin)
I do not believe it	Victor Meldrew (One Foot in the Grave)
I hate those meeces to pieces	Mr Jinks (The Huckleberry Hound Show, Pixie and Dixie segment)
I have a cunning plan	Baldric (Blackadder)
I heard that, pardon?	Uncle Staveley (I Didn't Know You Cared)
I know nathing	Manuel (Fawlty Towers)
I love me rabbits	Lucien Boswell (The Liver Birds)
I must get a little hand put on this watch	Nellie Pledge (Nearest and Dearest)
I only arsked	Popeye Popplewell (The Army Game)
I'll stay on me own	Old Tommy (Early Doors)
I'll have a half	Jacko (Love Thy Neighbour)

I'll scream, scream and scream until I'm sick	Violet Elizabeth Bott (Just William)
I'm a lady	Emily Howard (Little Britain)
I'm free!	Mr Humphreys (Are You Being Served?)
I'm listening	Dr Frasier Crane (Frasier)
I'm not a number: I'm a free man	No. 6 (The Prisoner)
I'm the only gay in the village	Dafydd Thomas (Little Britain)
It's just a bit of fun	Keith Barret (The Keith Barret Show)
Just one more thing	Lt Columbo (Columbo)
Just the facts	Sgt Joe Friday (Dragnet)
Katanga!	Joshua Yarlog (The Lenny Henry Show)
Leesten very carefully: I shall say zis only wance	Michelle Dubois ('Allo 'Allo)
Let's be careful out there	Sgt Phil Esterhaus (Hill Street Blues)
Lovely jubbly	Del Boy Trotter (Only Fools and Horses)
Magic!	Selwyn Froggitt (Oh No – It's Selwyn Froggitt)
Morning campers	Gladys Pugh (Hi-De-Hi!)
My arse!	Jim Royle (The Royle Family)
No, no, no, no, no ... yes	Jim Trott (The Vicar of Dibley)
Oh boy!	Dr Sam Beckett (Quantum Leap)
Oh go on	Mrs Doyle (Father Ted)
Oh my God, they killed Kenny	South Park characters
Oh you are awful, but I like you	Mandy (Dick Emery Show)
Ooh Betty!	Frank Spencer (Some Mothers Do 'Ave 'Em)
Perfick!	Pop Larkin (The Darling Buds of May)
Permission to speak, sir	Cpl Jones (Dad's Army)
Power to the people!	Wolfie Smith (Citizen Smith)
Shoulders back, lovely boy	RSM Williams (It Ain't Half Hot Mum)
Sorry about that, Chief	Maxwell Smart (Get Smart)
Stupid boy	Capt. Mainwaring (Dad's Army)
Ten-Four	Chief Dan Mathews (Highway Patrol)
There you go	Sam McCloud (McCloud)
They don't like it up 'em	Cpl Jones (Dad's Army)
This time next year we'll be millionaires	Del Boy Trotter (Only Fools and Horses)
Very interesting, but stupid	Arte Johnson (Rowan & Martin's Laugh-in)
We're doomed, doomed	Pte Fraser (Dad's Army)
Who loves you, baby	Theo Kojak (Kojak)
Yabba Dabba Do!	Fred Flintstone (The Flintstones)
Yeah but no but yeah but ...	Vicky Pollard (Little Britain)
Yeah I know	Andy (Little Britain)
You dirty old man	Harold Steptoe (Steptoe and Son)
You rang?	Lurch (The Addams Family)
You silly moo!	Alf Garnett (Till Death Us Do Part)
Yus, m'lady	Parker (Thunderbirds)

See also lists of catchphrases from The Fast Show and Rowan and Martin's Laugh-In.

UK TV Firsts

	FIRST
BBC NEWSREADER	Richard Baker, 5 July 1954
CHILDREN'S PROGRAMME	For the Children, 7 July 1946
COLOUR BROADCASTS (REGULAR)	BBC 2, 1 July 1967
COMMERCIAL TELEVISION BROADCAST	Associated-Rediffusion/ATV, 22 September 1955
COMMERCIAL	Gibbs SR toothpaste, 22 September 1955
COOKERY PROGRAMME	BBC, 9 December 1936
CORONATION	King George VI and Queen Elizabeth, 12 May 1937
ELECTION BROADCAST	Rochdale by-election, 12 February 1958
FA CUP FINAL	BBC, 30 April 1938
FEMALE ANNOUNCER	Elizabeth Cowell, BBC, 31 August 1936
FEMALE NEWSREADER	Barbara Mandell, ITV, 23 September 1955
HOUSE OF COMMONS BROADCAST	BBC, 21 November 1989
ITN NEWSCASTER	Christopher Chataway, 22 September 1955
LIVE TRANS-ATLANTIC BROADCAST	BBC, 11 July 1962 (via Telstar)
MONARCH'S CHRISTMAS BROADCAST	Queen Elizabeth II, BBC/ITV, 25 December 1957
NATIONAL BREAKFAST TELEVISION	BBC 1, 17 January 1983
NATIONAL LOTTERY DRAW	BBC 1, 19 November 1994
NEWS PROGRAMME	BBC, 21 March 1938
OPEN UNIVERSITY PROGRAMME	BBC 2, 3 January 1971
OXFORD AND CAMBRIDGE BOAT RACE	BBC, 2 April 1938
PARTY POLITICAL BROADCAST	BBC, 2 May 1953
REGULAR TELEVISION SERVICE	BBC, 2 November 1936
SATELLITE BROADCASTS (DIRECT TO HOME)	Sky, 16 January 1989
SCHOOLS' PROGRAMME	ITV, 13 May 1957
TEXT SERVICE	CEEFAX, BBC 1, 23 September 1974
WEATHER FORECAST	BBC, 20 November 1936
WEATHERMAN (IN VISION)	George Cowling, BBC, 11 January 1954
WELSH LANGUAGE CHANNEL	Sianel Pedwar Cymru (S4C), 1 November 1982
WORLDWIDE LIVE SATELLITE BROADCAST	Our World, BBC 1, 25 June 1967

Making a Monkee out of Advertising

In September 1965 local trade papers The Hollywood Reporter and The Daily Variety both ran the following advertisement:

MADNESS!!

AUDITIONS

Folk & Roll Musicians/Singers for acting roles in new TV series

Running parts for 4 insane boys, age 17–21

Want spirited Ben Frank's types

Have courage to work

Must come down for interview

CALL: HO. 6-5188

The result was the gathering together of Davy Jones, Mickey Dolenz, Peter Tork and Michael Nesmith and the launch of the TV series The Monkees the following year.

(Ben Frank's was a 24-hour coffee house on Sunset Boulevard, Los Angeles, used by young music fans.)

....

Top of the Pops Dance Troupes

The Go-jos   Pan's People

Ruby Flipper   Legs and Co   Zoo

....

The Blue Peter Summer Expeditions

1965	Norway	1985	Australia
1966	Singapore and Borneo	1986	No expedition
1967	Jamaica and New York	1987	Soviet Union
1968	Morocco	1988	West Coast USA
1969	Ceylon	1989	Zimbabwe
1970	Mexico	1990	The Caribbean
1971	Iceland and Scandinavia	1991	Japan
1972	Fiji and Tonga	1992	Hungary and New Zealand
1973	Ivory Coast	1993	Argentina
1974	Thailand	1994	USA (New England)
1975	Turkey	1995	South Africa
1976	Brunei	1996	Hong Kong and China
1977	Brazil	1997	Canada
1978	USA	1998	Mexico
1979	Egypt	1999	Australia
1980	Malaysia	2000	Spain
1981	Japan	2001	Vietnam
1982	Canada	2002	Mozambique
1983	Sri Lanka	2003	Brazil
1984	Kenya	2004	India

The UK by Programme

Real-life settings for TV dramas and comedies

TOWN/CITY/AREA	PROGRAMME
Belfast	Harry's Game
Birmingham	Crossroads
	Empire Road
	Gangsters
Blackpool	Blackpool
	September Song
Bolton	Peter Kay's Phoenix Nights
Bradford	Band of Gold
Bridlington	Constant Hot Water
Brighton	Brighton Belles
Bristol	A Respectable Trade
	Shoestring
Cambridge	Cambridge Spies
	The Glittering Prizes
	Porterhouse Blue
Cardiff	Dirty Work
	Jack of Hearts
Chelmsford	Chelmsford 123
Chester	Hollyoaks
Derby	The Hello Girls
Dudley	The Grimleys
Edinburgh	Murder Rooms: The Dark Beginnings of Sherlock Holmes
	Rebus
Forest of Dean	Blue Remembered Hills
	The Singing Detective
Glasgow	Rab C Nesbitt
	Sea of Souls
	Taggart
	Takin' Over the Asylum
	Your Cheatin' Heart
Guernsey	Enemy at the Door
Hastings	Foyle's War
Jersey	Bergerac
Leeds	The Beiderbecke Affair
	North Square

Liverpool	Boys from the Blackstuff
	Bread
	Brookside
	A Family at War
	GBH
	The Liver Birds
	Merseybeat
Luton	Days Like These
Manchester	A&E
	Cold Feet
	Coronation Street
	Cracker
	dinnerladies
	The Dustbinmen
	Early Doors
	Queer as Folk
	The Royle Family
Middlesbrough	Steel River Blues
Newcastle-upon-Tyne	Auf Wiedersehen, Pet
	Byker Grove
	55 Degrees North
	The Likely Lads
	Our Friends in the North
	Spender
Norwich	I'm Alan Partridge
Nottingham	Paradise Heights/The Eustace Brothers
	Resnick
Oxford	Brideshead Revisited
	Inspector Morse
Penzance	Wycliffe
Sheffield	Threads
Shrewsbury	Cadfael
Slough	The Office
Southampton	Target
Stoke-on-Trent	Clayhanger
Swansea	Mine All Mine
Torquay	Fawlty Towers
Truro	Poldark
Ullswater	The Lakes
Warwick	Dangerfield
York	Bloomin' Marvellous

CURIOUS FACT

Our Friends in
the North star
Gina McKee
featured in
the first ever
TV advert for
condoms

Animals Farmed by Tom and Barbara Good in *The Good Life*

Brian, a horse
Geraldine, a goat
Glenda and Olivia, chickens
Lenin, a cockerel
Margo, a goat
Pinky and Perky, pigs

Tex Tucker's Magic Feathers

In the puppet series Four Feather Falls, Sheriff Tex Tucker is endowed with four feathers, each with its own magical property: one allows Tex's dog, Dusty, to speak; one allows Tex's horse, Rocky, to speak; the other two allow Tex's twin pistols to fire automatically when he is in danger.

Famous TV Acronyms

ACRONYM (SERIES)	EXPLANATION
BISHOP (The Secret Service)	British Intelligence Secret Headquarters, Operation Priest
CI5 (The Professionals)	Criminal Intelligence 5
CTU (24)	Counter Terrorist Unit
IMF (Mission: Impossible)	Impossible Mission Force
KITT (Knight Rider)	Knight Industries Two Thousand
OSI (The Six Million Dollar Man)	Office of Scientific Information
SHADO (UFO)	Supreme Headquarters, Alien Defence Organization
SIF (The Sandbaggers)	Special Intelligence Force
TARDIS (Doctor Who)	Time And Relative Dimensions In Space
TITCO (Only Fools and Horses)	Trotters Independent Trading Company
UNCLE (The Man from UNCLE)	United Network Command for Law and Enforcement
WASP (Stingray)	World Aquanaut Security Patrol
WIN (Joe 90)	World Intelligence Network

Fawlty Towers Hotel Signs

At the start of most episodes of Fawlty Towers, the hotel sign has been re-arranged by meddling hands to present a series of anagrams, listed below. Other episodes simply have letters missing from the 'Fawlty Towers' name.

Farty Towels   Fatty Owls
Flay Otters   Flowery Twats   Watery Fowls

Back in the Saddle

HORSE	COWBOY (SERIES)
Beauty	Adam Cartwright (Bonanza)
Blue Boy	Mark McCain (The Rifleman)
Brandy	Cheyenne Bodie (Cheyenne)
Buck	Ben Cartwright (Bonanza)
Buck	Marshal Matt Dillon (Gunsmoke)
Buckshot	Wild Bill Hickok
Buttermilk	Dale Evans (The Roy Rogers Show)
Champion	Gene Autry
Charger	Heath Barkley (The Big Valley)
Chub	Hoss Cartwright (Bonanza)
Cochise	Little Joe Cartwright (Bonanza)
Coco	Nick Barkley (The Big Valley)
Diablo	Manolito Montoya (The High Chaparral)
Diablo	The Cisco Kid
El Loaner	Bret Maverick (Maverick)
Gumlegs	Cousin Beauregard Maverick (Maverick)
Hannibal	Ben Calhoun (Iron Horse)
Joker	Jingles (The Adventures of Wild Bill Hickok)
Jubilee	Jim Hardie (Tales of Wells Fargo)
Loco	Pancho (The Cisco Kid)
Lucky	Dick West (The Range Rider)
Midnight	Rowdy Yates (Rawhide)
Misty Girl	Victoria Barkley (The Big Valley)
Rafter	Paladin (Have Gun Will Travel)
Rawhide	The Range Rider
Razor	Lucas McCain (The Rifleman)
Rebel	Buck Cannon (The High Chaparral)
Rex	Sgt Preston (Sergeant Preston of the Yukon)
Rocky	Tex Tucker (Four Feather Falls)
Scout	Tonto (The Lone Ranger)
Silver	The Lone Ranger
Soapy	Blue Cannon (The High Chaparral)
Sport	Adam Cartwright (Bonanza)
Stardust	Bat Masterson (Bat Masterson)
Topper	Hopalong Cassidy
Trigger	Roy Rogers

Some Unusual Implements Maliciously Employed in Midsomer Murders

Ashtray	Liquid nicotine
Billhook	Ornamental sword
Bottles of fine wine	Pillow
Bow and arrow	Pitchfork
Candlestick	Plough
Cricket bat	Slide projector
Desk	Spade
Doped horse	Stanley knife
Drinks cabinet	Switch blade razor
Electricity	Syringe
Fork-lift truck	Walking stick
Hemlock	Wrench

The Original Blake's 7

Roj Blake

Kerr Avon

Jenna Stannis

Vila Restal

Cally

Gan Olag

Zen (computer)

A Question of Sport Regulars

HOSTS	TEAM CAPTAINS*
David Vine	Cliff Morgan
David Coleman	Henry Cooper
Sue Barker	Fred Trueman
	Brendan Foster
	Gareth Edwards
	Emlyn Hughes
	Willie Carson
	Bill Beaumont
	Ian Botham
	Ally McCoist
	John Parrott
	Frankie Dettori
	Matt Dawson

* Excludes guests and stand-ins

Ten Unexpected TV Moments

Irish writer Desmond Leslie interrupting a live broadcast of That Was the Week That Was in 1963 to punch theatre critic Bernard Levin, who had previously rubbished a one-woman show featuring Leslie's wife, Agnes Bernelle.

Jack Ruby shooting Lee Harvey Oswald, the accused assassin of President John F Kennedy, as he was being transferred between jails in 1963.

Baby elephant Lulu making a mess on the Blue Peter floor in 1969.

Bill Grundy rising to The Sex Pistols' bait and encouraging the punk pioneers to swear on a live edition of Today in 1976.

Actress/singer Grace Jones whacking Russell Harty in 1980 when she considered she was being ignored by the chat show host.

Tory minister John Nott walking off the set in 1982 after being described by interviewer Robin Day as a 'here today, gone tomorrow' politician. (Nott later used the words as the title of his autobiography.)

The Challenger space shuttle exploding in 1986.

Oliver Reed appearing drunk on Aspel and Company in 1986 (and George Best conveying the same impression on Wogan in 1990).

Gay rights activists invading a BBC studio in 1988 as the Six O'Clock News was being broadcast live.

The Bee Gees walking off Clive Anderson's show in 1997 after he joked about one of their earliest stage names (apparently Les Tosseurs).

....

Trainspotting

TRAIN	PROGRAMME
532 Blue Peter	Blue Peter
Bessie	Chigley
Blossom	Oh Doctor Beeching!
Cannonball Express	Casey Jones
Cannonball	Petticoat Junction
Flockton Flyer	The Flockton Flyer
Green Dragon	The Railway Children
Ivor	Ivor the Engine
Nimrod (carriage)	The Wild, Wild West
Thomas	Thomas the Tank Engine and Friends
The Train	The Magic Roundabout

TV Quiz and Game Show Hosts

PROGRAMME	HOST(S)
All Clued Up	David Hamilton
Animal, Vegetable, Mineral?	Lionel Hale, Glyn Daniel
Ask the Family	Robert Robinson, Alan Titchmarsh, Dick & Dom
Back in the Day	Clive Anderson
Backdate	Valerie Singleton
Beat the Nation	Graeme Garden, Tim Brooke-Taylor
Beat the Teacher	Howard Stableford, Paul Jones
Big Break	Jim Davidson
Blankety Blank	Terry Wogan, Les Dawson, Lily Savage
Blind Date	Cilla Black
Blockbusters	Bob Holness, Michael Aspel, Liza Tarbuck
Bob's Full House	Bob Monkhouse
Bob's Your Uncle	Bob Monkhouse
Bullseye	Jim Bowen
Busman's Holiday	Julian Pettifer, Sarah Kennedy, Elton Welsby
Call My Bluff	Robin Ray, Joe Melia, Peter Wheeler, Robert Robinson, Bob Holness, Fiona Bruce
Carry on Campus	Will MacDonald
Catchphrase	Roy Walker, Nick Weir, Mark Curry
Celebrity Squares	Bob Monkhouse
The Chair	John McEnroe
Cluedo	James Bellini, Chris Tarrant, Richard Madeley
Connections	Sue Robbie, Bob Carolgees, Richard Madeley, Simon Potter
Countdown	Richard Whiteley
Criss Cross Quiz	Jeremy Hawk
The Crystal Maze	Richard O'Brien, Edward Tudor-Pole
Dog Eat Dog	Ulrika Jonsson
Don't Forget Your Toothbrush	Chris Evans
Dotto	Robert Gladwell, Jimmy Hanley, Shaw Taylor
Double Your Money	Hughie Green
Eggheads	Dermot Murnaghan
Every Second Counts	Paul Daniels
Everybody's Equal	Chris Tarrant
Face the Music	Joseph Cooper
Families at War	Vic Reeves, Bob Mortimer, Alice Beer

Family Fortunes	Bob Monkhouse, Max Bygraves, Les Dennis, Andy Collins
Fifteen to One	William G Stewart
Film Buff of the Year	Robin Ray
Fort Boyard	Melinda Messinger, Jodie Penfold
Gambit	Fred Dinenage, Tom O'Connor
Give Us a Clue	Michael Aspel, Michael Parkinson, Tim Clark
Going for a Song	Max Robertson, Michael Parkinson, Michael Aspel
Going for Gold	Henry Kelly
The Golden Shot	Jackie Rae, Bob Monkhouse, Norman Vaughan, Charlie Williams
The Great British Quiz	Janice Long, Philip Hayton
Hard Spell	Eamonn Holmes
Headjam	Vernon Kay
Hitman	Nick Owen
Interceptor	Annabel Croft
It's a Knockout	David Vine, Eddie Waring, Stuart Hall, Keith Chegwin, Frank Bruno
The Krypton Factor	Gordon Burns, Penny Smith
Lose a Million	Chris Tarrant
The Main Event	Chris Tarrant
Man O Man	Chris Tarrant
Mastermind	Magnus Magnusson, Clive Anderson, John Humphrys
Masterteam	Angela Rippon
Matchpoint	Angela Rippon
Mr and Mrs	Alan Taylor, Derek Batey, Julian Clary
Name That Tune	Tom O'Connor, Lionel Blair
Odd One Out	Paul Daniels
One to Win	Andrew O'Connor
Pop Quest	Steve Merike, Kid Jensen, Sally James, Mike Read, Megg Nicol
Pop Quiz	Mike Read, Chris Tarrant
The Price is Right	Leslie Crowther, Bruce Forsyth
The Pyramid Game	Steve Jones
A Question of Entertainment	Tom O'Connor
A Question of Pop	Jamie Theakston
A Question of Sport	David Vine, David Coleman, Sue Barker
Quiz Ball	David Vine, Barry Davies, Stuart Hall

TV Quiz and Games Show Hosts

PROGRAMME	HOST(S)
Runaround	Mike Reid, Leslie Crowther, Stan Boardman
Runway	Chris Serle, Richard Madeley
Sale of the Century	Nicholas Parsons
Screen Test	Michael Rodd, Brian Trueman, Mark Curry
Shafted	Robert Kilroy-Silk
The $64,000 Question	Bob Monkhouse
Sporting Triangles	Nick Owen, Andy Craig
Spot the Tune	Ken Platt, Ted Ray, Jackie Rae, Pete Murray
The Sky's the Limit	Hughie Green
Strike It Lucky	Michael Barrymore
Supermarket Sweep	Dale Winton
Take a Letter	Bob Holness
Take Your Pick	Michael Miles, Des O'Connor
Takeover Bid	Bruce Forsyth
Talking Telephone Numbers	Phillip Schofield, Emma Forbes, Claudia Winkelman
Television Top of the Form	Geoffrey Wheeler, David Dimbleby, Paddy Feeny, John Edmunds, John Dunn
Telly Addicts	Noel Edmonds
3-2-1	Ted Rogers
Through the Keyhole	David Frost, Loyd Grossman, Catherine Gee
Top of the World	Eamonn Andrews
University Challenge	Bamber Gascoigne, Jeremy Paxman
The Vault	Davina McCall, Melanie Sykes, Gabby Logan
We Are the Champions	Ron Pickering
We Love TV	Gloria Hunniford
The Weakest Link	Anne Robinson
Whatever You Want	Gaby Roslin
What's My Line?	Eamonn Andrews, David Jacobs, Penelope Keith, Angela Rippon, Emma Forbes
Wheel of Fortune	Michael Miles
Wheel of Fortune	Nicky Campbell, Bradley Walsh, John Leslie, Paul Hendy
Who Wants to Be a Millionaire?	Chris Tarrant
Whodunnit?	Edward Woodward, Jon Pertwee
Winner Takes All	Jimmy Tarbuck, Geoffrey Wheeler
Wipeout	Paul Daniels, Bob Monkhouse
You Bet!	Bruce Forsyth, Matthew Kelly, Darren Day, Diane Youdale

Sibling Stars

James Arness and Peter Graves
Hywel Bennett and Alun Lewis
Duggie Brown and Lynne Perrie
Simon Cadell and Selina Cadell
Keith Chegwin and Janice Long
Charlotte Coleman and Lisa Coleman
Sinead, Sorcha, Niamh and Catherine Cusack
David Dimbleby and Jonathan Dimbleby
Colin Firth and Jonathan Firth
Steve Forrest and Dana Andrews
Edward Fox and James Fox
Philip Glenister and Robert Glenister
Caroline Harker and Susannah Harker
David Jason and Arthur White
Kevin Lloyd and Terry Lloyd
Joe, Paul, Mark and Stephen McGann
John Mills and Annette Mills
Juliet Mills and Hayley Mills
Robin Ray and Andrew Ray
Brian Rix and Sheila Mercier
Jonathan Ross and Paul Ross
Carol Royle and Amanda Royle
Julia Sawalha and Nadia Sawalha
Jeremy Sinden and Mark Sinden
David Suchet and John Suchet
Clive Swift and David Swift
Emma Thompson and Sophie Thompson
Michael Troughton and David Troughton
Jeremy Vine and Tim Vine
Honeysuckle Weeks and Perdita Weeks

....

The Play School Toys

Big Ted (bear)
Dapple (rocking horse)
Hamble (doll)*
Humpty (egg)
Jemima (doll)
Little Ted (bear)

* Replaced in 1986 by a black doll called Poppy

A Gift of God

'Television is a gift of God, and God will hold those who utilize his divine instrument accountable to him.' - Philo T Farnsworth, television pioneer

Real Settings for Fictional TV Towns

FICTIONAL TOWN (SERIES)	REAL SETTING
Aidensfield (Heartbeat)	Goathland, North Yorkshire
Balamory	Tobermory, Argyll & Bute
Ballykissangel	Avoca, County Wicklow
Beckindale (Emmerdale)	Esholt, West Yorkshire*
Bridehaven (Harbour Lights)	West Bay, Dorset
Capeside (Dawson's Creek)	Wilmington, North Carolina
Cardale (Peak Practice)	Crich, Derbyshire
Causton (Midsomer Murders)	Wallingford, Oxfordshire
Cicely (Northern Exposure)	Roslyn, Washington State
Cooper's Crossing (The Flying Doctors)	Minyip, Victoria
Darrowby (All Creatures Great and Small)	Askrigg, North Yorkshire
Dibley (The Vicar of Dibley)	Turville, Buckinghamshire
Fogburrow (Dead Man Weds)	Bradwell, Derbyshire
Glendarroch (Take the High Road)	Luss, Argyll & Bute
Hatley (Oh Doctor Beeching!)	Arley, Worcestershire
Kingsmarkham (The Ruth Rendell Mysteries)	Romsey, Hampshire
Lochdubh (Hamish Macbeth)	Plockton, Highland
Ormston (Born and Bred)	Downham, Lancashire
Portwenn (Doc Martin)	Port Isaac, Cornwall
Royston Vasey (The League of Gentlemen)	Hadfield, Derbyshire
St Gweep (Wild West)	Portloe, Cornwall
Skelthwaite (Where the Heart Is)	Slaithwaite, West Yorkshire
Stanton (The Cops)	Bury, Greater Manchester
Tannochbrae (Doctor Finlay)	Auchtermuchty, Fife
Tannochbrae (Dr Finlay's Casebook)	Callendar, Stirling
Tarrant (Howards' Way)	Bursledon, Hampshire
Tilling-on-Sea (Mapp & Lucia)	Rye, East Sussex
Twin Peaks	Snoqualmie Falls, Washington State
The Village (The Prisoner)	Portmeirion, Gwynedd
Walmington-on-Sea (Dad's Army)	Thetford, Norfolk

* Now no longer used: a special set has been constructed.

French Titles of English Language Series

SERIES	FRENCH TITLE
The Avengers	Chapeau Melon et Bottes de Cuir
Bewitched	Ma Sorcière Bien Aimée
The Big Easy	Le Flic de Mon Coeur
Buffy the Vampire Slayer	Buffy contre les Vampires
Burke's Law	L'Homme à la Rolls
Chicago Hope	La Vie à Tout Prix
CSI: Crime Scene Investigation	Les Experts
Dangerfield	Le Docteur Mène L'Inquête
The Dukes of Hazzard	Shérif Fais Moi Peur
Family Ties	Sacrée Famille
The Hammer House of Horror	Hammer La Maison de Tous Les Cauchemars
Hart to Hart	Pour l'Amour de Risque
Hawaii Five-O	Hawaï, Police d'Etat
Hetty Wainthropp Investigates	Les Inquêtes d'Hetty
Hill Street Blues	Capitaine Furillo
I Dream of Jeannie	Jinny de Mes Rêves
I Love Lucy	L'Extravagante Lucy
Ironside	L'Homme de Fer
The League of Gentlemen	Le Club des Gentlemen
The Life and Times of Grizzly Adams	La Légende de James Adams et de l'Ours Benjamin
The Man from UNCLE	Des Agents Très Spéciaux
Miami Vice	Deux Flics à Miami
Midnight Caller	Jack Killian, L'Homme au Micro
Midsomer Murders	Inspecteur Barnaby
Police Woman	Sergent Anderson
Queer as Folk	Histoires Gays
The Quest	Sur la Piste des Cheyennes
The Six Million Dollar Man	L'Homme qui Valait Trois Milliards
Thirtysomething	Génération Pub
The Thorn Birds	Les Oiseaux se Cachent Pour Mourir
The Untouchables	Les Incorruptibles
The West Wing	A la Maison Blanche

....

Immovable Object

'Television has changed a child from an irresistible force to an immovable object.'

– Dr Laurence J Peter, educationalist

Films Derived From TV Programmes

PROGRAMME	FILM
The Addams Family	The Addams Family (1991)
	Addams Family Values (1993)
	Addams Family Reunion (1998)
The Adventures of Robin Hood	Sword of Sherwood Forest (1960)
The Army Game	I Only Arsked (1958)
The Brady Bunch	The Brady Bunch Movie (1995)
	A Very Brady Sequel (1996)
	A Very Brady Christmas (1998)
Charlie's Angels	Charlie's Angels (2000)
	Charlie's Angels: Full Throttle (2003)
Colonel March of Scotland Yard	Colonel March Investigates (1953)
Doctor Who	Dr Who and the Daleks (1965)
	Daleks: Invasion Earth 2150 AD (1966)
Emergency – Ward 10	Life in Emergency Ward 10 (1959)
Fabian of the Yard	Fabian of the Yard (1954)
	Handcuffs, London (1955)
The Flintstones	A Man Called Flintstone (1966)
	The Flintstones (1994)
	The Flintstones in Viva Rock Vegas (2000)
The Fugitive	The Fugitive (1993)
	US Marshals (1998)
George of the Jungle	George of the Jungle (1997)
The Grove Family	It's a Great Day (1955)
Harry Enfield and Chums	Kevin & Perry Go Large (2000)
He-Man and the Masters of the Universe	Masters of the Universe (1987)
HR Pufnstuf	Pufnstuf (1970)
The Incredible Hulk	Hulk (2003)
The Jetsons	Jetsons: the Movie (1990)
Josie and the Pussycats	Josie and the Pussycats (2001)
The Larkins	Inn for Trouble (1960)
The Life and Loves of a She Devil	She-Devil (1989)
The Magic Roundabout	Dougal and the Blue Cat (1970)
	The Magic Roundabout (2005)

The Man From UNCLE	To Trap a Spy (1964)
	The Spy With My Face (1965)
	The Spy in the Green Hat (1966)
	One of Our Spies is Missing (1966)
	One Spy Too Many (1966)
	The Karate Killers (1967)
	The Helicopter Spies (1968)
	How To Steal the World (1968)
McHale's Navy	McHale's Navy (1964)
	McHale's Navy Joins the Airforce (1965)
	McHale's Navy (1997)
Mighty Morphin Power Rangers	Mighty Morphin Power Rangers: the Movie (1995)
Mission: Impossible	Mission: Impossible (1996)
	Mission: Impossible II (2000)
The Monkees	Head (1968)
Monty Python's Flying Circus	And Now For Something Completely Different (1971)
	Monty Python and the Holy Grail (1975)
	Monty Python's Life of Brian (1979)
	Monty Python's Meaning of Life (1983)
Mr Bean	Bean – the Ultimate Disaster Movie (1997)
The Munsters	Munster, Go Home! (1966)
The Muppet Show	The Muppet Movie (1979)
	The Great Muppet Caper (1981)
	The Muppets Take Manhattan (1984)
	A Muppet Christmas Carol (1992)
	Muppet Treasure Island (1996)
	Muppets from Space (1999)
My Favorite Martian	My Favorite Martian (1999)
On The Buses	On the Buses (1971)
	Mutiny on the Buses (1972)
	Holiday on the Buses (1973)
The Phil Silvers Show	Sgt Bilko (1996)
Police Squad	The Naked Gun (1988)
	The Naked Gun $2\frac{1}{2}$: the Smell of Fear (1991)
	Naked Gun $33\frac{1}{3}$: the Final Insult (1994)

Films Derived From TV Programmes

PROGRAMME	FILM
The Quatermass Experiment	The Quatermass Experiment (1955)
	Quatermass II (1957)
	Quatermass and the Pit (1967)
Rocky and His Friends	The Adventures of Rocky and Bullwinkle (2000)
Scooby Doo, Where Are You?	Scooby-Doo (2002)
	Scooby-Doo 2 Monsters Unleashed (2004)
Six-Five Special	6.5 Special (1958)
The Six Wives of Henry VIII	Henry VIII and His Six Wives (1972)
South Park	South Park: Bigger, Longer & Uncut (1999)
Steptoe and Son	Steptoe and Son (1972)
	Steptoe and Son Ride Again (1973)
The Sweeney	Sweeney! (1976)
	Sweeney 2 (1978)
Thunderbirds	Thunderbirds Are Go (1966)
	Thunderbird Six (1968)
	Thunderbirds (2004)
Till Death Us Do Part	Till Death Us Do Part (1969)
	The Alf Garnett Saga (1972)
The Twilight Zone	Twilight Zone: The Movie (1983)
Whack-O!	Bottoms Up (1959)
The Wombles	Wombling Free (1977)

The following programmes have all had film spin-offs with exactly the same title:

Are You Being Served? (1977), The Avengers (1998), Batman (1966), The Beverly Hillbillies (1993), Bless This House (1972), Callan (1974), Dad's Army (1971), Doomwatch (1972), Dragnet (1954, 1987), Father, Dear Father (1972), For the Love of Ada (1972), George and Mildred (1980), I Spy (2002), Josie and the Pussycats (2001), Kojak (2005), Leave It to Beaver (1997), The Likely Lads (1976), Lost in Space (1998), Love Thy Neighbour (1973), The Lovers (1972), Man about the House (1974), Man at the Top (1973), Maverick (1994), The Mod Squad (1999), Nearest and Dearest (1972), Pennies from Heaven (1981), Porridge (1979), The Railway Children (1970), Rising Damp (1980), S.W.A.T. (2003), Starsky and Hutch (2004), The Untouchables (1987), Up Pompeii! (1971), The Wild, Wild West (1999), The X Files (1998)

For Star Trek, see separate list.

TV Personalities Featured on the Cover of Paul McCartney and Wings' Band on the Run Album

James Coburn (actor)
John Conteh (boxer)
Clement Freud (humorist)
Christopher Lee (actor)
Kenny Lynch (actor)
Michael Parkinson (chat show host)

....

Bizarre Answers Given by Contestants on Family Fortunes

WHEN ASKED TO NAME:	THEY SAID:
A dangerous race	The Arabs
A part of the body beginning with N	Knee
Something with a hole in it	A window
Something you put on walls	Roofs
A domestic animal	A leopard
Something that floats in the bath	Water
Something red	My cardigan
A famous cowboy	Buck Rogers
A famous Scotsman	Jock
A song with the word 'moon' in the title	Blue Suede Moon
Something you do in the bathroom	Decorate
Something made of wool	A sheep
A song from The Sound of Music	Dancing Queen
A yellow fruit	An orange
Some famous brothers	Bonnie and Clyde
Something you would find in a garage	A grand piano
A sign of the zodiac	April
A famous Phil or Philip	Phil Johnson
Something slippery	A conman
A bird with a long neck	Naomi Campbell
Something a blind person might use	A sword
Something you wear on the beach	A deckchair
Something that flies without an engine	A bicycle with wings
A wild animal native to Britain	A bear
Something made to be wheeled around	A hammer
A type of ache	Filet o'fish
A well-known TV soap	Dove
An animal that makes people scream	A squirrel
Something a trainspotter might keep in his pocket	A magnifying glass
An animal with a long tail	A rabbit

First Night: Channel 4's Opening Schedule (2 November 1982)

4.45pm Countdown. The first edition of Richard Whiteley's words and numbers game.

5.15 Preview 4. Channel 4's continuity announcers – Paul Coia, Olga Hubicka, David Stranks and Keith Harrison – introduce themselves and highlights of Channel 4's programming.

5.30 The Body Show. An exercise programme presented by Yvonne Ocampo.

6.00 People's Court. Real-life criminal cases from Los Angeles are settled not in the courtroom but in a TV studio.

6.30 Book Four. Literary review hosted by Hermione Lee.

7.00 Channel 4 News. Presented by Peter Sissons.

8.00 Brookside. First episode of the Merseyside soap.

8.30 The Paul Hogan Show. Australian comedy sketch show.

9.00 Film on Four: Walter. Ian McKellen stars in a drama about a mentally-challenged man.

10.15 The Comic Strip Presents … Five Go Mad in Dorset. First outing for series of send-up comedies starring Adrian Edmondson, Dawn French, Peter Richardson and Jennifer Saunders.

10.45–11.50 In the Pink. The Raving Beauties celebrate women's lives through music, poetry and dance.

....

Camberwick Green, Trumpton and Chigley characters

CAMBERWICK GREEN (1966)

The soldiers of Pippin Fort headed by Capt Snort and Sgt Major Grout

Windy Miller, the miller

Roger Varley, the chimney sweep

Mr Carraway, the fishmonger

Mrs Honeyman, the chemist's wife, and her baby

Dr Mopp

Jonathan Bell, the farmer

Mr Crockett, the garage owner

Mickey Murphy, the baker, and his children, Paddy and Mary

Mr Dagenham, the salesman

Thomas Tripp, the milkman

Peter Hazel, the postman

Mrs Dingle, the postmistress, and her puppy, Packet

PC McGarry

Firemen Pugh, Pugh, Barney McGrew, Cuthbert, Dibble and Grubb, led by Captain Flack

Miss Lovelace, the hat maker, and her dogs Mitzi, Daphne and Lulu

The Mayor

Mr Troop, the Town Clerk

Philby, the mayor's driver

Mrs Cobbit, the flower seller

Mr Platt, the clock maker

Mr Craddock, the park keeper

Mr Wantage and Fred, telephone engineers

Mr Munnings, the printer

Policeman Potter

Walter Harkin, the decorator

Raggy Dan, the rag and bone man

Mr Robinson, the window cleaner

Mr Rumpling, the bargee

Mr Antonio, the ice cream man

Mr Clamp, the greengrocer

Chippy Minton, the carpenter, his wife, Dora, and their son, Nibs

Mr Wilkins, the plumber

Mr Bolt, the borough engineer

Nick Fisher, the bill sticker

CHIGLEY (1969)

Lord Belborough

Mr Brackett, Lord Belborough's butler

Mr Bilton, Lord Belborough's gardener

Mr Swallow, the wharf manager

Mr Cresswell, the biscuit factory owner, and his employees

Harry Farthing, the potter, and his daughter, Winnie

Mr Clutterbuck, the builder

Cyril and Horace, the bricklayers

Willie Munn, the biscuit stamper

Note: characters were known to cross over between series.

....

Pop Up TV

'Television is like the American toaster, you push the button and the same thing pops up everytime.'

– Alfred Hitchcock

Animal Adventures

ANIMAL/SERIES	TYPE	BEST FRIEND
The Adventures of Black Beauty	Horse	Vicky Gordon (Judi Bowker)
The Adventures of Rin-Tin-Tin	Dog	Rusty (Lee Aaker)
Champion the Wonder Horse	Horse	Ricky North (Barry Curtis)
Flipper	Dolphin	Sandy Ricks (Luke Halpin)
Fury	Horse	Joey Newton (Bobby Diamond)
Gentle Ben	Bear	Mark Wedloe (Clint Howard)
Lassie	Dog	Jeff Miller (Tommy Rettig)
		Timmy Martin (Jon Provost)
		Corey Stuart (Robert Bray)
The Littlest Hobo	Dog	
Mr Ed	Horse	Wilbur Post (Alan Young)
My Friend Flicka	Horse	Ken McLaughlin (Johnny Washbrook)
Salty	Sea lion	Taylor Reed (Mark Slade)
Skippy, the Bush Kangaroo	Kangaroo	Sonny Hammond (Garry Parkhurst)

....

The Presenters of Blue Peter and Magpie

BLUE PETER

Leila Williams	Peter Duncan	Stuart Miles
Christopher Trace	Janet Ellis	Katy Hill
Anita West	Michael Sundin	Romana D'Annunzio
Valerie Singleton	Mark Curry	Richard Bacon
John Noakes	Caron Keating	Konnie Huq
Peter Purves	Yvette Fielding	Simon Thomas
Lesley Judd	John Leslie	Matt Baker
Simon Groom	Diane-Louise Jordan	Liz Barker
Christopher Wenner	Anthea Turner	Zoe Salmon
Tina Heath	Tim Vincent	Gethin Jones
Sarah Greene		

MAGPIE

Susan Stranks	Douglas Rae	Tommy Boyd
Pete Brady	Mick Robertson	
Tony Bastable	Jenny Hanley	

Alter-egos of TV Superheroes

SUPERHERO	ALTER-EGO
Bananaman	Eric Twinge
Batgirl	Barbara Gordon
Batman	Bruce Wayne
The Flash	Barry Allen
The Green Hornet	Britt Reid
He-Man	Prince Adam
Highlander	Duncan MacLeod
Hong Kong Phooey	Penry Pooch
The Incredible Hulk	Dr David Banner
Joe 90	Joe McClaine
The Lone Ranger	John Reid
Robin	Dick Grayson
The Saint	Simon Templar
Captain Scarlet	Paul Metcalfe
The Scarlet Pimpernel	Sir Percy Blakeney
She-Ra	Princess Adora
Spiderman	Peter Parker
Supergran	Granny Smith
Superman/Superboy	Clark Kent
Tarzan	Lord Greystoke
Thermoman	George Sunday
Wonder Woman	Diana Prince
Zorro	Don Diego de la Vega

Famous Guest Callers to Frasier Crane's Radio Programme (*Frasier*)

Gillian Anderson
Kevin Bacon
Halle Berry
Pat Boone
Matthew Broderick
Mel Brooks
Cyd Charisse
Rosemary Clooney
Cindy Crawford
Billy Crystal
Macaulay Culkin
Sandra Dee

Phil Donahue
David Duchovny
Olympia Dukakis
Anthony Edwards
Gloria Estefan
Carrie Fisher
Jodie Foster
Art Garfunkel
Daryl Hannah
Ron Howard
Eric Idle
Stephen King

Jay Leno
Henry Mancini
Malcolm McDowell
John McEnroe
Helen Mirren
Mary Tyler Moore
Christopher Reeve
Carly Simon
Neil Simon
Ben Stiller
Lily Tomlin
Elijah Wood

The 100 Greatest Cartoons

As selected by viewers for the Channel 4 programme broadcast on 27 February 2005.

1   The Simpsons
2   Tom and Jerry
3   South Park
4   Toy Story/Toy Story 2
5   Family Guy
6   Shrek/Shrek 2
7   The Lion King
8   Spirited Away
9   The Incredibles
10 Bugs Bunny
11 The Flintstones
12 The Iron Giant
13 The Nightmare Before Christmas
14 Finding Nemo
15 Wallace and Gromit
16 Akira
17 Aladdin
18 The Ren and Stimpy Show
19 Who Framed Roger Rabbit?
20 Looney Tunes/Merrie Melodies
21 Princess Mononoke
22 Monsters, Inc
23 Popeye
24 Danger Mouse
25 Pinocchio
26 Futurama
27 Teenage Mutant Ninja Turtles
28 Spongebob Squarepants
29 Dungeons and Dragons
30 Daffy Duck
31 Mickey Mouse
32 Beavis and Butthead
33 Beauty and the Beast
34 He-Man and the Masters of the Universe
35 Sylvester and Tweetie Pie

CURIOUS FACT

The character of Aunt Harriet in Batman did not appear in the original comic strip but was added to the TV series to deflect suspicion over three grown men sharing a house

....

'Television' in Different Languages

Czech	Televize	Latvian	Televizija
Danish	Fjernsyn	Lithuanian	Televizija
Dutch	Televisie	Malaysian	Televisyen
Esperanto	Televido	Norwegian	Fjernsyn
Estonian	Televisioon	Polish	Telewizji
Finnish	Televisio	Portuguese	Televisão
French	Télévision	Serbo-Croat	Televizija
Gaelic	Telefís	Spanish	Televisión
German	Fernsehen	Swedish	Television
Hungarian	Televizió	Turkish	Televizyon
Italian	Televisione	Welsh	Teledu

ITV Franchise Holders

The companies that have run ITV since its launch in 1955.

COMPANY	REGION	ON AIR
ABC	Midlands (weekends)	18 Feb 1956–28 Jul 1968
	North of England (weekends)	5 May 1956–28 Jul 1968
Anglia	East of England	27 Oct 1959–
Associated-Rediffusion	London (weekdays)	22 Sep 1955–29 Jul 1968
ATV	London (weekends)	24 Sept 1955–28 Jul 1968
	Midlands (weekdays)	17 Feb 1956–26 Jul 1968
	Midlands (all week)	19 Jul 1968–31 Dec 1981
Border	The Borders	1 Sep 1961–
Carlton	London (weekdays)	1 Jan 1993–
Central	Midlands (all week)	1 Jan 1982–
Channel	Channel Islands	1 Sep 1962–
GMTV	National Breakfast Service	1 Jan 1993–
Grampian	North of Scotland	30 Sep 1961–
Granada	North of England (weekdays)	3 May 1956–26 Jul 1968
	North-west England	29 Jul 1968–
HTV	Wales and West of England	4 Mar 1968–
LWT	London (weekends)	2 Aug 1968–
Meridian	South of England	1 Jan 1993–
Scottish	Central Scotland	31 Aug 1957–
Southern	South of England	30 Aug 1958–31 Dec 1981
Thames	London (weekdays)	30 Jul 1968–31 Dec 1992
TSW	South-west England	12 Aug 1981–31 Dec 1992
TV-am	National Breakfast Service	1 Feb 1983–31 Dec 1992
TVS	South of England	1 Jan 1982–31 Dec 1992
TWW	Wales and West of England	14 Jan 1958–3 Mar 1968
Tyne Tees	North-east England	15 Jan 1959–
Ulster	Northern Ireland	31 Oct 1959–
Wales West and North	West and North Wales	14 Sep 1962–26 Jan 1964*
Westcountry	South-west England	1 Jan 1993–
Westward	South-west England	29 Apr 1961–11 Aug 1981
Yorkshire	Yorkshire	29 Jul 1968–

Note: Mergers and take-overs have seen ITV's federal network of regional broadcasters now largely subsumed into one company called ITV.

* The only ITV franchisee ever to go bust (the transmission area was unrealistically small and was absorbed later into the Wales and West of England area).

Bagpuss's Helpers

Emily, the girl who brings items to the shop for repair
Gabriel, the toad
Madeleine, the rag doll
Prof. Yaffle, the woodpecker bookend
The mice (Charliemouse, Eddiemouse, Janiemouse, Jenniemouse, Lizziemouse and Williemouse)

More Fictional TV Towns

FICTIONAL TOWN	SERIES
Angleton	The Newcomers
Auchnacluchnie	All Along the Watchtower
Bedrock	The Flintstones
Broadstone	Hunter's Walk
Cabot Cove, Maine	Murder, She Wrote
Castlefield	Playing the Field
Cwmderi	Pobol y Cwm
Denton	A Touch of Frost
Dunn's River	Soap
Elsinby	The Royal
Erinsborough	Neighbours
Fairwater	Bless Me, Father
Fulchester	Crown Court
Gallowshield	When the Boat Comes In
Gasforth	The Thin Blue Line
Gotham City	Batman
Greendale	Postman Pat
Gunnershaw	Cluff
Hartley	Juliet Bravo
Hepworth	Common as Muck
Holby	Casualty, Holby City
Hooterville	Petticoat Junction, Green Acres
King's Oak	Crossroads
Lanford	Roseanne
Limanaki	Sunburn
Los Barcos	Eldorado
Luxton	On the Buses
Marineville	Stingray
Market Wetherby	We'll Meet Again
Mayberry	The Andy Griffith Show
Mayfield	Leave It to Beaver
Melton	Noah's Ark

Nether Hopping	The Army Game
Nettlebridge	Oh Happy Band!
New Rochelle	The Dick Van Dyke Show
Newtown	Z Cars
Norbridge	Press Gang
North Fork	The Rifleman
Nouvion	'Allo 'Allo
Oakleigh	Down to Earth
Orbit City	The Jetsons
Oxbridge	Emergency – Ward 10
Palisades	Saved by the Bell
Pencwm	The District Nurse
Ramsden	Foxy Lady
Raven's Bay	Rosie
Roseville	The Phil Silvers Show
Scarsdale	Oh No It's Selwyn Froggitt
Skellerton	Sam
Space City	Fireball XL5
Springfield	Father Knows Best, The Simpsons
Springwood	Sixpenny Corner
St Mary Mead	Miss Marple
St Oswald	Timeslip
Stackton Tressel	Dear Ladies
Stipton	After Henry
Stray Town	The Adventures of Twizzle
Sullbridge	Starr and Company
Summer Bay	Home and Away
Sunnydale	Buffy the Vampire Slayer
Utterley	Brass
Waltons' Mountain	The Waltons
Weatherfield	Coronation Street
Wetherton	Dalziel and Pascoe
Woodbridge	Here's Harry
Woodley	Spooner's Patch

CURIOUS FACT

Erinsborough, the town featured in Australia's most successful soap, is an anagram of 'Or Neighbours'

First TV Play

The first play to be televised was The Man with the Flower in His Mouth, transmitted as part of John Logie Baird's television trials on 14 July 1930. This play, by the Italian dramatist Luigi Pirandello, was staged with the help of the BBC and was chosen because it had only three characters and was therefore easy to capture with one camera.

Zones in The Crystal Maze

In the Channel 4 game show The Crystal Maze, contestants had to solve puzzles and face challenges in four 'zones':

Aztec
Futuristic
Medieval
Industrial*

* Later replaced by Ocean.

....

Groundbreaking TV

Twenty programmes that changed our lives and our viewing:

CATHY COME HOME (1966)
A play with an innovative documentary feel; shaped our views on homelessness and led to the setting up of the charity Shelter.

CORONATION STREET (1960–)
Not the first British soap, but the first with staying power; an inspiration to every soap since.

THE FAMILY (1974)
A docu-soap years before the term was invented, offering fly-on-the-wall voyeurism of a Reading family.

THE FORSYTE SAGA (1967)
Not only turned period drama into a prime time hit but also made BBC 2 relevant to a previously unconvinced audience.

GRANGE HILL (1978–)
Placed a new slant on children's television through a far more realistic view of school life than seen in previous school dramas.

HILL STREET BLUES (1981–7)
The pioneer of ensemble drama with hand-held camera work and human failure among the characters added to remove the gloss.

I LOVE LUCY (1951–61)
The series that blazed the trail for the all-conquering American domestic sitcom.

INSPECTOR MORSE (1987–2000)
A beautifully-filmed crime drama that drove the two-hour format, allowing for complex plots and in-depth characterisation.

MONTY PYTHON'S FLYING CIRCUS (1969–74)
Anarchic and surreal: TV comedy has never been the same since.

THE QUATERMASS EXPERIMENT (1953)
The first programme to reveal how TV could scare its audience; the forerunner of great sci-fi.

READY, STEADY, GO! (1963–6)
The first programme truly to reveal the edge and excitement of pop and rock music, without patronising its young audience.

THE ROYLE FAMILY (1998–2000)
Took sitcoms in a new direction through a comedy with no twists, set-ups or punchlines, confident enough to abandon the studio audience and canned laughter.

THE SIMPSONS (1989–)
Wicked animation with multi-dimensional appeal for both kids and grown-ups.

THAT WAS THE WEEK THAT WAS (1962–3)
Satire made for television, eons before Spitting Image and Have I Got News for You.

TILL DEATH US DO PART (1965–75)
A shocking comedy that raised questions about the country's views on race, religion and politics.

TISWAS (1974–82)
Introduced madness and mayhem to the previously ordered and condescending world of kids' TV: superficially funny for children, addictively subversive for adults.

WHO WANTS TO BE A MILLIONAIRE? (1998–)
Put the zing back into TV quiz shows and inspired a raft of tense, big-money, blue-lit clones.

WORLD IN ACTION (1963–98)
Pushed back the boundaries of TV journalism, challenging authority and changing attitudes; now sorely missed in the age of simplistic, sound-bite reporting.

THE YOUNG ONES (1982–4)
A kick up the rear of the cosy, domestic sitcom, bringing the alternative humour of the 1980s to television.

Z CARS (1962–78)
The days of the cuddly copper were numbered when these patrol cars and their fallible, not-so-virtuous drivers hit the crime-ridden streets.

The BBC's First-Ever Continuity Announcers

Leslie Mitchell   Jasmine Bligh   Elizabeth Cowell

First Night: Channel 5/Five's Opening Schedule (30 March 1997)

6.00pm   This is 5! Stars introduce Channel 5's offerings.

6.30   Family Affairs. First episode of the Hart family soap.

7.00   Two Little Boys. The childhood influences of PM John Major and Leader of the Opposition Tony Blair.

8.00   Hospital! One-off comedy staring Greg Wise, Bob Peck, Hywel Bennett and Celia Imrie.

9.00   Beyond Fear. Dramatisation of the kidnap of estate agent Stephanie Slater, starring Gina McKee and Sylvester McCoy.

10.30   The Jack Docherty Show. Late-night chat show.

11.10   The Comedy Store Special. Humour from the stand-up specialists.

11.40   Turnstyle. Look back at the weekend's sporting action.

12.10   Live and Dangerous. Includes a preview of US baseball coverage.

....

Not for Looking at

'Television is for appearing on, not looking at.'

– Noël Coward

....

Colour Pioneers

Colour television was pioneered by CBS in the USA. Although John Logie Baird had experimented with colour, and made the first ever colour transmission way back in 1928, the first formal colour broadcasts only came in 1941 through CBS in New York. It was CBS who also started the world's first regular colour service, in June 1951. However, as the CBS colour broadcasts could not be picked up on black and white receivers, the corporation soon lost out in the colour TV race to NBC, whose more compatible system was officially approved as the standard in 1953.

....

Villages in Murderous Midsomer

Aspern Tallow	Martyr Warren	Midsomer Mere
Badger's Drift	Midsomer Barrow	Midsomer Parva
Causton (county town)	Midsomer Deverell	Midsomer St Michael
Fletcher's Cross	Midsomer Florey	Midsomer Wellow
Goodman's Land	Midsomer Magna	Midsomer Worthy
Lower Warden	Midsomer Malham	Morton Fendle
Malham Bridge	Midsomer Mallow	Newton Magna
Marshwood	Midsomer Market	Upper Warden

Fifteen Minutes of Fame: Stars Discovered by Docu-soaps

DOCU-SOAP	'STAR(S)'
Airline	Leo Jones
Airport	Jeremy Spake
Castaway 2000	Ben Fogle
Driving School	Maureen Rees
Hotel	Eileen Downey
Lakesiders	Emma Boundy
Paddington Green	Jackie McAuliffe
The Clampers	Ray Brown
The Cruise	Jane McDonald
The Family	The Wilkins family
The House	Keith Cooper
The Salon	Paul Merritt
Vets' School	Trude Mostue

The 14-Day Rule

Until July 1957, broadcasters in the UK were unable to report or discuss any matter due for debate in Parliament for 14 days beforehand. The rule was introduced voluntarily by the BBC in 1944, as a means of ensuring the corporation's political independence, but, by the mid-1950s and the arrival of ITV, the rule was under increasing pressure. The Suez Crisis of 1956, which split Parliament, proved to be the breaking point. Unable to report a matter of such major concern to the nation, the broadcasters pushed for a repeal of the rule, which was granted a year later by the new prime minister, Harold Macmillan.

Long-running US Sitcoms Never Screened on UK TV

The Adventures of Ozzie and Harriet (1952–66)
Alice (1976–85)
The Andy Griffith Show (1960–8)
The Danny Thomas Show (1953–71)
The Donna Reed Show (1958–66)
The Facts of Life (1979–88)
Family Matters (1989–98)
Father Knows Best (1954–63)
Full House (1987–95)
The Jeffersons (1975–85)
Leave It to Beaver (1957–63)
One Day at a Time (1975–84)

'Bilko's' Famous Guest Stars

Among the numerous guests appearing in The Phil Silvers Show were:

Alan Alda	George Kennedy
Lucille Ball	Dean Martin
Yogi Berra	Mickey Rooney
Sammy Cahn	Sam Snead
Dick Cavett	Ed Sullivan
Bing Crosby	Dick Van Dyke

Ken Dodd's Diddymen

Harry Cott
Evan
Wee Hamish McDiddy
Mick the Marmalizer
Dicky Mint
Hon. Nigel Ponsonby-Smallpiece
Sid Short
Weany Wally

Mind over Matter

One edition of The Dimbleby Talk-in lives long in many viewers' memories. The programme of Friday, 23 November 1973, provided the UK's first good look at spoon-bending Israeli Uri Geller. During the programme Geller, using his mental powers, successfully mangled cutlery and stopped watches. The BBC was later inundated with calls from spooked viewers who experienced the same happenings at home.

The Magic Roundabout

Voices featured in the 2005 film of the classic 1960s animation series:

CHARACTER	VOICE
Brian	Jim Broadbent
Dougal	Robbie Williams
Dylan	Bill Nighy
Ermintrude	Joanna Lumley
Florence	Kylie Minogue
The Train	Lee Evans
Zebedee	Ian McKellen

The film also introduced two new characters, Zeebadee, voiced by Tom Baker, and Soldier Sam, voiced by Ray Winstone.

Ahead with The Jetsons

Some 21st-century gadgets from Orbit City:

Foodarackacycle (meal machine)
Moving sidewalks
Nuclear-powered car
Nuclear-powered knitting machine
Rosie the domestic robot
Seeing-eye vacuum cleaner
Solar-powered stamp licker
Supersonic skateboard
Talking diary
Video phone
Voice-operated washing machine

Four-Letter First

The first instance of the use of the 'F' word on British television came on 13 November 1965 in an edition of the BBC satirical magazine, BBC-3 (a sequel to That Was The Week That Was). The perpetrator was arts critic Kenneth Tynan, who used the word in a debate about theatre censorship. His surprised interviewer was Robert Robinson.

The Week According to Play School

Monday	Useful Box Day
Tuesday	Dressing-up Day
Wednesday	Pets' Day
Thursday	Ideas Day
Friday	Science Day

BBC Regional News Segments of Nationwide

Look East
Look North
Midlands Today
Points West
Reporting Scotland
Scene Around Six (Ulster)
South Today
Spotlight South West
Wales Today

Note: Look North West and South East at Six were later additions.

The Mavericks Move In

The Maverick family of gamblers wandered the Wild West in search of easy prey. The towns they visited often had rather eccentric names, such as:

Bent City
Duck 'n' Shoot
Hollow Rock
Hound Dog
Oblivion
Stop Gap
Ten Strike

First Outside Broadcast

Less than a year after the BBC's regular high resolution television service was launched, the corporation staged its first outside broadcast. This was to cover the coronation of King George VI and Queen Elizabeth on 12 May 1937. Such were the limitations of this early exercise that only three cameras were used and only the procession was covered, cameras not being permitted inside Westminster Abbey to witness the crowning of the new king. The estimated audience for the coverage was just 50,000.

From TV to MP

TV contributors turned politicians:

Martin Bell	journalist: BBC News
Ben Bradshaw	journalist: BBC News
Gyles Brandreth	panel game star and presenter: GMTV
Tim Brinton	newscaster: ITN
Christopher Chataway	newscaster: ITN
Andrew Faulds	actor: The Protectors
Clement Freud	humorist and dog food advertiser
Bryan Gould	journalist: TV Eye*
Glenda Jackson	actor: Elizabeth R
Boris Johnson	journalist and panel game star
Geoffrey Johnson-Smith	journalist: Tonight
Gerald Kaufman	writer: That Was the Week That Was
Stephen Milligan	journalist: BBC News
Austin Mitchell	presenter: Calendar
Shaun Woodward	producer: That's Life

* Had been an MP prior to moving into television.

Doctor Who?

ACTOR	**William Hartnell**
ERA	1963–6
FIRST STORY	An Unearthly Child
LAST STORY	The Tenth Planet
COMPANIONS	Susan , Ian , Barbara , Vicki, Steven, Katarina, Dodo, Polly, Ben

ACTOR	**Patrick Troughton**
ERA	1966–9
FIRST STORY	The Power of the Daleks
LAST STORY	The War Games
COMPANIONS	Polly, Ben, Jamie , Victoria , Zoe

ACTOR	**Jon Pertwee**
ERA	1970–4
FIRST STORY	Spearhead from Space
LAST STORY	Planet of the Spiders
COMPANIONS	Brig. Lethbridge-Stewart, Liz, Jo, Sarah Jane

ACTOR	**Tom Baker**
ERA	1974–81
FIRST STORY	Robot
LAST STORY	Logopolis
COMPANIONS	Sarah Jane, Harry, Leela, K9, Romana, Adric, Nyssa, Tegan

ACTOR	**Peter Davison**
ERA	1982–4
FIRST STORY	Castrovalva
LAST STORY	The Caves of Androzani
COMPANIONS	Adric, Nyssa, Tegan, Turlough, Peri

ACTOR	**Colin Baker**
ERA	1984–6
FIRST STORY	The Twin Dilemma
LAST STORY	The Trial of a Time Lord
COMPANIONS	Peri, Melanie

ACTOR	**Sylvester McCoy**
ERA	1987–9
FIRST STORY	Time and the Rani
LAST STORY	Survival
COMPANIONS	Melanie, Ace

ACTOR	**Paul McGann**
ERA	1996
FIRST STORY	Doctor Who (TV movie)
LAST STORY	Doctor Who (TV movie)
COMPANIONS	Grace , Chang Lee

ACTOR	**Christopher Eccleston**
ERA	2005
FIRST STORY	Rose
LAST STORY	The Parting of the Ways
COMPANIONS	Rose , Captain Jack Harkness

ACTOR	**David Tennant**
ERA	2005–
FIRST STORY	n/a
LAST STORY	n/a
COMPANION	Rose

A £1,000,000 Question

This was the final question correctly answered by Judith Keppel, first winner of the ITV Who Wants to Be a Millionaire? top prize:

'Which king was married to Eleanor of Aquitaine?'

A: Henry I   B: Henry II
C: Richard I   D: Henry V

ANSWER: B: Henry II

The First TV Star

He said no words, not even a 'gottle of geer', but Stukey Bill, a ventriloquist's dummy, provided television's first recognisable face. His head was used by pioneer John Logie Baird as a model in his early experiments with television in the 1920s.

Saturday Night Live Discoveries

The US series Saturday Night Live, a live comedy showcase, gave important regular exposure to up-and-coming stars. These included:

Dan Aykroyd
John Belushi
Chevy Chase
Billy Crystal
Robert Downey Jr
Eddie Murphy
Bill Murray
Mike Myers
Adam Sandler
Rob Schneider

No Ringing Endorsement

The fondly-remembered, 1960s European fairy story, The Singing Ringing Tree (screened as part of the BBC's Tales from Europe series) was not so popular with some residents in its native country of East Germany. The eerie story of a bad-tempered princess, her suitor prince and the wicked dwarf who turns him into a bear was slated by ruling Communists for being 'dangerously bourgeois'. They felt such stories should not be set among the aristocracy but in a working-class environment.

TV Channel Opening Dates

BBC (1)	2 November 1936
ITV	22 September 1955
BBC 2	20 April 1964
Channel 4	2 November 1982
Channel 5/Five	30 March 1997
ITV 2	7 December 1998
BBC 4	2 March 2002
BBC 3	9 February 2003
ITV 3	1 November 2004

Catchphrases Popularised by Rowan and Martin's Laugh-In

Beautiful Downtown Burbank
Here comes de judge
I'll drink to that
Look that up in your Funk and Wagnalls
Ring my chimes
Say goodnight, Dick
Sock it to me
Very interesting, but stupid
You bet your sweet bippy

Some Items Furnishing Steptoe and Son's Living Room

Skeleton	Hat stand
Stuffed bear	Skull
Mounted fish and animal heads	Bagpipes
Cased birds	Bureau
Guitar	Bell
Grandfather clock	Chamber pot
Statuettes	Wireless set
Set of optics	Bed warmer
Bugle	Ship in a bottle
Bust of Beethoven	Assorted bottles and jars
Walking stick	Wind-up gramophone
Potted plant	Filing cabinet

Euphemisms Used by TV Channels for 'Repeat'

Another chance to see
Archive footage
A classic episode
First shown on...
Re-run
A retrospective season
A tribute to...
A vintage episode

Royal First

The first member of the royal family to be interviewed on television was HRH The Duke of Edinburgh. He appeared alongside Richard Dimbleby on the BBC's Panorama programme on 29 May 1961 to discuss Commonwealth Technical Training Week, which he was inaugurating.

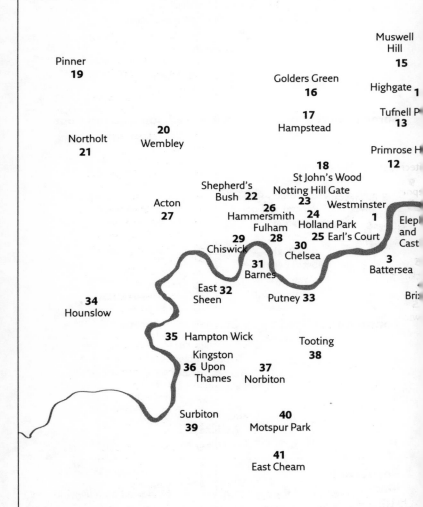

London by Sitcom

Muswell
Hill
15

Pinner
19

Golders Green
16

Highgate **1**

17
Hampstead

Tufnell P
13

20
Wembley

Northolt
21

Primrose H
12

18
St John's Wood

Shepherd's
Bush **22**

Notting Hill Gate
23

Acton
27

26
Hammersmith
Fulham

Westminster
1

24
Holland Park

Elep
and
Cast

29
Chiswick

28

25 Earl's Court

30
Chelsea

3

31
Barnes

Battersea

East **32**
Sheen

Putney **33**

Bri

34
Hounslow

35 Hampton Wick

Tooting
38

Kingston
36 Upon
Thames

37
Norbiton

Surbiton
39

40
Motspur Park

41
East Cheam

Chigwell
11

1 My Dad's the Prime Mimister
The New Statesman
No Job for a Lady
Yes, Minister
2 Up the Elephant and Round the Castle
3 Game On
4 The Lenny Henry Show
5 The Gnomes of Dulwich
6 Desmond's
Only Fools and Horses
7 Till Death Us Do Part
8 Down the Gate
9 Goodnight Sweetheart
10 Never Mind the Quality, Feel the Width
11 Birds of a Feather
12 Life without George
13 Spaced
14 Keep It in the Family
15 Beggar My Neighbour
Going Straight
16 Alexander the Greatest
17 Father, Dear Father
18 Babes in the Wood
19 May to December
20 The Kumars at No. 42
21 My Hero
22 Steptoe and Son
23 Hippies
24 Absolutely Fabulous
25 Marriage Lines
26 Bottom
27 'Orrible
28 Not on Your Nellie
Robin's Nest
29 2 Point 4 Children
30 Girls on Top
31 Fresh Fields
32 Pig in the Middle
33 Bless This House
34 Is It Legal?
35 George and Mildred
36 Side by Side
37 The Fall and Rise of Reginald Perrin
38 Citizen Smith
Hugh and I
39 The Good Life
40 Brush Strokes
41 Hancock's Half Hour
42 Terry and June

techapel
9
pney   **8** Billingsgate
sle of
Dogs
7

6
ckham

5
wich

42
Purley

Shadow Boxing

The casting director for The Phil Silvers Show was ex-world boxing champion Rocky Graziano, whose real name, incidentally, was Rocco Barbella, the same as one of Bilko's corporals.

....

Serial Soap Stars

Characters played by the same actors in various soap operas.

ACTOR	CORONATION STREET	EMMERDALE	EASTENDERS
Rachel Ambler	Gill Collins	Emma Nightingale	
Kathryn Apanowicz		Helen Ackroyd	Mags Czajkowski
Debbie Arnold	Sylvie Hicks	Debbie Wilson	April Branning
John Bardon	Ernie Lumsden		Jim Branning
Tony Barton	Pat Hegarty	Desmond Burtenshaw	
Roy Boyd	Mr Franklyn	Dryden Hogben	
Tracy Brabin	Tricia Armstrong		Roxy Drake
John Branwell	Ed Malone	DI Tom Keysel	
June Brown	Mrs Parsons		Dot Cotton
Beverly Callard	Liz McDonald	Angie Richards	
Brian Capron	Richard Hillman		Jerry Mackenzie
Jane Cox	Mrs Shaw	Lisa Dingle	
David Crellin	Graham Baxter	Billy Hopwood	
Diana Davies	Norma Ford	Caroline Bates	
Rachel Davies	Donna Parker	Shirley Foster	
Peter Dean	Jeff Bateman		Peter Beale
Elizabeth Estensen	Pam Middleton	Diane Blackstock	
Ken Farrington	Billy Walker	Tom King	
Siobhan Finneran	Josie Phillips	Heather Hutchinson	
Paul Fox	Mark Redman	Will Cairns	
Anna Friel	Belinda Johnson	Poppy Bruce	
Sandra Gough	Irma Barlow	Nellie Dingle	
Jill Halfpenny	Rebecca Hopkins		Kate Mitchell
John Hallam		Terry Prince	'Barnsey' Barnes
Sherrie Hewson	Maureen Holdsworth	Leslie Meredith	
Michelle Holmes	Tina Fowler	Britt Woods	
Annie Hulley	Gwen Davies	Karen Moore	
Louise Jameson		Sharon Crossthwaite	Rosa di Marco
Judi Jones	Pam Hargreaves	Barbara Kirk	
Gorden Kaye	Bernard Butler	Gerry	
Ross Kemp		Graham Lodsworth	Grant Mitchell
Roberta Kerr	Wendy Crozier	Jan Glover	

ACTOR	CORONATION STREET	EMMERDALE	EASTEnders
Bobby Knutt	Ron Sykes	Albert Dingle	
Sally Knyvette	Margi Quigley	Kate Sugden	
Johnny Leeze	Harry Clayton	Ned Glover	
Lesley Manville	Jill Mason	Rosemary Kendall	
Jim Millea	Carl Armstrong	Pete Whiteley	
Lesley Nightingale	Josie Clark		Ronnie Bains
Helen Pearson		Carol Wareing	April McIntosh
Arthur Pentelow	George Greenwood	Henry Wilks	
Jacqueline Pirie	Linda Baldwin	Tina Dingle	
Mark Powley	Rob Lucas	Liam Hammond	
Nicholas R Bailey	Lee Middleton		Anthony Trueman
Stan Richards	Arthur Stokes	Seth Armstrong	
David Roper	Bob Bradshaw		Geoff Barnes
Alan Rothwell	David Barlow	John Kenyon	
Ken Sharrock	A mayor		Derek Taylor
Pam St Clement		Mrs Eckersley	Pat Evans
Kathy Staff	Vera Hopkins	Winnie Purvis	
Shirley Stelfox	Shirley Henderson	Edna Birch	
Teddy Turner	Chalky Whiteley	Bill Whiteley	
Joanne Whalley	Pamela Graham	Angela Read	
Nicola Wheeler	Melanie Tindell	Nicola Blackstock	
Stuart Wolfenden	Mark Casey	Darren Pearce	

....

In a Previous Life

TV chef Ainsley Harriott, host of the BBC's Ready Steady Cook, was once a supporting comedian on Bobby Davro's ITV series, Davro.

In 1959, future soccer legend Bobby Charlton appeared as a contestant in the ITV quiz show Double Your Money. He won the top prize of £1,000 by answering questions on pop music.

When he created The X-Files, Chris Carter was working as a writer on a surfing magazine.

Actor/comedian Hugh Laurie rowed for Cambridge in the 1980 Boat Race.

The Addams Family's Uncle Fester once appeared alongside Charlie Chaplin. Actor Jackie Coogan played the little boy in the 1921 silent classic, The Kid.

Top of the Pops and Great British Quiz presenter Janice Long once appeared as a contestant in the game show 3-2-1.

New Broadcasters Wanted

In 1954 The Times ran the following advertisement:

INDEPENDENT TELEVISION AUTHORITY

The Independent Television Authority invites applications from those interested in becoming PROGRAMME CONTRACTORS in accordance with the provisions of the Television Act. Applicants should give a broad picture of the types of programme they would provide, their proposals for network or local broadcasting of their programmes, some indication of their financial resources, and the length of contract they would desire.

All applications will be treated in the strictest confidence.

Replies to the Chairman, care of General Post Office Headquarters, E.C.1.

TV the Medium

'Television – a medium.
So called because it is neither rare nor well-done.'

– Ernie Kovacs, US comedian

Longest Name

Very probably the longest name ever given to a TV programme was:

Why don't you just switch off your television set
and go and do something less boring instead?

For ease of use, this children's magazine programme was usually abbreviated to Why Don't You... ? or, as it was billed in the Radio Times for its first airing in 1973:

Wdyjsoytsagadslbi?

Those Meddling Kids!

The Mystery Machine travellers:
Scooby-Doo   Shaggy
Velma   Fred   Daphne

Early to Bed

Forget the Midnight Movie. In the winter of 1973–4 UK television was forced off air at 10.30 every night by Government edict. This move to conserve energy was deemed necessary after a sharp increase in oil prices and major industrial action by coal miners and power workers that led to most industries being confined to working a three-day week.

A Few Goodbyes

Bye bye, everybody, bye, bye.
Harry Corbett, The Sooty Show

Don't have nightmares. Do sleep well.
Nick Ross, Crimewatch UK

It's goodnight from me,
and it's goodnight from him.
The Two Ronnies

Say goodnight, Gracie
George Burns, The Burns and Allen Show

See you next weeeek.
Here Come the Double Deckers

The next Tonight will be tomorrow night.
Cliff Michelmore, Tonight

There are eight million stories in the Naked City.
This has been one of them.
Naked City

'Time for bed', said Zebedee.
The Magic Roundabout

Time to go home.
Andy Pandy

Auf Wiedersehen, Pet.

Further Reading

Baily, Kenneth (ed.): *The Television Annual*, Odhams, various editions

Betts, Graham: *Complete UK Hit Singles*, Collins, 2005

Blacknell, Steve: *The Story of Top of the Pops*, PSL, 1985

Brandt, George (ed.): *British Television Drama in the 1980s*, Cambridge University Press, 1993

Brooks, Tim, and Earle Marsh: *The Complete Directory to Prime Time Network and Cable TV Shows*, Ballantine Books, 2003

Brooks, Tim: *The Complete Directory to Prime Time TV Stars*, Ballantine Books, 1987

Brown, Les: *Les Brown's Encyclopedia of Television*, Visible Ink, 1992

Cain, John: *The BBC: 70 Years of Broadcasting*, BBC 1992

Castleman, Harry, and Walter J. Podrazik: *Harry and Wally's Favorite TV Shows*, Prentice Hall Press, 1989

Clark, Steve: *The Only Fools and Horses Story*, BBC 1998

Cooke, Alistair: *Masterpieces*, Bodley Head, 1982

Cornell, Paul, Martin Day and Keith Topping: *The Guinness Book of Classic British TV*, Guinness Publishing, 1996

Crowther, Bruce, and Mike Pinfold: *Bring Me Laughter*, Columbus Books, 1987

Crystal, David (ed.): *The Cambridge Biographical Encyclopedia*, Cambridge University Press, 1998

Davis, Anthony: *TV's Greatest Hits*, Boxtree, 1988

Donovan, Paul: *The Radio Companion*, Grafton, 1992

Down, Richard, and Christopher Perry: *The British Television Drama Research Guide*, Kaleidoscope Publishing, 1997

Down, Richard, and Christopher Perry: *The British Television Music & Variety Research Guide*, Kaleidoscope Publishing, 1997

Down, Richard, Richard Marson and Christopher Perry: *The British Television Children's Research Guide*, Kaleidoscope Publishing, 1999

Editors of TV Guide: *TV Guide Guide to TV*, Barnes & Noble, 2004

Evans, Jeff: *Midsomer Murders: the Making of an English Crime Classic*, Batsford, 2002

Evans, Jeff: *The Penguin TV Companion*, Penguin, 2003

Fane-Saunders, Kilmeny (ed.): *Radio Times Guide to Films*, BBC Books, 2004

Fischer, Stuart: *Kids' TV The First 25 Years*, Facts on File, 1983

Freeman, Mickey, and Sholom Rubinstein: *Bilko*, Virgin, 2000

Fulton, Roger: *The Encyclopedia of TV Science Fiction*, Boxtree, 1995

Gambaccini, Paul, and Rod Taylor: *Television's Greatest Hits*, Network Books, 1993

Garner, Joe: *Stay Tuned*, Andrews McMeel, 2002

Gearing, Brian and Phil McNeil (ed.): *Seventy Years of BBC Sport*, André Deutsch, 1999

Grade, Lew: *Still Dancing*, Fontana, 1987

Greenfield, Jeff: *Television, The First Fifty Years*, Crescent Books, 1981

Halliwell, Leslie, and Philip Purser: *Halliwell's Television Companion*, Granada, 1986

Harbord, Jane, and Jeff Wright: *40 Years of British Television*, Boxtree, 1992

Hayward, Anthony and Deborah: *TV Unforgettables*, Guinness Publishing, 1993

Hayward, Anthony, et al.: *Who's Who on Television*, various editions

Hayward, Anthony: *The Guinness Who's Who of Soap Operas*, Guinness Publishing, 1995

Hill, Tom (ed.): *Nick at Nite's Classic TV Companion*, Simon & Schuster, 1996

Home, Anna: *Into the Box of Delights*, BBC Books, 1993

Housham, David, and John Frank-Keyes: *Funny Business*, Boxtree, 1992

Hunter, Allan (ed.): *Chambers Film & TV Handbook*, Chambers, 1991

Jarvis, Peter: *Teletalk*, BBC Television Training, 1991

Jasper, Tony: *Fab! The Sounds of the Sixties*, Blandford, 1984

Javna, John: *Cult TV*, St Martin's Press, 1985

Javna, John: *The Best of Science Fiction TV*, Harmony Books, 1987

Javna, John: *The Best of TV Sitcoms*, Harmony Books, 1988

Jeffries, Stuart: *Mrs Slocombe's Pussy*, Flamingo, 2001

Kalter, Suzy: *The Complete Book of M*A*S*H*, Abrams, 1984

Kay, Graeme: *Life in the Street*, Boxtree, 1991

Kingsley, Hilary, and Geoff Tibballs: *Box of Delights*, Macmillan, 1989

Kingsley, Hilary: *Soap Box*, Macmillan, 1988

Lasswell, Mark: *Fifty Years of Television*, Crown, 2002

Lewis, Richard: *The Encyclopedia of Cult Children's TV*, Allison & Busby, 2001

Lewisohn, Mark: *Radio Times Guide to TV Comedy*, BBC Worldwide, 2003

Little, Daran: *40 Years of Coronation Street*, Granada, 2000

Marschall, Rick: *The Golden Age of Television*, Bison Books, 1987

McGown, Alistair, and Mark J Docherty: *The Hill and Beyond*, BFI, 2003

McNeil, Alex: *Total Television*, Penguin, 1996

Miall, Leonard: *Inside the BBC*, Weidenfeld & Nicolson, 1994

Monaco, James: *The Virgin International Encyclopedia of Film*, Virgin Books, 1991

Morton, Alan: *The Complete Directory to Science Fiction, Fantasy and Horror Television Series*, Other Worlds Books, 1997

Passingham, Kenneth: *The Guinness Book of TV Facts and Feats*, Guinness, 1984

Penney, Edmund F.: *The Facts on File Dictionary of Film and Broadcast Terms*, Facts on File, 1991

Podmore, Bill, with Peter Reece: *Coronation Street, The Inside Story*, Macdonald, 1990

Postgate, Oliver: *Seeing Things*, Pan, 2001

Preston, Mike: *Tele-Tunes, Mike Preston Music*, various editions

Roberts, David (ed.): *British Hit Singles and Albums*, Guinness World Records, 2005

Rogers, Dave: *The ITV Encyclopedia of Adventure*, Boxtree, 1988

Ross, Robert: *The Complete Goodies*, Batsford, 2000

Sachs, John, and Piers Morgan: *Secret Lives*, Blake Publishing, 1991

Sangster, Jim, and David Bailey: *Friends Like Us*, Virgin, 1998

Schwartz, David, Steve Ryan and Fred Wostbrock: *The Encyclopedia of TV Game Shows*, Facts on File, 1995

Sheridan, Simon: *The A–Z of Classic Children's Television*, Reynolds & Hearn, 2004

Simpson, Paul (ed.): *The Rough Guide to Cult TV*, Rough Guides, 2002

Taylor, Rod: *The Guinness Book of Sitcoms*, Guinness Publishing, 1994

Terrace, Vincent: *The Ultimate TV Trivia Book*, Faber and Faber, 1991

Tibballs, Geoff: *The Boxtree Encyclopedia of TV Detectives*, Boxtree, 1992

Tibballs, Geoff: *The Golden Age of Children's Television*, Titan Books, 1991

Vahimagi, Tise: *British Television*, Oxford University Press, 1994

Walker, John (ed.): *Halliwell's Film*, Video & DVD Guide, HarperCollins, 2004

Walker, John (ed.): *Halliwell's Who's Who in the Movies*, HarperCollins, 2003

Warner, Hannah: *Fascinating TV Facts*, Virgin, 2004

Webber, Richard: *Dad's Army: a Celebration*, Virgin, 1997

Webber, Richard: *A Celebration of The Good Life*, Orion, 2000

Webber, Richard: *Rising Damp: a Celebration*, Boxtree, 2001

Wheen, Francis: *Television*, Century, 1985

Woolery, George W.: *Children's Television: The First Thirty-Five Years* (2 volumes), Scarecrow Press, 1983 and 1985

Index

A

B

C

R

S

T